Catalogue of Manuscripts on Performing Arts

Catalogue of Manuscripts on Performing Arts is a compiling information of manuscripts on dance, music and drama. Such compilation reflects years of efforts in gathering information from the institutional libraries and private collections. This will not be just a copy of the music, dance, drama material in Aufrecht or Raghavan but it will update or rather fill the gap of existing knowledge in these fields.

Dr Kaushalya Gupta, (b. 1929) is former professor, Department of Sanskrit, Miranda House, University of Delhi. She has published a number of articles in leading journals. She has participated in many National and International conferences. Her doctoral thesis is on Women in Buddhism. In 2004 she was awarded Sanskrit Sewa Samman by Sanskrit Akademi. She as also contributed in the research of "Plants in Sanskrit Literature". Currently she is engaged in writing poetry in Hindi. Some of them Alok Sparsh, Man Batayan etc have been published.

Catalogue of Manuscripts on Performing Arts

(Music, Dance and Drama)

Compiled by
Kaushalya Gupta

राष्ट्रीय पाण्डुलिपि मिशन
॥ विज्ञानमुपास्व ॥
National Mission for Manuscripts
Dev Publishers & Distributors

Published by:
National Mission for Manuscripts
Indira Gandhi National Centre for the Arts
11, Man Singh Road
New Delhi-110 001
Phone: 91 11 2307 3387
E-mail: directornamami@nic.in
Website: www.namami.nic.in

and Co-published by:
Dev Publishers & Distributors
2nd Floor, Prakash Deep,
22, Delhi Medical Association Road,
Darya Ganj,
New Delhi-110002
Phone : 011-43572647
E-mail: devbooks@hotmail.com
*Website:*www.devbooks.co.in

ISBN 978-93-80829-45-6
First published 2016

Price : ₹ 800

Contents

Preface vii

Foreword ix

Abbreviations xi

List of Transliteration xvi

Catalogue 1—224

Preface

There is almost an inexhaustible and unexplored treasure of manuscripts on Indian music and dance, in classical as well as in modern Indian languages, lying buried across the world. Only a very limited number of these have been published or made use of by some scholars, while doing research in Indian music or allied subjects, but most of them still wait to see the light of the day and be avaliable to those who want to consult them. These manuscripts are either in the collections of the institutional libraries or in private collections. Some individuals treasure these as antique, without realising the extent of damage they do by depriving the world to have glimpse of these and gather the knowledge therein.

While looking for some materials related to music and dance in the library of Sangeet Natak Aacademy, I came across some references and manuscripts on the subjects. Since, in many cases, I found that even the catalogues of the manuscript collections were not complied, in some cases where the catalogues were available, they were not in the alphabetical order, what to say to their being descriptive. Not all the manuscripts mentioned in the catalogues from the other countries of the world were avaliable (to this can be added the limitation of my knowledge of various scripts in which the titles were mentioned in the catalogues). It gave me an inspiration to take up the task of collecting information of the manuscripts pertaining to music, dance and dramaturgy.

From the Catalogus Catalogorum by Theodor Aufrecht. Wiesbaden, 1962 (first published in 1896, prepared on the basis of the catalogues and lists of manuscripts in Sanskrit available to him at that time) there could have been more or less an exhaustive bibliography of works in Sanskrit language on the said subjects. A new volume of the Catalogus Catalogorum published by V. Raghavan, University of Madras was also very helpful in peparing the intended bibliography, which at present is based on the extracts from various catalogues. I am sure this publication will throw some new light to these existing ones.

Though it took a long time to accomplish the work, but I hope the result of my efforts would serve the purpose of the research scholars of Indian music, drama and dance. Since some of the titles are really very tantallizing, their critical study should yield fruitful result and original contribution in the field.

Dr. Shankar Dutt Pandey has brought together all the materials collected by me in the form of this catalogue. It could not have been possible without his dedicated help.

This work would not have seen the light of the day without the encouragement of Dr. Dipti S. Tripathi, Former Director of the National Mission for Manuscripts and sincere cooperation of Dr. Sanghamtra Basu, Coordinator Research and Publication, NMM. I am really grateful to National Mission for Manuscripts for bringing out this publication.

Kaushalya Gupta

Foreword

Dr. Kaushalya Gupta is a Sanskrit scholar and former Professor of University of Delhi. The present catalogue of music, dance and drama appears to be the result of her years of patient compilation of available original manuscripts in various languages in different parts of the country and abroad.

Dr. Gupta has gathered information from the Govt. Oriental Library, Mysore, State Central Library-Hyderabad, Persian manuscripts in Aligarh University Library, Lucknow University Library, Govt. Oriental Library, Madras etc. She has also included the manuscripts of the Indian Office Library in London. These manuscripts are written in a wide range of scripts from Devanagari to Telugu, Grantha, Tamil, Marathi, Persian, etc.

This catalogue, as compiled by Dr. Kaushalya Gupta is going to update the already existing inventory and fill in the lacunae in the currently available catalogue of Aufrecht and Raghavan and facilitate new research.

I do hope that this publication will be useful to specialists and researchers in all these three areas.

VEENA JOSHI
Director and Joint-Secretary
National Mission for Manuscripts,
New Delhi

Abbreviations

A C of Ms in the A B S P, Lucknow	:	A Catalogue of Manuscripts in the Akhila Bharatiya Sanskrit Parisad, Compiled by Daulat Ram Juyal, Lucknow, 1963.
C of Ms in the L of H H the M of U, Udaipur, 1943, S B L	:	Catalogue of Manuscripts in the Library of H. H. the Maharana of Udaipur, by M.L. Menaria, Udaipur,1943, Saraswati Bhandar Library.
A C of P & S P Ms D L, Nepal, Calcutta,1905	:	A Catalogue of Palmleaf & Selected Paper Manuscripts, Darbar Library, Nepal, Calcutta, 1905, by H. P. Shastri.
A C of S I S Ms C, London, M. Winternitz, 1902	:	A Catalogue of South Indian Sanskrit Manuscript, London, compiled by M. Winternitz, 1902.
A D C of the O Ms in the D L, Bahawalpur	:	A Descriptive Catalogue of the Oriental Manuscripts in the Durgah Library, Bahawalpur, by Ghulam Sarwar, 1959–60.
A D C of S Ms in the C O L, Trivandrum	:	A Descriptive Catalogue of Sanskrit Manuscripts in the Curator's Office Library, Trivandrum, Edited by Vaidyasastranipuna L. A. Ravi Varma, 1946, Volume-VII.
A D C of the S Ms in the G O M L, Madras, V-XXVIII :	:	A Descriptive Catalogue of the Sanskrit Manuscripts in the Government Oriental Manuscripts Library, Madras, Volume-XXVIII, (Supplemental), by S. K. Shastri, 1939.
A D C of the S Ms in the H H M P L, Trivandrum	:	A Descriptive Catalogue of the Sanskrit Manuscripts in the H. H. Maharajahs Palace Library, Trivandrum, 1938, Volume-VII.
A D C of the T Ms in the T M S S M L, Waltair, 1933, A U S-11	:	A Descriptive Catalogue of the Telugu Manuscripts in the Tanjore Maharaja Serfojis Saraswati Mahal Library, Waltair, 1933, Andhra University Series No. 11.

Andhra Univ. Lib., A. P.	:	Andhra University Library, Andhra Pradesh.
Asiatic Society of Bengal, Cal., 1924, V-I	:	Catalogue of the Persian Manuscripts in the Collection of the Asiatic Society of Bengal, Calcutta, 1924, Volume-I.
Asiatic Society of Bengal, Calcutta, 1926, V-II	:	Catalogue of the Persian Manuscripts in the Collection of the Asiatic Society of Bengal, Calcutta, 1926, Volume-II.
Asiatic Society of Bengal, Calcutta, 1926	:	Descriptive Catalogue of the Persian Manuscripts in the Curzon Collection, Volume –II, Asiatic Society of Bengal by Wladimir Ivanow, Calcutta, 1926.
B H U, Varanasi	:	Banaras Hindu University, Sanskrit Manuscript Catalogue, Varanasi.
B I S M H G C, Poona	:	Bhārata Itihāsa Samśodhaka Maṇḍalastha Hastalikhita Grantha Catalogue, Edited by Hari Sūnu Gaṇeśa, Poona, 1960.
Bodleian LIB., Oxford, U.K.	:	Catalogue of the Persian, Turkish, Hindustani & Pushtu manuscripts in the Bodleian Library, Part-II, by H. Ethe, Oxford at the Clarendon Press, U.K.
B O R I, Poona	:	Bhandarkar Oriental Research Institute, Poona.
British Museum, London	:	Supplementry Catalogue of Sanskrit, Pali & Prakrta Manuscripts in the British Museum, London, 1892-1966.
C of P & A Ms in the G O M L, Madras	:	Catalogue of Persian & Arabic Manuscripts in the Government Oriental Manuscript Library, Madras, by T. Chandrasekharan.
C of P Ms in the I O L, London, V-I, Pt-II	:	Catalogue of Persian Manuscripts in the India Office Library, London, Volume-I, Part-II.
C of S Ms in the I O L, London, V-I, Pt-II	:	Catalogue of Sanskrit Manuscripts in the India Office Library, London, Volume-I, Part-II.
C of S Ms in the I O L, London, V-II	:	Catalogue of Sanskrit Manuscripts in the India Office Library, London, Volume-II.
C of S & P Ms in M S P C, L D B S V, Ahmedabad	:	Catalogue of Sanskrit & Prakrita Manuscripts in Muniraja Sri Punyavijayaji's Collection, Lalbhai Dalapatbhai Bhartiya Sanskrit Vidyamandir, Ahmedabad, Compiled by Muniraja Sri Punyavijayaji's, Edited by Pt. A. P. Shah, 1965.

C of the H Ms in the I O L, London	:	Catalogue of the Hindustani Manuscripts in the India Office Library, London
C of the P Ms in the Būhār Library, V-I	:	Catalogue of the Persian manuscripts in the Būhār Library by Maulavī Qāsin Hasīr Raḍavī & Maulavī Abdul-Muqtadir, Volume -I.
C of the P Ms in the B M, London, 1881, V-II	:	Catalogue of the Persian Manuscripts in the British Museum, London, 1881, Volume-II, by Charles Rieu.
D C of the S Ms in the T M S S M L, Tanjore, V-XVI	:	Descriptive Catalogue of the Sanskrit Manuscripts in the Tanjore Maharajaha Serfojis Saraswati Mahal Library, Tanjore,Vol-XVI, by Shastri.
D C of T M in M D U V S, I L, Adyar, Madras-26	:	Descriptive Catalogue of Tamil Manuscripts in Mahāmahopādhyāya Dr. U.V. Svāmināthana Iyer Library, Adyar, Madras-26.
G O M L, Triplicane, Madras	:	Government Oriental Manuscript Library, Triplicane, Madras.
Gujrat Vidya Sabha, Ahmedabad	:	A Descriptive Catalogue of Sanskrit Manuscripts, Gujrat Vidya Sabha, Ahmedabad, 1964, Compiled & Edited by Priyabala Shah.
Kerala Univ. Lib., Trivandrum	:	Kerala University Library, Trivandrum.
K M U H H G K S T V, Kashi	:	"Khoja" Me Upalabdha Hastalikhita Hindi Grantho Ka Satrahavā Traivārṣika Vivaraṇa, Edited by – Pt. Vidyābhūṣaṇa Miśra, 1926-43.
L of S Ms in P L of S I, Madras, 1880, V-I	:	List of Sanskrit Manuscripts in Private Library of Southern India, Madras, by Gustov Oppert, 1880, Volume-I.
Lucknow Univ. Lib., Lucknow	:	A Catalogue of Oriental Manuscripts in Lucknow University Library, Lucknow, by Kali Prasad, 1951.
Maulana Azad Lib., A M U, Aligarh	:	Maulana Azad Library, Aligarh Muslim University, Aligarh.
Nagpur Univ. Lib., 1957	:	Catalogue of Sanskrit Manuscripts in the Nagpur University Library, Edited by V.W. Karambdlar, 1957.
Nagari Pracharini Sabha, Varanasi	:	Hastalikhita Hindi Pustakon ka Sankshipta Vivarana, Nagari Pracharini Sabha, Varanasi, 1900-1955 A.D. हस्तलिखित हिन्दी पुस्तकों का संक्षिप्त विवरण, नागरी प्रचारिणी सभा, वाराणसी,1900 1905 ई०

National Lib., Belvedere, Calcutta-27	:	National Library, Belvedere, Calcutta-27.
N of S Ms Pub. by G of B, Calcutta, 1871	:	Notices of Sanskrit Manuscripts published by Government of Bengal, Calcutta, by Rajendra lāla mitrā, Volume-I, 1871.
O I, Baroda	:	Oriental Institute, Baroda.
Oriental Public Lib., Bankipore, Patna	:	Supplement to the Catalogue of the Persian Manuscripts in the Oriental Public Library, Bankipore, Patna, Volume-II, by Maulavi Abdul Muqtadir, Calcutta, 1933.
O R I, Mysore	:	Oriental Research Institute, Mysore.
Patna Univ. Lib., Bihar	:	Patna University Library, Bihar.
Prachina Sahitya Shodh Sansthana, Udaipur	:	Rajasthan Me Hindi Ke Hastalikhita Grantho Ki Khoj (sec. Part) (Cha) Sangita-grantha, by Agarachand Nahta, Prachina Sahitya Shodh Sansthana, Udaipur.
R O I, Jodhpur, Pt.-I	:	Catalogue of Sanskrit & Persian Manuscripts in the Rajasthan Oriental Institute, Jodhpur, Part-I, Jaipur Collection, 1966.
R O I, Jodhpur, Pt.-II	:	A Catalogue of Sanskrit & Persian Manuscripts in the Rajasthan Oriental Institute, Jodhpur, Part-II, Jaipur Collection, 1966.
R on the S for S Ms. in the B P, Bombay	:	Report on the Search for Sanskrit Manuscripts in the Bombay Presidency, Bombay, 1897, by R. G. Bhandarkar.
R P G V-II, O R I, Jodhpur	:	Rajasthan Puratana Granthamala Volume-II, by Jin Vijaymuni, Oriental Research Institute, Jodhpur, Hastalikhita Grantha Suchi, Jodhapur.
Skt. College Banarasa, Allahabad, 1902	:	List of Sanskrit, Jain & Hindi Manuscripts Sanskrit College Banaras, Allahabad, 1902.
Skt. College Banarasa, Allahabad, 1911	:	Catalogue of the Sanskrit Manuscripts in the Sanskrit College Banaras, Allahabad, 1911.
State Central Lib., Hyderabad	:	State Central Library, Hyderabad, Andhra Pradesh.
T A C C, Wiesbaden, 1962, Pt-	:	Theodor Aufrecht Catalogus Catalogorum , Wiesbaden, 1962, Part-I.
T T R on the S of H Ms, Allahabad	:	The Twelfth Report on the Search of Hindi Manuscripts Volume-I, by Hiralāla, Allahabad-1944.

Utkal Univ. Lib., Bhuvaneswar	: Utkal University Library, Vani Vihar, Bhuvaneswar.
Varanaseya Skt. Visvavidyalaya Lib., Varanasi	: A Descriptive Catalogue of the Sanskrit Manuscripts, Varanaseya Sanskrit Visvavidyalaya Library, Varanasi, 1965, Volume-XII.
Venkatesvara Univ., Tirupati	: Venkatesvara University, Tirupati.
V V R I, Hoshiarpur	: Catalogue of V V R I Manuscripts Collection, Visvesvaranand Vedic Research Institute, Hoshiarpur, by Visvabandhu, Part-I, 1956

B. No.	:	Burnell Number
cm.	:	Centimeter
Cond.	:	Condition
C.O.L. No.	:	Curator's Office Library Number
D O C	:	Date of Composition
D O T	:	Date of transcription
Edi. by	:	Edited by
G. No.	:	General Number
Gra.	:	Granth
Incomp.	:	Incomplete
Lang.	:	Language
Mat.	:	Material
Opp. No.	:	Oppert Number
Oxf. No.	:	Oxford Number
Pub. By	:	Published by
P. Year	:	Publication Year
Sam.	:	Samvat
Te.	:	Telugu
V. S.	:	Vikram Samvat

Key to Transliteration

VOWELS

अ a	आ ā	इ i	ई ī = ī	उ u	ऊ ū
(but)	(palm)	(it)	(beet)	(put)	(pool)
ऋ ṛ	ए e	ऐ ai	ओ o	औ au	
(rhythm)	(play)	(air)	(toe)	(loud)	

CONSONANTS

Guttural	क ka	ख* kha	ग ga	घ gha	ङ ṅa
	(skate)	(blockhead)	(gate)	(ghost)	(sing)
Palatal	च ca	छ cha	ज ja	झ jha	ञ ña
	(chunk)	(catchhim)	(john)	(hedgehog)	(bunch)
Cerebral	ट ṭa	ठ* ṭha	ड/ड़ ḍa	ढ*/ढ़ ḍha	ण* ṇa
	(start)	(anthill)	(dart)	(godhead)	(under)
Dental	त ta	थ tha	द da	ध dha	न na
	(path)	(thunder)	(that)	(breathe)	(numb)
Labial	प pa	फ* pha	ब ba	भ bha	म ma
	(spin)	(philosophy)	(bin)	(abhor)	(much)
Semi-vowels	य ya	र ra	ल la	व va	
	(young)	(drama)	(luck)	(vile)	
Sibilants	श śa	ष ṣa	स sa	ह ha	
	(shove)	(bushel)	(so)	(hum)	
Others	क्ष kṣa	त्र tra	ज्ञ jña	ळ* l	ॠ* ṝ
	(*kṣātriya*)	(*triśūla*)	(*jñānī*)	(play)	

अं (—) *ṁ* or *ṃ amusūra* (nasalisation of preceding vowel) like *saṁskṛti/or soṃskṛti*

अः *visarga* = *ḥ* (aspiration of preceding vowel like (*prātaḥ*)

ऽ *Avagraha* consonant #' consonant (like-*imé vasthitā*)

Anusvāra at the end of a line is presented by m (म्) and not *ṁ*

*No exact English equivalents for these letters.

Note on Diacritical Marks

Standard diacritical marks for Devanagari script have been used throughout. However long and short syllables for "e" and "o" as "ē" and "ō" are distinguished only for the words in Telugu and Tamil languages.

A

Title	: ***Abhijñānaśākuntalam with Sanskrit Ṭīkā***
	अभिज्ञानशाकुन्तलम् संस्कृत टीका के साथ
Author	: Kālidāsa
Size	: 14.3″ × 1.3″
Folios	: 37
Language	: Sanskrit
Source	: Bhuvaneswar Museum, Bhuvaṇeswar

Title	: ***Abhilaṣitārtha Cintāmaṇiḥ***
	अभिलषितार्थचिन्तामणिः
Author	: Someśvaraḥ
Source	: Venkatesvara Univ., Tirupati

Title	: ***Abhinavabharatasārasaṅgrahaḥ***
	अभिनवभरतसारसंग्रहः
Source	: O R I, Mysore
No.	: A 65

Title	: ***Abhinavabharatasārasaṅgraha***
	अभिनवभरतसारसंग्रह
Author	: Mummaḍi Cikka Bhūpāla
Mat.	: Paper
Size	: 7½″ × 12⅞″
Pages	: 208
Script	: Devanāgarī
Cond.	: Bad
Dated	: 1900 AD
Source	: C of S mss in the I O L, London, Vol II
Ms. No.	: 7902
Acc. No.	: 3740

A treatise on Music, Singing etc. The manuscript is a very bad copy of an inaccurate and often defective or illegible original. Many lacunae are indicated and the copies often misread the original.

Title	: ***Abhinavabhāratī***
	अभिनवभारती
Author	: Abhinavagupta
Size	: 22 × 2 cm.
Folios	: 130
Illustration	: 8
Script	: Malayalam

Source : A D C of the S mss in the H H M P L, Trivandrum

S. No. : 1404

Title : ***Abhinavabhāratī***

अभिनवभारती

Author : Abhinavagupta

Size : 21½ × 2 cm.

Folios : 118

Illustration : 10

Script : Malayalam

Source : A D C of the S mss in the H H M P L, Trivandrum

S. No. : 1405

Title : ***Abhinavabhāratī***

अभिनवभारती

Author : Abhinavagupta

Source : British Museum, London

No. : 14055 b 36(1)

The commentary on "Bharatanā-yaśāstra".

Title : ***Abhinavabhāratī***

अभिनवभारती

Author : Abhinavagupta

Source : Lucknow Univ. Lib.

Call. No. : 891.22 A14A

Acc. No. : 45205, 4521-16

Title : ***Abhinavabhāratī***

अभिनवभारती

Author : Abhinavagupta

Source : Venkatesvara Univ., Tirupati

Title : ***Abhinavābjodaya-sulocanāni***

अभिनवाब्जोदयसुलोचनानि

Author : Aruṇācala Pillai

Source : British Museum, London

No. : 14053 b 45

A treatise in verse on the actor's art with Telugu interpretation. It was published from Madras in 1907 AD

Title : ***Abhinavarāgamañjarī***

अभिनवरागमंजरी

Author : Viṣṇuśarmā

Edi. by : Bhālacandra Sītārāma Sukthaṅkara

Dated : 1921 AD

Source : British Museum, London

No. : 14055 e 5 (2)

A manual of musical modes.

Title : ***Abhinavatālamañjarī***

अभिनवतालमंजरी

Author : Kāśīnātha

Pages : 14

Pub. by : Viṣṇu Nārāyaṇa Mātakhaṇḍe

Pub. from : Bombay

Dated : 1914 AD

Source : British Museum, London

A metrical work on musical rhythms.

Its English translation done by "Ānandakumāra Svāmī and Gopal Kṛṣṇāyyara Duggirala with introduction.

Title : ***Abhinayabharataśāstraṃ***

अभिनयभरतशास्त्रम्

Source : O R I, Mysore

No. : 4758

Title : ***Abhinayadarpaṇa***

अभिनयदर्पण

Author : Nandikeśvara

Size : 6⅞″ × 1⅝″

Folios : 46

Illustration : 7

Script : Grantha

Source : A C of S I S Ms, London,1902

S. No. : 110

Title : ***Abhinayadarpaṇa***

अभिनयदर्पण

Author : Abhinava Nandikeśvar

Source : British Museum, London

No. : 14055 f 2

Title : ***Abhinayadarpaṇa***

अभिनयदर्पण

Mat. : European paper

Size : 9″ × 7⅜″

Folios : 17

Lines : 20

Script : Devanāgarī

Source : C of S mss in the I O L, London, Vol I, Pt-II

S. No. : 1248

Acc. No. : 3090

A Treatise on the gestures and motions of the hands, as practised by dancers, for the purpose of mimic representation.

(Cf. Aufrecht, Cat., p. 879; 202)

Title : ***Abhinayadarpaṇa***

अभिनयदर्पण

Size : 13½″ × 8½″

Folios : 65

Lines : 20 - 22

Script : Telugu

Source : C of S mss in the I O L, London, Vol I, Pt-II

S. No. : 1249

Acc. No. : 3028
With a brief Telugu explanation.
(Cf. Burnell, Index of Tanjore mss, p. 60)

Title : ***Abhinayadarpaṇa***
अभिनयदर्पण
Size : 6½" × 8¼"
Folios : 18
Lines : 18 - 21
Script : Telugu
Dated : 1870 AD
Source : C of S mss in the I O L, London, Vol I, Pt-II
S. No. : 5270
Acc. No. : 436 C
A treatise on the use of gesture by singers, dancers to express the feelings of the subject of their representation, in three sections. There are several copies of a work of this name given in Burnell, Tanjore Cat. p. 60, but of the descriptions agree with this work.

Title : ***Abhinayadarpaṇa***
अभिनयदर्पण
Author : Unknown
Source : Lucknow Univ. Lib.
Call. No. : 891.22 A14
Acc. No. : 45298

Title : ***Abhinayadarpaṇa***
अभिनयदर्पण
Author : Nandikeśvara
Leaves : 15
Granths : 600
Source : O I, Baroda
Acc. No. : 9996 (b)

Title : ***Abhinayadarpaṇa***
अभिनयदर्पण
Author : Nṛsiṁhācāra
Size : 300 × 12 mm.
Script : Grantha
Ms. W P : Mysore with Arcaka Yogānanda Bhaṭṭa
Source : L of S mss in P L of S I, Madras, 1880, Vol I
S. No. : 15

Title : ***Abhinayadarpaṇa***
अभिनयदर्पण
Author : Vīrarāghava
Size : 200 × 8 mm.
Script : Grantha
Ms. W P : Mysore with Arcaka Yogānanda Bhaṭṭa
Source : L of S mss in P L of S I, Madras, 1880, Vol I
S. No. : 950

Title : ***Abhinayadarpaṇa***

अभिनयदर्पण

Author : Vīrāsma Ayaṅgara

Script : Grantha

Ms. W P : Mysore with Arcaka Yogānanda Bhaṭṭa

Source : L of S mss in P L of S I, Madras, 1880, Vol I

S. No. : 2503

Title : ***Abhinayadarpaṇa***

अभिनयदर्पण

Author : Unknown

Ms. W P : With Library of H.H. the R. of Vizagpataṃ

Source : L of S mss in P L of S I, Madras, 1880, Vol I

S. No. : 7264

Title : ***Abhinayadarpaṇa***

अभिनयदर्पण

Author : Unknown

Ms. W P : With Subramaṇya Dīkṣita

Source : L of S mss in P L of S I, Madras, 1880, Vol I

S. No. : 450

Title : ***Abhinayadarpaṇa***

अभिनयदर्पण

Author : Unknown

Ms. W P : D. Śāmaṇācārī of Śrīmuṣṇaṃ

Source : L of S mss in P L of S I, Madras, 1880, Vol I

S. No. : 500

Title : ***Abhinayadarpaṇa***

अभिनयदर्पण

Author : Unknown

Ms. W P : Anantarāma Śāstrī

Source : L of S mss in P L of S I, Madras, 1880, Vol I

S. No. : 2205

Title : ***Abhinayadarpaṇa***

अभिनयदर्पण

Author : Unknown

Ms. W P : Gopāla Bhārgava

Source : L of S mss in P L of S I, Madras, 1880, Vol I

S. No. : 5473

Title : ***Abhinayadarpaṇa***

अभिनयदर्पण

Author : Jadunātha Sinha Mahāpātrā

Size : 10.5″ × 1.2″

Pages : 64

Language : Oriya

Source : Utkal Univ. Lib., Bhuvaneswar

Title : *Abhinayadarpaṇaḥ*

अभिनयदर्पणः

Author : Unknown

Size : $16^{1\backslash 8''} \times 1\frac{1}{4}''$

Leaves : 85

Granths : 1275

Script : Grantha

Source : D C of the S mss in the T M S S M L, Tanjore, Vol XVI

S. No. : 10685

B. No. : 11516

Title : *Abhinayadarpaṇaḥ*

अभिनयदर्पणः

Author : Unknown

Script : Grantha

Text : Incomplete

Source : D C of the S mss in the T M S S M L, Tanjore, Vol XVI

S. No. : 10686

B. No. : 11519

Title : *Abhinayadarpaṇaḥ*

अभिनयदर्पणः

Author : Unknown

Script : Tamil/Grantha

Text : Incomplete

Source : D C of the S mss in the T M S S M L, Tanjore, Vol XVI

S. No. : 10687

B. No. : 11521 a

Title : *Abhinayadarpaṇaḥ*

अभिनयदर्पणः

Author : Unknown

Script : Grantha

Text : Incomplete

Source : D C of the S mss in the T M S S M L, Tanjore, Vol XVI

S. No. : 10688

B. No. : 11533

Title : *Abhinayadarpaṇaḥ*

अभिनयदर्पणः

Author : Unknown

Script : Grantha

Text : Incomplete

Source : D C of the S mss in the T M S S M L, Tanjore, Vol XVI

S. No. : 10689

B. No. : 14177

Title : *Abhinayadarpaṇaḥ*

अभिनयदर्पणः

Author : Unknown

Script : Telugu

Text : Incomplete

Source : D C of the S mss in the T M S S M L, Tanjore, Vol XVI

S. No. : 10690

B. No. : 11518

Title	: ***Abhinayadarpaṇaḥ***
	अभिनयदर्पणः
Author	: Unknown
Script	: Devanāgarī
Text	: Incomplete
Source	: D C of the S mss in the T M S S M L, Tanjore, Vol XVI
S. No.	: 10691
B. No.	: 6651

Title	: ***Abhinayadarpaṇaḥ***
	अभिनयदर्पणः
Author	: Unknown
Script	: Telugu
Text	: Incomplete
Source	: D C of the S mss in the T M S S M L, Tanjore, Vol XVI
S. No.	: 10692
B. No.	: 11536 a

Title	: ***Abhinayadarpaṇaḥ***
	अभिनयदर्पणः
Author	: Unknown
Script	: Telugu
Text	: Incomplete
Source	: D C of the S mss in the T M S S M L, Tanjore, Vol XVI
S. No.	: 10693
B. No.	: 11536 b

Title	: ***Abhinayadarpaṇaḥ***
	अभिनयदर्पणः
Author	: Unknown
Script	: Telugu
Text	: Incomplete
Source	: D C of the S mss in the T M S S M L, Tanjore, Vol XVI
S. No.	: 10694
B. No.	: 11524

Title	: ***Abhinayadarpaṇaṃ with Āndhra Ṭīkā***
	अभिनयदर्पणम् आन्ध्र टीका के साथ
Author	: Unknown
Size	: 17½ × 1¾ cm.
Folios	: 17
Illustration	: 8
Script	: Telugu
Source	: A D C of the S mss in the G O M L, Madras, Vol XXVIII
No.	: 15864

Title	: ***Abhinayadarpaṇam***
	अभिनयदर्पणम्
Author	: Nandikeśvara
Mat.	: Palmleaf
Size	: 41 × 3.5 cm.
Pages	: 20
Script	: Grantha

Source : G O M L, Triplicane, Madras

Title : ***Abhinayadarpaṇam***
अभिनयदर्पणम्
Author : Nandikeśvara
Mat. : Paper
Size : 31.5 × 21.3 cm.
Pages : 18
Script : Telugu
Source : G O M L, Triplicane, Madras

Title : ***Abhinayadarpaṇam***
अभिनयदर्पणम्
Author : Nandikeśvara
Mat. : Paper
Size : 27 × 24.6 cm.
Pages : 15
Script : Devanāgarī
Source : G O M L, Triplicane, Madras

Title : ***Abhinayadarpaṇam***
अभिनयदर्पणम्
Author : Nandikeśvara
Mat. : Paper
Size : 33.5 × 21 cm.
Pages : 8
Script : Telugu
Source : G O M L, Triplicane, Madras

Title : ***Abhinayadarpaṇam***
अभिनयदर्पणम्
Author : Nandikeśvara
Mat. : Palmleaf
Size : 43 × 4 cm.
Script : Nandināgarī
Source : G O M L, Triplicane, Madras

Title : ***Abhinayadarpaṇam with Telugu Ṭīkā***
अभिनयदर्पणम् तेलुगू टीका के साथ
Author : Nandikeśvara
Mat. : Palmleaf
Size : 37 × 3.6 cm.
Pages : 5
Script : Telugu
Source : G O M L, Triplicane, Madras

Title : ***Abhinayadarpaṇam with Telugu Ṭīkā***
अभिनयदर्पणम् तेलुगू टीका के साथ
Author : Nandikeśvara
Mat. : Palmleaf
Size : 44 × 3.6 cm.
Script : Telugu
Source : G O M L, Triplicane, Madras

Title : ***Abhinayadarpaṇam***
अभिनयदर्पणम्
Author : Nandikeśvara
Mat. : Palmleaf
Size : 36 × 3.5 cm.
Pages : 6

Script : Telugu
Source : G O M L, Triplicane, Madras

Title : ***Abhinayadarpanam***
अभिनयदर्पणम्
Author : Nandikeśvara
Mat. : Palmleaf
Size : 24 × 4.6 cm.
Pages : 4
Script : Kannada
Source : G O M L, Triplicane, Madras

Title : ***Abhinayadarpaṇam with Telugu Ṭīkā***
अभिनयदर्पणम् तेलुगू टीका के साथ
Author : Nandikeśvara
Mat. : Palmleaf
Size : 38.3 × 3 cm.
Script : Telugu
Source : G O M L, Triplicane, Madras

Title : ***Abhinayadarpaṇam with Telugu Ṭīkā***
अभिनयदर्पणम् तेलुगू टीका के साथ
Author : Nandikeśvara
Mat. : Palmleaf
Size : 31 × 20 cm.
Pages : 1
Script : Telugu
Source : G O M L, Triplicane, Madras

Title : ***Abhinayadarpaṇam***
अभिनयदर्पणम्
Author : Unknown
Mat. : Paper
Size : 21 × 15.5 cm.
Pages : 11
Script : Telugu
Source : G O M L, Triplicane, Madras

Title : ***Abhinayadarpaṇam***
अभिनयदर्पणम्
Author : Unknown
Mat. : Palmleaf
Size : 38.1 × 4.2 cm.
Pages : 28
Language : Sanskrit/Tamil
Script : Tamil/Grantha
Source : G O M L, Triplicane, Madras

Title : ***Abhinayadarpaṇaṃ***
अभिनयदर्पणम्
Source : O R I , Mysore
No. : C 287

Title : ***Abhinayadarpaṇamu***
अभिनयदर्पणमु
Author : Vicitrarāyavataṃsa
Size : $18^{3/4''} \times 1^{3/10''}$
Lines : 28
Granths : 425

Source : A D C of the T mss in the T M S S M L, Waltair, 1933, A U S-11

No. : 718

B. No. : 11537

Title : ***Abhinayadarpaṇamu***

अभिनयदर्पणमु

Author : Vicitrarāyavataṃsa

Pages : 52

Language : Telugu

Source : Andhra Univ. Lib.

Title : ***Abhinayadarpaṇa Prakāśa***

अभिनयदर्पण प्रकाश

Author : Jadunātha Mahāpātra

Size : 16.2″ × 1.3″

Folios : 81

Language : Sanskrit & Oriya Translation

Source : Bhuvaneswar Museum, Bhuvaneswar

Title : ***Abhinayādivicāraḥ***

अभिनयादिविचारः

Author : Unknown

Leaves : 49

Size : $19^{1/8}$″ × 1¾″

Script : Telugu

Granths : 1400

Source : D C of the S mss in the T M S S M L, Tanjore, Vol XVI

S. No. : 10695

B. No. : 11523

Title : ***Abhinayalakṣaṇādi***

अभिनयलक्षणादि

Author : Unknown

Size : $10^{7/8}$″ × $1^{3/8}$″

Leaves : 42

Granths : 250

Script : Grantha /Telugu

Source : D C of the S mss in the T M S S M L, Tanjore, Vol XVI

S. No. : 10699

B. No. : 14178

Title : ***Abhinayalakṣaṇam***

अभिनयलक्षणम्

Source : O R I , Mysore

No. : 3494

Title : ***Abhinayalakṣaṇam***

अभिनयलक्षणम्

Source : O R I, Mysore

No. : 4121

Title : ***Abhinayalakṣaṇam***

अभिनयलक्षणम्

Author : Śṛṅgāraśekhara

Size : 16⅞″ × 1¾″

Leaves : 54

Granths : 1650

Script : Telugu

Source : D C of the S mss in the T M S S M L, Tanjore, Vol XVI

S. No. : 10684

B. No. : 11531

Title : *Abhinayalakṣaṇam with Āndhra Ṭīkā*

अभिनयलक्षणम् आंध्र टीका के साथ

Author : Unknown

Size : 16¼″ × 1½″

Leaves : 17

Granths : 350

Script : Telugu

Source : D C of the S mss in the T M S S M L, Tanjore, Vol XVI

S. No. : 10696

B. No. : 11530

Title : *Abhinayalakṣaṇam*

अभिनयलक्षणम्

Author : Unknown

Size : 19⅝″ × 1½″

Leaves : 10

Granths : 300

Script : Telugu

Source : D C of the S mss in the T M S S M L, Tanjore, Vol XVI

S. No. : 10697

B. No. : 11543 a

Title : *Abhinayalakṣaṇam*

अभिनयलक्षणम्

Author : Unknown

Size : 9½″ × 1 1\3″

Leaves : 135

Granths : 1040

Script : Telugu

Source : D C of the S mss in the T M S S M L, Tanjore, Vol XVI

S. No. : 10698

B. No. : 11542

Title : *Abhinayalakṣaṇam*

अभिनयलक्षणम्

Author : Śivadāsa Kavi

Source : Venkatesvara Univ., Tirupati

Title : *Abhinayamukuraḥ*

अभिनयमुकुरः

Source : O R I , Mysore

No. : SV 116

Title : *Abhinayaprakaraṇam*

अभिनयप्रकरणम्

Source : O R I , Mysore

No. : 24

Title	: ***Abhinayaśāstram (Kohalīyam) with Telugu Ṭīkā***
	अभिनयशास्त्रम् (कोहलीयम्) तेलुगू टीका के साथ
Author	: Kohala
Mat.	: Paper
Size	: 31 × 20 cm.
Script	: Telugu
Source	: G O M L, Triplicane, Madras

Title	: ***Abhinayaśāstram***
	अभिनयशास्त्रम्
Author	: Unknown
Mat.	: Paper
Size	: 20 × 16 cm.
Script	: Telugu
Source	: G O M L, Triplicane, Madras

Title	: ***Abhinayaśāstraṃ***
	अभिनयशास्त्रम्
Author	: Unknown
Mat.	: Paper
Size	: 24 × 17.5 cm.
Script	: Telugu
Source	: G O M L, Triplicane, Madras

Title	: ***Abhinayaśāstram with Telugu Ṭīkā***
	अभिनयशास्त्रम् तेलुगू टीका के साथ
Author	: Unknown
Mat.	: Paper
Size	: 31 × 20 cm.
Script	: Telugu
Source	: G O M L, Triplicane, Madras

Title	: ***Abun Nagmā***
	अबुन नगमा
Author	: Unknown
Size	: 9.1″ × 6:6″ × 3.5″
Folios	: 76
Dated	: 1130 AH
Source	: A D C of the O mss in the D L, Bahawalpur
No.	: 267

Title	: ***A Collection of Treatises on Indian Music***
	अ कलेक्शन ऑफ ट्रीटाइजेस् ऑन इंडियन म्यूजिक
Size	: 8¾″ × 5½″ ; 7″ × 4″
Illustration	: 13
Pub. by	: Imperial Lib., Calcutta
Source	: C of the P mss in the Būhār Library, Vol I
No.	: 236
	(I) Usūl-i-Ginā, Folios 1b – 4a, On different tunes and melodies by Rai Dāl Chand Sāha Sāhil on Dated - 1178 AH (1764 AD).
	(II) Risālah-i-Mūsīqī , Folios 17b – 38b, Rāgas and

Rāgiṇīs have been described in this book.

(III) Usūl-Un-Nagmāt , Folios 40b – 99b, Dated – 18th century.

Title : ***Ādibharataṃ***

आदिभरतम्

Author : Unknown

Size : 18⅞″ × 1¼″

Leaves : 3 - 83

Granths : 900

Script : Telugu

Source : D C of the S mss in the T M S S M L, Tanjore, Vol XVI

S. No. : 10661

B. No. : 11534

Title : ***Ādibharataṃ***

आदिभरतम्

Author : Unknown

Script : Grantha

Text : Incomplete

Source : D C of the S mss in the T M S S M L, Tanjore, Vol XVI

S. No. : 10662

B. No. : 11569 b

Title : ***Ādimular-noṇḍi-nāṭakaṃ***

आदिमूलर नोण्डि नाटकम्

Author : Māri Muttu

Mat. : Palmleaf

Size : 45.7 × 2.5 cm.

Pages : 74

Language : Tamil

Script : Tamil

Source : G O M L, Triplicane, Madras

Title : ***A Fragment of a Large Treatise on Indian Music***

अ फ्राग्मेन्ट् ऑफ अ लार्ज ट्रीटाइज ऑन इंडियन म्यूजिक

Size : 8½″ × 6″ ; 6″ × 3½″

Folios : 63

Lines : 11–17

Dated : 18th century

Pub. By : Imperial Lib., Calcutta

Source : C of the P mss in the Būhār Library, Vol I

No. : 237

Title : ***A Fragment of the Saṅgītadarpaṇa (Chapter II)***

अ फ्राग्मेन्ट् ऑफ दी संगीतदर्पण (अध्याय *II*)

Size : 9″ × 4⅛″

Folios : 1

Lines : 12

Script : Devanāgarī

Dated : 19th century

Source : C of S mss in the I O L, London, Vol II

Ms. No. : 7901

Acc. No. : 3955 W

Title : ***A List of Rāgās or Tunes***
अ लिस्ट् ऑफ रागाज और ट्यून्स्

Size : 6⅞" × 8½"
Folios : 2
Lines : 23
Script : Devanāgarī
Dated : 1875 AD
Source : C of S mss in the I O L, London, Vol II
Ms. No. : 5195
B. No. : 487 f

List of Rāgās or Tunes. It begins folio 1: कर्नाटक राग, घनराग 1, नाटराग 2, गौलराग 3, 124 of these are indicated, ending with गोडुमल्लार 123, हंसक 124. There two and no. 121, 122 being121 and 122 being classified under the Sub-head मध्ययमामराग. There comes हिन्दुस्थानीराग, रामकलीराग 1, गुणकली राग 2, भैरवराग 3, The are 38 ending— कुकुमी 37, दीपक 38. This is apparently Transcript of some unspecified Tanjore list.

Title : ***Amudamathananāṭakam***
अमुदमथननाटकम्

Author : Nīlāyatākai Amthā
Mat. : Palmleaf
Size : 33 × 3.2 cm.
Pages : 238
Language : Tamil
Script : Tamil
Source : G O M L, Triplicane, Madras

Title : ***Anagharāghava Nāṭaka***
अनघराघव नाटक

Author : Murāri Miśra
Size : 14" × 1.3"
Folios : 103
Language : Sanskrit
Source : Bhuvaneswar Museum, Bhuvaneswar

Title : ***Ānandasañjīvana***
आनन्दसंजीवन

Author : Madanapāla
Size : 10½" × 3½"
Folios : 40
Language : Sanskrit
Source : Asiatic Society, 1, Park Street, Calcutta-16

Title : ***Ānandasañjīvanam***
आनन्दसंजीवनम्

Author : Unknown
Source : Venkatesvara Univ., Tirupati

Title : *Aṅgadarpaṇa*

अंगदर्पण

Author : Gulām Nabī 'Rasalīn' Bilgrāmī

Size : 21 × 15 cm.

Pages : 16

Language : Hindi

Script : Urdu

Dated : Samvat 1829

Source : State Central Lib., Hyderabad Consists of 179 Hindi Dohās on Śikha-Nakha.

Title : *Aṅgahāralakṣanam*

अंगहारलक्षणम्

Author : Unknown

Size : 11 × 2 cm.

Folios : 64

Illustration : 10

Script : Grantha

Source : A D C of the S mss in the H H M P L, Trivandrum

S. No. : 1403

Title : *Aṅgahāravartikam*

अंगहारवर्तिकम्

Author : Unknown

Source : Venkatesvara Univ., Tirupati

Title : *Anītanāṭakam*

अनीतनाटकम्

Author : Tillaivitaṅkan Mārimuttappillai

Mat. : Palmleaf

Size : 42 × 3.2 cm.

Pages : 74

Language : Tamil

Script : Tamil

Source : G O M L, Triplicane, Madras

Title : *Anūpasaṅgītaratnākara (Dvitīya Rāgādhyāya)*

अनूपसंगीतरत्नाकर (द्वितीय रागाध्याय)

Author : Bhāvabhaṭṭa

Folios : 259

Dated : 18th century

Source : R P G Vol II, O R I, Jodhpur

S. No. : 6741

Title : *Arcunantavam*

अर्चुनन्तवम्

Author : Pūśari Muttan

Mat. : Palmleaf

Size : 42 × 3.2 cm.

Pages : 40

Language : Tamil

Script : Tamil

Source : G O M L, Triplicane, Madras

Title : *Aricandrannāṭakam*

अरिचन्द्रन्नाटकम्

Author : Unknown

Mat. : Palmleaf
Size : 42 × 3.8 cm.
Pages : 344
Language : Tamil
Script : Tamil
Source : G O M L, Triplicane, Madras

Title : ***Arjunabharatam***
अर्जुनभरतम्
Author : Arjuna
Size : 16″ × 7″
Leaves : 34
Granths : 1125
Script : Devanāgarī
Source : D C of the S mss in the T M S S M L, Tanjore, Vol XVI
S. No. : 10663
B. No. : 6643 a

Title : ***Arjunabharataṃ***
अर्जुनभरतम्
Author : Arjuna
Script : Telugu
Source : D C of the S mss in the T M S S M L, Tanjore, Vol XVI
S. No. : 10664
B. No. : 11510

Title : ***Arjunabharatam***
अर्जुनभरतम्
Author : Arjuna
Script : Devanāgarī
Source : D C of the S mss in the T M S S M L, Tanjore, Vol XVI
S. No. : 10665
B. No. : 14174

Title : ***Arjunabharataṃ***
अर्जुनभरतम्
Author : Arjuna
Script : Telugu
Source : D C of the S mss in the T M S S M L, Tanjore, Vol XVI
S. No. : 10666
B. No. : 11510 b

Title : ***Arjunādimatsaraḥ***
अर्जुनादिमत्सरः
Author : Suddhasattva Venkatācārya
Mat. : Paper
Size : 27.5 × 24.5 cm.
Script : Devanāgarī
Source : G O M L, Triplicane, Madras

Title : ***Arjunādimatsaraḥ***
अर्जुनादिमत्सरः
Author : Suddhasattva Venkatacāryaḥ
Source : Venkatesvara Univ., Tirupati

Title : ***Aṣl-Al-Usūl***
अस्ल–अल–उसूल
Author : Mohammad Nāsir “Rañja”

Size : 10 3/8″ × 6 1/8″

Folios : 55

Illustration : 15

Dated : 1806 AD

Source : C of P mss in the I O L, London, Vol I, Pt-II

S. No. : 2975

Acc. No. : 3162

Title : ***Asl-Ul-Usūl***

अस्ल–उल–उसूल

Author : Khwāzā Mohammad Nāsīr 'Rañj'

Size : 21.5 × 15.5 cm.

Pages : 56

Language : Persian

Text : Incomplete at end

Source : State Central Lib., Hyderabad The author of this treatise was the grand-son of the famous Urdu poet 'Mīr Dard'. This consists of two chapters, the first with 'Tāla' and second with 'Dai'.

Title : ***Aṣṭottaraśatatālanāma-prakaraṇa***

अष्टोत्तरशततालनामप्रकरण

Author : Unknown

Mat. : European paper

Size : 6 7/8″ × 8½″

Folios : 5

Lines : 19

Script : Devanāgarī

Dated : 1875 AD

Source : C of S mss in the I O L, London, Vol II

Ms. No. : 5194

B. No. : 487 e

This book is an account of 108 Tāla. The mss is incorrect. It appears from a note on folio 2 to be a copy of the Tanjore mss No. 6625 (Tanjore Cat., p. 60b).

Title : ***Aumāpata***

औमापत

Author : Unknown

Pages : 140

Lines : 6

Script : Malayalam

Ms. W P : H. H. The Ciria Anujan Rājā

Source : Private Libraries of Southern India, Madras

S. No. : 2568

Title : ***Aumāpata***

औमापत

Author : Umāpati

Source : T A C C , Wiesbaden, 1962, Pt-I

Opp. No. : 2568

Title	: ***Aumāpataṃ***
	औमापतम्
Author	: Umapati
Size	: 8⅞″ × 5½″
Folios	: 128
Illustration	: 9
Script	: Devanāgarī
Dated	: 14th century
Source	: B O R I, Poona
Acc. No.	: 78/1919-24

Title	: ***Aumāpataṃ***
	औमापतम्
Mat.	: Paper
Size	: 27.8 × 20.5 cm.
Pages	: 42
Script	: Devanāgarī
Source	: G O M L, Triplicane, Madras

Title	: ***Auraṅgajebavilāsa***
	औरंगजेबविलास
Author	: Payandabega
P. Year	: 1922 AD
Source	: Nagari Pracarini Sabha, Varanasi, Vol I
S. No.	: 83

Title	: ***Auraṅgajeba Bilās***
	औरंगजेब बिलास
Author	: Husaini
Size	: 17.5 × 13 cm.
Pages	: 90
Language	: Hindi
Script	: Urdu
Source	: State Central Lib., Hyderabad

B

Title	: ***Bālacaritam***
	बालचरितम्
Mat.	: Palmleaf
Size	: 41 × 3 cm.
Pages	: 5
Script	: Grantha
Source	: G O M L, Triplicane, Madras

Title	: ***Bālacaritam***
	बालचरितम्
Mat.	: Palmleaf
Size	: 41 × 3 cm.
Pages	: 5
Script	: Grantha
Source	: G O M L, Triplicane, Madras

Title	: ***Balarāmabhāratam***
	बलरामभारतम्
Author	: Balarāma Kulaśekhara
Mat.	: Paper
Size	: 33.1 × 21.5 cm.
Pages	: 158
Script	: Devanāgarī
Source	: G O M L, Triplicane, Madras

Title	: ***Balarāmabhāratam***
	बलरामभारतम्
Author	: Balarāma-varmā Mahārāja
Size	: 13 × 2 cm.
Folios	: 133
Illustration	: 7
Script	: Grantha
Dated	: 1724 -1798 AD
Source	: D C of the S mss in the H H M P L, Trivandrum
S. No.	: 1413

Title	: ***Balarāmayaśobhūṣaṇam***
	बलरामयशोभूषणम्
Author	: Sadāśiva Dīkṣita
Size	: 12 ½ × 8 ½ cm.
Folios	: 78
Illustration	: 20
Script	: Devanāgarī
Source	: A D C of S mss in the C O L, Trivandrum
S. No.	: 1200
C.O.L. No.	: 946

Title	: ***Bārajātak Tarjumā***
	बारजातक तर्जुमा
Author	: Mirzā Rośan Zamīr
Size	: 25 × 15 cm.
Pages	: 344
Language	: Persian
Source	: State Central Lib., Hyderabad
	This is a translation of Ahobala's (Probably of Ahobala's Saṅgīta Parijāta)

Title	: ***Bhajanaikkīrttanaikal***
	भजनैकीर्तनैकल्
Author	: Unknown
Mat.	: Palmleaf
Size	: 23.8 × 3.2 cm.
Pages	: 246
Language	: Tamil
Script	: Tamil
Source	: G O M L, Triplicane, Madras

Title	: ***Bhajankīrtanāni***
	भजनकीर्तनानि
Author	: Nāmadeva
Mat.	: Śrītāla
Size	: 18.5 × 4 cm.
Pages	: 8
Script	: Grantha
Source	: G O M L, Triplicane, Madras

Title	: ***Bhaktivaibhava Nāṭaka***
	भक्तिवैभव नाटक
Author	: Kavidiṇḍima Jīvadevācārya
Size	: 12.5″ × 8″
Pages	: 268
Language	: Sanskrit
Source	: Bhuvaneswar Museum, Bhuvaneswar

Title	: ***Bhaktivaibhava Nāṭaka***
	भक्तिवैभव नाटक
Author	: Bahnipati Jībācārya Rājaguru
Size	: 14.5″ × 1.2″
Pages	: 145
Language	: Oriya
Source	: Utkal Univ. Lib., Bhuvaneswar

Title	: ***Bhaktivaibhava Nāṭaka***
	भक्तिवैभव नाटक
Author	: Bahnipati Jībācārya Rājaguru
Size	: 13.5" × 1.1"
Pages	: 64
Lang	: Oriya
Source	: Utkal Univ. Lib., Bhuvaneswar

Title	: ***Bharatabhāṣya (Sarasvatī hṛdayālaṁkāra)***
	भरतभाष्य (सरस्वती हृदयालंकार)
Author	: Nānyadeva

Size : 11½″ × 4⅞″

Folios : 211

Illustration : 11

Dated : 11th or 12th Century AD

Source : B O R I, Poona

Acc. No. : 111/1869-70

Title : ***Bharatacandrikā***

भरतचन्द्रिका

Extent : 1500

Source : O R I, Mysore

No. : A 618

Title : ***Bharatalakṣaṇam***

भरतलक्षणम्

Author : Unknown

Size : 9¾″ × 4½″

Leaves : 13

Granths : 160

Script : Devanāgarī

Source : D C of the S mss in the T M S S M L, Tanjore, Vol XVI

S. No. : 10678

B. No. : 6624

Title : ***Bharatalakṣaṇam***

भरतलक्षणम्

Author : Unknown

Script : Devanāgarī

Source : D C of the S mss in the T M S S M L, Tanjore, Vol XVI

S. No. : 10679

B. No. : 6649

Title : ***Bharatalakṣaṇam***

भरतलक्षणम्

Author : Unknown

Script : Grantha

Source : D C of the S mss in the T M S S M L, Tanjore, Vol XVI

S. No. : 10680

B. No. : 11521 b

Title : ***Bharatalakṣaṇam***

भरतलक्षणम्

Author : Unknown

Script : Telugu

Source : D C of the S mss in the T M S S M L, Tanjore, Vol XVI

S. No. : 10681

B. No. : 11532 c

Title : ***Bharatalakṣaṇam***

भरतलक्षणम्

Author : Unknown

Script : Grantha

Source : D C of the S mss in the T M S S M L, Tanjore, Vol XVI

S. No. : 10682

B. No. : 14175

Title : ***Bharatalakṣaṇam***

भरतलक्षणम्

Author : Unknown

Script : Grantha

Source : D C of the S mss in the T M S S M L, Tanjore, Vol XVI

S. No. : 10683

B. No. : 14176

Title : ***Bharatanāṭakam***

भरतनाटकम्

Author : Unknown

Mat. : Palmleaf

Size : 33.3 × 2.8 cm.

Pages : 308

Language : Tamil

Script : Tamil

Source : G O M L, Triplicane, Madras

Title : ***Bharatanāṭyasaṅgrahaḥ***

भरतनाट्यसंग्रहः

Author : Unknown

Mat. : Palmleaf

Size : 41 × 3 cm.

Script : Telugu

Source : G O M L, Triplicane, Madras

Title : ***Bharatanāṭyaśāstra***

भरतनाट्यशास्त्र

Author : Bharatamuni

Leaves : 100

Grantha : 2200

Source : O I, Baroda

S. No. : 59

Acc. No. : 7104

Title : ***Bharatanāṭyaśāstra***

भरतनाट्यशास्त्र

Author : Bharatamuni

Leaves : 4 - 222

Extent : 2500

Source : O I, Baroda

S. No. : 60

Acc. No. : 11629

Title : ***Bharatanāṭyaśāstra***

भरतनाट्यशास्त्र

Author : Bharatamuni

Leaves : 100

Extent : 2200

Source : O I, Baroda

S. No. : 59

Acc. No. : 7104

Title : ***Bharatanāṭyaśāstra***

भरतनाट्यशास्त्र

Author : Bharatamuni

Leaves : 78 - 79

Granths : 20

Source : O I, Baroda

S. No. : 61

Acc. No. : 13751(e)

Title : ***Bharatanāṭyaśāstram***

भरतनाट्यशास्त्रम्

Source : O R I , Mysore

No. : 472

Title : ***Bharatanaṭyaśāstra-vyākhyā 'Abhinavabhāratī'***

भरतनाट्यशास्त्रव्याख्या 'अभिनवभारती'

Author : Abhinavagupta

Leaves : 137

Granths : 2250

Source : O I, Baroda

S. No. : 62

Acc. No. : 13282

Title : ***Bharatārṇava***

भरतार्णव

Author : Nandikeśvara

Size : 13½" × 8¼"

Folios : 69

Illustration : 20

Dated : 1915 AD

Source : B O R I, Poona

Acc. No. : 42/1916 -18

Title : ***Bharatārṇava***

भरतार्णव

Author : Bharataśāstra

Ms. W P : With Paravastu Veṅkataraṅgācārayār of Vizagpatam

Source : L of S mss in P L of S I, Madras, 1880, Vol I

S. No. : 8128

Title : ***Bharatārṇavaḥ***

भरतार्णवः

Author : Nandikeśa

Mat. : Paper

Size : 22.2 × 14.1 cm.

Script : Devanāgarī

Source : G O M L, Triplicane, Madras

Title : ***Bharatārṇavaḥ***

भरतार्णवः

Author : Nandikeśa

Mat. : Paper

Size : 26.7 × 23.3 cm.

Script : Telugu

Source : G O M L, Triplicane, Madras

Title : ***Bharatārṇavaḥ***
भरतार्णवः
Author : Nandikeśa
Mat. : Palmleaf
Size : 38.5 × 3 cm.
Script : Telugu
Source : G O M L, Triplicane, Madras

Title : ***Bharatārṇavaḥ with Telugu commentary***
भरतार्णवः तेलुगू व्याख्या के साथ
Author : Nandikeśvara
Mat. : Palmleaf
Size : 40.7 × 3.8 cm.
Pages : 80
Script : Telugu
Source : G O M L, Triplicane, Madras

Title : ***Bharatārṇavaḥ with Telugu meaning***
भरतार्णवः तेलुगू अर्थ के साथ
Author : Nandikeśa
Mat. : Paper
Size : 20 × 16 cm.
Script : Telugu
Source : G O M L, Triplicane, Madras

Title : ***Bharatārṇavaḥ with Telugu meaning***
भरतार्णवः तेलुगू अर्थ के साथ
Author : Nandikeśvara
Mat. : Paper
Size : 20 × 16 cm.
Script : Telugu
Source : G O M L, Triplicane, Madras

Title : ***Bharatārṇavaḥ***
भरतार्णवः
Author : Nandikeśvara
Mat. : Paper
Size : 24 × 17.5 cm.
Script : Telugu
Source : G O M L, Triplicane, Madras

Title : ***Bharatārṇavaḥ***
भरतार्णवः
Source : O R I , Mysore
No. : 5279

Title : ***Bharatārṇavaḥ***
भरतार्णवः
Source : O R I , Mysore
No. : 5257

Title : ***Bharatārṇavaḥ***
भरतार्णवः
Author : Nandikeśvara
Size : 9″ × 5½″
Leaves : 12 - 51
Granths : 709
Script : Devanāgarī
Source : D C of the S mss in the T M S

S M L, Tanjore, Vol XVI

S. No. : 10653

B. No. : 14843

Title : ***Bharatārṇavaḥ***

भरतार्णवः

Author : Nandikeśvara

Script : Telugu

Source : D C of the S mss in the T M S S M L, Tanjore, Vol XVI

S. No. : 10654

B. No. : 11515

Title : ***Bharatārṇavaḥ***

भरतार्णवः

Author : Nandikeśvara

Script : Telugu

Source : D C of the S mss in the T M S S M L, Tanjore, Vol XVI

S. No. : 10655

B. No. : 11530 a

Title : ***Bharatārṇavaḥ***

भरतार्णवः

Author : Nandikeśvara

Script : Telugu

Source : D C of the S mss in the T M S S M L, Tanjore, Vol XVI

S. No. : 10656

B. No. : 11598 b

Title : ***Bharatārṇavaḥ***

भरतार्णवः

Author : Nandikeśvara

Script : Telugu

Source : D C of the S mss in the T M S S M L, Tanjore, Vol XVI

S. No. : 10657

B. No. : 11538 b

Title : ***Bharatārṇavaḥ***

भरतार्णवः

Author : Nandikeśvara

Script : Telugu

Source : D C of the S mss in the T M S S M L, Tanjore, Vol XVI

S. No. : 10658

B. No. : 11538 d

Title : ***Bharatārṇavaḥ***

भरतार्णवः

Author : Nandikeśvara

Source : Venkatesvara Univ., Tirupati

Title : ***Bharatārṇavaṃ***

भरतार्णवम्

Source : O R I , Mysore

No. : 3809

Title : ***Bharatārṇavasaṅgrahaḥ***

भरतार्णवसंग्रहः

Author : Unknown

Size : 16″ × 1¼″

Leaves : 11

Granths : 200

Script : Grantha

Source : D C of the S mss in the T M S S M L, Tanjore, Vol XVI

S. No. : 10659

B. No. : 11516 c

Title : ***Bharatārṇavasaṅgrahaḥ***

भरतार्णवसंग्रहः

Author : Unknown

Script : Telugu

Source : D C of the S mss in the T M S S M L, Tanjore, Vol XVI

S. No. : 10660

B. No. : 11525 c

Title : ***Bharatārṇavasāra-saṅgrahaḥ***

भरतार्णवसारसंग्रहः

Author : Unknown

Source : Venkatesvara Univ., Tirupati

Title : ***Bharatārthacandrikā***

भरतार्थचन्द्रिका

Mat. : Paper

Size : 24 × 17.5 cm.

Pages : 5

Script : Telugu

Source : G O M L, Triplicane, Madras

Title : ***Bharatasaṅgīta***

भरतसंगीत

Author : Laghujana (Vikramajīta)

Dated : Sam.-1881

P. Year : 1906 AD

Source : Nagari Pracarini Sabha, Varanasi, Vol II

S. No. : 67

Title : ***Bharatasārasaṅgraha***

भरतसारसंग्रह

Author : Candraśekhara

Size : 7½″ × 12³⁄₈″

Pages : 11 & 77

Lines : 24 - 29

Script : Devanāgarī

Dated : 1900 AD

Source : C of S mss in the I O L, London, Vol II

S. No. : 7914

Acc. No. : 3742

A treatise on dramatology.

Adhyāya I - Pīṭhikāprakaraṇa

Adhyāya II - Asaṃyuta-hastaprakaraṇa

Adhyāya III - Tālanirṇaya

Title : ***Bharatasārasaṅgrahaḥ***

भरतसारसंग्रहः

Source : O R I , Mysore

No. : A 69

Title : ***Bharatasārasaṅgrahaḥ***

भरतसारसंग्रहः

Source : O R I, Mysore

No. : A 66

Title	:	***Bharatasārasaṅgrahamu***
		भरतसारसंग्रहमु
Author	:	Cillakuri Divākarakavi
Mat.	:	Paper
Size	:	21 × 16.5 cm.
Pages	:	48
Language	:	Telugu
Script	:	Telugu
Source	:	G O M L, Triplicane, Madras

Title	:	***Bharatasarvārthasaṅgraha with Āndhra Ṭīkā***
		भरतसर्वार्थसंग्रह आन्ध्र टीका के साथ
Folios	:	96
Illustration	:	8
Source	:	A D C of the S mss in the G O M L, Madras, Vol XXVIII
S. No.	:	15865

Title	:	***Bharatasarvārthasāra-saṅgrahaḥ***
		भरतसर्वार्थसारसंग्रहः
Author	:	Mudumba Nṛsiṁhācārya
Mat.	:	Paper
Size	:	27.5 × 23.5 cm.
Script	:	Devanāgarī
Source	:	G O M L, Triplicane, Madras

Title	:	***Bharatasarvārtha-sārasaṅgrahaḥ with Telugu meaning***
		भरतसर्वार्थसारसंग्रहः तेलुगू अर्थ के साथ
Author	:	Mudumba Nṛsiṁhācārya
Mat.	:	Palmleaf
Size	:	44 × 3.6 cm.
Pages	:	4
Script	:	Grantha
Source	:	G O M L, Triplicane, Madras

Title	:	***Bharataśāstra***
		भरतशास्त्र
Size	:	13⅝" × 1¾"
Leaves	:	46
Lines	:	7 - 12
Script	:	Telugu
Source	:	C of S mss in the I O L, London, Vol II
S. No.	:	5196
Acc. No.	:	122
		A number of sections of a work on music and dancing, claiming the title of भरतशास्त्र, consisting of Skt. Verses and Telugu interpretations, the latter for more extensive.

Title	:	***Bharataśāstra***
		भरतशास्त्र
Author	:	Raghunātha
Ms. W P	:	Mysore with Arcaka Yogānanda Bhaṭṭa
Source	:	L of S mss in P L of S I, Madras, 1880, Vol I
S. No.	:	4099

Title	: ***Bharataśāstra***
	भरतशास्त्र
Author	: Raghunātha
Source	: T A C C, Wiesbaden, 1962, Pt-I
S. No.	: 27 C
B. No.	: 60 b

Title	: ***Bharataśāstragrantha***
	भरतशास्त्रग्रन्थ
Author	: Unknown
Size	: 13¼″ × 8½″
Folios	: 30
Illustration	: 20
Dated	: 1916 AD
Source	: B O R I, Poona
Acc. No.	: 40/1916 -18

Title	: ***Bharataśāstraṃ***
	भरतशास्त्रम्
Author	: Unknown
Folios	: 109
Language	: Tamil
Source	: National Lib., Belvedere, Calcutta-27

Title	: ***Bharataśāstraṃ***
	भरतशास्त्रम्
Source	: O R I, Mysore
No.	: B 1062

Title	: ***Bharataśāstraṃ***
	भरतशास्त्रम्
Author	: Raghunātha
Size	: 8⅝″ × 6¾″
Leaves	: 63
Granths	: 520
Script	: Devanāgarī
Source	: D C of the S mss in the T M S S M L, Tanjore, Vol XVI
S. No.	: 10669
B. No.	: 6643

Title	: ***Bharataśāstraṃ***
	भरतशास्त्रम्
Author	: Unknown
Size	: 10¼″ × 4″
Leaves	: 21
Granths	: 400
Script	: Devanāgarī
Source	: D C of the S mss in the T M S S M L, Tanjore, Vol XVI
S. No.	: 10670
B. No.	: 6648

Title	: ***Bharatasattīraṃ***
	भरतसत्तीरम्
Author	: Unknown
Mat.	: Palmleaf

Size : 24.1 × 2.8 cm.
Pages : 50
Language : Tamil
Script : Tamil
Source : G O M L, Triplicane, Madras

Title : ***Bharatasiddhāntam***
भरतसिद्धान्तम्
Author : Unknown
Mat. : Paper
Size : 34.3 × 22.2 cm.
Pages : 354
Language : Tamil
Script : Tamil & Grantha
Source : G O M L, Triplicane, Madras

Title : ***Bharatavyākhyā***
भरतव्याख्या
Author : Unknown
Size : 21¾ × 2 cm.
Folios : 11
Illustration : 19
Script : Malayālama
Source : A D C of S mss in the C O L, Trivandrum
S. No. : 1192 C
C.O.L. No. : 2357

Title : ***Bhāratīya***
भारतीय
Author : Bhaṭṭācārya
Ms. W P : With Paravastu Veṅkataraṅgācārayār of Vizagpatam
Source : L of S mss in P L of S I, Madras, 1880, Vol I
S. No. : 8133

Title : ***Bhārtīyanāṭyaśāstra***
भारतीयनाट्यशास्त्र
Author : Bharatamuni
Source : British Museum, London
Acc. No. : 365

Title : ***Bhāratīyanāṭyaśāstraṃ***
भारतीयनाट्यशास्त्रम्
Source : British Museum, London
No. : 14055 bb 2

Title : ***Bhāratīyanāṭyaśāstraṃ***
भारतीयनाट्यशास्त्रम्
Author : Bharatamuni
Size : 18¾″ × 1½″
Leaves : 243
Granths : 5500
Script : Telugu
Source : D C of the S mss in the T M S S M L, Tanjore, Vol XVI
S. No. : 10650
B. No. : 11571

Title	: ***Bhāratīyanāṭyaśāstraṃ***
	भारतीयनाट्यशास्त्रम्
Author	: Bharatamuni
Script	: Telugu
Source	: D C of the S mss in the T M S S M L, Tanjore, Vol XVI
S. No.	: 10651
B. No.	: 14570 A

Title	: ***Bhāratīyanāṭyaśāstraṃ***
	भारतीयनाट्यशास्त्रम्
Author	: Bharatamuni
Script	: Telugu
Source	: D C of the S mss in the T M S S M L, Tanjore, Vol XVI
S. No.	: 10652
B. No.	: 14570 b

Title	: ***Bhāvaprakāśanaṃ***
	भावप्रकशनम्
Author	: Śāradātanaya
Mat.	: Paper
Size	: 33 × 21 cm.
Pages	: 102
Script	: Telugu
Source	: G O M L, Triplicane, Madras

Title	: ***Bhāvaprakāśanaṃ***
	भावप्रकाशनम्
Author	: Śāradātanaya
Size	: 9¾ × 1¾ cm.
Folios	: 196
Illustration	: 9
Script	: Malayalam
Dated	: 11th - 13th century
Source	: A D C of the S mss in the H H M P L, Trivandrum
S. No.	: 1414
	Its based on Tāla, Svara & Bhāvas.

Title	: ***Bhāvaprakāśanaṃ***
	भावप्रकाशनम्
Author	: Śāradātanaya
Size	: 9½ × 1¾ cm.
Folios	: 195
Illustration	: 9
Script	: Grantha
Dared	: 11th - 13th century
Source	: A D C of the S mss in the H H M P L, Trivandrum
S. No.	: 1415

Title	: ***Bhāvaprakāśanaṃ***
	भावप्रकाशनम्
Author	: Śāradātanaya
Size	: 9½ × 1¾ cm.
Folios	: 88
Illustration	: 12
Script	: Grantha

Dated : 11th - 13th century

Source : A D C of the S mss in the H H M P L, Trivandrum

S. No. : 1416

Title : *Bhūvaprakāśanaṃ*

भावप्रकाशनम्

Author : Śāradātanaya

Source : Venkatesvara Univ., Tirupati

Title : *Bhāvaprakāśanavyākhyā*

भावप्रकाशनव्याख्या

Author : Unknown

Source : Venkatesvara Univ., Tirupati

Title : *Bidagdhamādhaba Nāṭaka*

बिदग्धमाधब नाटक

Author : Rūpagosvāmī

Size : 13.2" × 1.2"

Pages : 208

Language : Oriya

Source : Utkal Univ. Lib., Bhuvaneswar

Title : *Bodhakaśobhanappadal*

बोधकषोभनपाडल्

Author : Māduarapperumāl

Mat. : Palmleaf

Size : 35 × 25 cm.

Pages : 20

Language : Tamil

Script : Tamil

Source : G O M L, Triplicane, Madras

Title : *Bṛjarasa Jībatu Nāṭaka*

बृजरस जीबतु नाटक

Author : Unknown

Size : 14.5" × 1.1"

Pages : 50

Language : Oriya

Source : Utkal Univ. Lib., Bhuvaneswar

Title : *Bṛhaddeśī*

बृहद्देशी

Author : Mataṅgmuni

Size : 13 × 9 cm.

Folios : 180

Illustration : 20

Script : Devanāgrī

Source : A D C of S mss in the C.O.L., Trivandrum

S. No. : 1224

C.O.L. No. : 646

C

Title : *Caccapūta Veṇpā*

चच्चपूत वेण्पा

Author : Unknown

Size : 9 × 1¼ cm.

Folios : 24

Illustration : 11

Source : D C of T M in M D U V S, I L, Adyar, Madras-26

Accession no: 2067 (874 -A)

Title : *Caitanya Candrodaya Nāṭaka*

चैतन्य चन्द्रोदय नाटक

Author : Paramānanda Senākavi

Size : 11.8″ × 4.5″

Pages : 96

Language : Sanskrit

Source : Bhuvaneswar Museum, Bhuvaneswar

Title : *Caitanya Candrodaya Nāṭaka*

चैतन्य चन्द्रोदय नाटक

Author : Gopāla Dāsa

Size : 12″ × 1.5″

Pages : 89

Language : Oriya

Source : Utkal Univ. Lib., Bhuvaneswar

Title : *Caitanya Rasāyana with Oriya translation*

चैतन्य रसायन उड़िया अनुवाद के साथ

Author : Unknown

Size : 8.3″ × 1.3½″

Folios : 72

Language : Sanskrit

Source : Bhuvaneswar Museum, Bhuvaneswar

Title : *Campūrāmāyaṇa Nāṭaka*

चम्पूरामायण नाटक

Author : Unknown

Size : 11.4″ × 1.5″

Pages : 91

Language : Oriya

Source : Utkal Univ. Lib., Bhuvaneswar

Title : ***Candrakalā Nāṭikā***

चन्द्रकला नाटिका

Author : Viśvanātha Kavirāja

Size : 14.3″ × 1.5″

Folios : 38

Language : Sanskrit

Source : Bhuvaneswar Museum, Bhuvaneswar

Title : ***Caturadaṇḍiparīkṣā***

चतुरदण्डिपरीक्षा

Author : Veṅketeśvara Dīkṣita

Edited by : Dattātreya Keśava Jośī

Source : British Museum, London

No. : 14055 e 5 (1)

A manual of music. It contains only 2-5 prakaraṇas.

Its published from Bombay in 1918.

Title : ***Catvāriṁśacchatarāga-nirūpaṇa***

चत्वारिंशच्छतरागनिरूपण

Author : Nārada

Pages : 24

Edited by : Dattātreya Keśava Jośī

Pub. from : Bombay, Poona

Dated : 1914 AD

Source : British Museum, London

No. : 14055 e 3 (6)

A metrical description of 140 musical modes, ascribed to the mythical Nārada.

Title : ***Catvāriṁśacchatarāga-nirūpaṇa***

चत्वारिंशच्छतरागनिरूपण

Author : Nārada

Source : T A C C, Wiesbaden, 1962, Pt-I

S. No. : 7 b

B. No. : 60 b

Title : ***Catvāriṁśacchatarāga-nirūpaṇa***

चत्वारिंशच्छतरागनिरूपण

Author : Nārada

Source : T A C C, Wiesbaden, 1962, Pt-I

S. No. : 85

Title : ***Cautālākāmoharā***

चौतालाकामोहरा

Author : Unknown

Mat. : Paper

Size : 5″ × 5″

Folios : 1 - 4

Lines : 13

Letters : 16

Script : Devanāgarī

Source : Varanaseya Skt. Visvavidyalaya Lib., Varanasi

S. No. : 45516

Title : ***Cidambara Sabhānathar Kīrttanānai***

चिदम्बर सभानथर कीर्तनानै

Author : Muttutāndavar

Mat. : Palmleaf

Size : 29.8 × 3.2 cm.

Pages : 40

Language : Tamil

Script : Tamil

Source : G O M L, Triplicane, Madras

Title : ***Cila Kirtanaṅkal Muṭaliyaṇa***

चिल कीर्तनंगल मुतलियण

Author : Unknown

Size : 13½ × 1 cm.

Folios : 8

Illustration : 7

Source : D C of T M in M D U V S, I L, Adyar, Madras-26

Acc. No. : 2068 (751)

Title : ***Citrarāgiṇī***

चित्रारागिणी

Author : Unknown

Folios : 36 Portraits

Language : Hindī & Rājasthānī

Source : Nagpur Univ. Lib., Nagpur

Acc. No. : 767

Title : ***Cūdāmaṇi***

चूडामणि

Author : Unknown

Source : T A C C, Wiesbaden, 1962, Pt-I

S. No. : 7 d

Oxf. No. : 201 a

D

Title	:	***Daika Aur Gītasaṅgraha***
		दैक और गीतसंग्रह
Author	:	Ananta Dāsa and others
Size	:	11.7″ × 1.4″
Pages	:	150
Language	:	Oriya
Source	:	Utkal Univ. Lib., Bhuvaneswar

Title	:	***Dakṣiṇīrāgamālā***
		दक्षिणीरागमाला
Author	:	Unknown
Size	:	10″ × 4 3/8″
Folios	:	5
Illustration	:	19
Dated	:	Sam. 1729
Source	:	B O R I, Poona
Acc. No.	:	384/1895 - 98

Title	:	***Dampata Bilās***
		दम्पत बिलास
Author	:	Mirzā Abdurrahamān
Size	:	18 × 12 cm.
Pages	:	186
Language	:	Hindi
Script	:	Urdu
Source	:	State Central Lib., Hyderabad This consists of Dohās and Kavittas. Scribe -Ānānda Rāma.

Title	:	***Daśarūpa with Avaloka***
		दशरूप अवलोक के साथ
Author	:	Dhanika
Size	:	11¼″ × 4 5/8″
Folios	:	102
Illustration	:	8
Dated	:	Sam. 1683
Source	:	B O R I, Poona
Acc. No.	:	706/1886 - 92

Title	:	***Daśarūpa with Avaloka***
		दशरूप अवलोक के साथ
Author	:	Dhanika
Size	:	10¾″ × 5¼″
Folios	:	61
Illustration	:	14
Source	:	B O R I, Poona
S. No.	:	334
Acc. No.	:	592/1887 - 91

Title : ***Daśarūpa***
दशरूप
Author : Dhanañjaya
Size : 6⅜″ × 8⅛″
Pages : 317
Lines : 2 - 3
Script : Malayalam
Age : 1860 AD
Source : C of S mss in the I O L, London, Vol II
S. No. : 5211
Acc. No. : Burnell 280

Title : ***Daśarūpaka***
दशरूपक
Author : Dhanañjaya
Size : 26 × 8.1 cm.
Folios : 1-2, 13
Illustration : 14
Script : Devanāgarī
Source : A C of mss in the A B S P, Lucknow
No. : 977

Title : ***Daśarūpaka***
दशरूपक
Author : Dhanañjaya
Size : 11⅞″ × 1¾″
Folios : 15
Illustration : 10
Dated : 10th century
Source : B O R I, Poona
Acc. No. : 86/1919-24

Title : ***Daśarūpakam***
दशरूपकम्
Author : Dhanañjaya
Dated : Śaka 1747
Source : B I S M H G C, Poona
No. : 4152

Title : ***Daśarūpaka Nāṭakaprakaraṇa***
दशरूपक नाटकप्रकरण
Author : Pratāparudra-yaśobhuṣaṇa
Size : 14⅞″ × 1¼″
Folios : 9
Lines : 6 - 8
Script : Grantha
Dated : 19th century
Source : C of S mss in the I O L, London, Vol II
S. No. : 5246
Acc. No. : 3461 b

A treatise on the dramatic art, styled in the margin of folios 1, "Daśarūpaka Nātakaprakaraṇa", being an account of the subject based on the "Daśarūpaka" of "Dhanañjaya", and agreeing fairly closely with that in "Pratāparudra-yaśobhuṣaṇa" of Viśvanātha.

Cf. The Madras Catalogue, XXII, 8664,8665. It closely agrees in Pratāparudra-yaśobhuṣaṇa, Pages - 101–31 with Kumārsvāmin's commentary.

Cf. 1176-1177 & 5249-5251 for Pratāparudra-yaśobhuṣaṇa of India Office Catalogue.

Title : ***Daśarūpakaṭīkā***

दशरूपकटीका

Author : Dhanika

Size : 10½ × 2 cm.

Folios : 56

Illustration : 13

Script : Malayalam

Source : A D C of S mss in the C O L, Trivandrum

S. No. : 1182 A

C.O.L. No. : 1974 A

Title : ***Daśarūpakaṭīkāvyākhyā***

दशरूपकटीकाव्याख्या

Author : Bhaṭṭa Nṛsiṁha

Size : 10½ × 2 cm.

Folios : 27

Illustration : 13

Script : Malayalam

Source : A D C of S mss in the C O L, Trivandrum

S. No. : 1182 B

C.O.L. No. : 1974 B

Title : ***Daśarūpakaṭīkāvyākhyā***

दशरूपकटीकाव्याख्या

Author : Bahūrūpamiśra

Size : 13 × 1½ cm.

Folios : 46

Illustration : 7

Script : Malayalam

Source : A D C of S mss in the C O L, Trivandrum

S. No. : 1183 A

C.O.L. No. : 616 A

Title : ***Daśarūpakaṭīkāvyākhyā***

दशरूपकटीकाव्याख्या

Author : Bhaṭṭa Nṛsiṁha

Size : 12 × 1½ cm.

Folios : 61

Illustration : 6

Script : Malayalam

Source : A D C of S mss in the C O L, Trivandrum

S. No. : 1184 B

C.O.L. No. : 256 B

Title : ***Daśarūpakaṭīkāvyākhyā***

दशरूपकटीकाव्याख्या

Author : Bhaṭṭa Nṛsiṁha

Size : 13 × 8½ cm.

Folios : 90

Illustration : 18

Script : Malayalam
Source : A D C of S mss in the C O L, Trivandrum
S. No. : 1186
C.O.L. No. : 127

Title : ***Daśarūpakāvalokana-vyākhyā***
दशरूपकावलोकनव्याख्या
Author : Unknown
Size : 13½ × 1⅜ cm.
Folios : 11
Illustration : 7
Script : Malayalam
Source : A D C of S mss in the C O L, Trivandrum
S. No. : 1185 B
C.O.L. No. : 1855 B

Title : ***Daśarūpakavyākhyā***
दशरूपकव्याख्या
Author : Unknown
Size : 13½ × 1⅜ cm.
Folios : 64
Illustration : 7
Script : Malayalam
Source : A D C of S mss in the C O L, Trivandrum
S. No. : 1185 A
C.O.L. No. : 1855 A

Title : ***Daśarūpakavyākhyā***
दशरूपकव्याख्या
Author : Dhanika
Size : 12 × 1½ cm.
Folios : 126
Illustration : 6
Script : Malayalam
Source : A D C of S mss in the C O L, Trivandrum
S. No. : 1184 A
C.O.L. No. : 256 A

Title : ***Daśarūpakavyākhyā***
दशरूपकव्याख्या
Author : Dhanika
Size : 21¾ × 2 cm.
Folios : 28
Illustration : 9
Script : Malayalam
Source : A D C of S mss in the C O L, Trivandrum
S. No. : 1192
C.O.L. No. : 2357

Title : ***Daśarūpakavyākhyā (Rūpadīpika)***
दशरूपकव्याख्या (रूपदीपिका)
Author : Bhaṭṭa Mahopādhyāya Bahūrūpa
Size : 13 × 8½ cm.
Folios : 223
Illustration : 20
Script : Devanāgarī
Source : A D C of S mss in the C O L, Trivandrum

S. No. : 1187

C.O.L. No. : 34

Title : ***Daśarūpakavyākhyā (Rūpadīpikā)***

दशरूपकव्याख्या (रूपदीपिका)

Author : Unknown

Size : 18½ × 2 cm.

Folios : 44

Illustration : 11

Script : Malayalam

Source : A D C of S mss in the C O L, Trivandrum

S. No. : 1188 A

C.O.L. No. : 1658

Title : ***Daśarūpakavyākhyā (Rūpadīpikā)***

दशरूपकव्याख्या (रूपदीपिका)

Author : Bahurūpa

Size : 14 × 2 cm.

Folios : 40

Illustration : 10

Script : Malayalam

Source : A D C of S mss in the C O L, Trivandrum

S. No. : 1189

C.O.L. No. : 2242

Title : ***Daśarūpāvaloka***

दशरूपावलोक

Author : Dhanañjaya

Size : 12¼″ × 4½″

Folios : 70

Lines : 11

Script : Devanāgarī

Source : C of S mss in the I O L, London, Vol I, Pt-II

S. No. : 1129

Acc. No. : 396 c

A commentary by Dhanika, on Dhanañjaya's : Daśarūpaka or compendium of dramaturgy, the text of which is embodied in the comment. Edited by Jr. Fitg Edward Hall, in the Bihliotheca India, 1805.

Title : ***Dattila Kohalīyaṃ***

दत्तिल कोहलीयम्

Author : Dattīlaḥ

Source : Venkatesvara Univ., Tirupati

Title : ***Dhaneśvaranāṭakaṃ***

धनेश्वरनाटकम्

Author : Unknown

Mat. : Paper

Size : 20.4 × 14 cm.

Pages : 101

Language : Tamil

Script : Tamil

Source : G O M L, Triplicane, Madras

Title : ***Dīkṣitakṛtyaḥ***

दीक्षितकृत्यः

Mat. : Palmleaf

Size : 41 × 3 cm.
Pages : 6
Script : Grantha
Source : G O M L, Triplicane, Madras

Title : ***Dilabahalāva***
दिलबहलाव
Author : Unknown
Dated : Sam. 1940
P. Year : 1929 AD
Source : Nagari Pracariṇi Sabha, Varanasi, Vol I
S. No. : 366

Title : ***Dolotsavādigītam***
दोलोत्सवादिगीतम्
Material : Palmleaf
Size : 42.5 × 3.5 cm.
Pages : 12
Script : Grantha
Source : G O M L, Triplicane, Madras

Title : ***Drupad Lahari Vol 123***
द्रुपद लहरी
Language : Bengali
Source : Sangeet Natak Academy Lib.

Title : ***Duropadai Malai Yiḍu Nāṭakaṃ***
दुरौपदै मालै इडु नाटकम्
Author : Unknown
Mat. : Palmleaf
Size : 33 × 2.5 cm.
Pages : 196
Language : Tamil
Script : Tamil
Source : G O M L, Triplicane, Madras

Title : ***Duropada Tukil Uri Nāṭakaṃ***
दुरौपद तुगिल् उरि नाटकम्
Author : Unknown
Mat. : Palmleaf
Size : 37.5 × 2.5 cm.
Pages : 341
Language : Tamil
Script : Tamil
Source : G O M L, Triplicane, Madras

E

Title	: ***Ekkālakkaṇṇi***
	एक्कालकण्णि
Author	: Unknown
Mat.	: Palmleaf
Size	: 35 × 2.5 cm.
Pages	: 42
Language	: Tamil
Script	: Tamil
Source	: G O M L, Triplicane, Madras

Title	: ***Elunagarvanigar Peril Kuluvaināṭakaṃ***
	एलुनगरवनिगर् पेरिल् कुलुवैनाटकम्
Author	: Māśiramaṇippula
Mat.	: Paper
Size	: 31.7 × 26.7 cm.
Pages	: 4
Language	: Tamil
Script	: Tamil
Source	: G O M L, Triplicane, Madras

G

Title : ***Gānabhāskaramu***

गानभास्करमु

Author : Śrīnivāsa Āyaṅgara

Pages : 12

Source : British Museum, London

No. : 14174 e 44

A manual of music in Telugu with Sanskrit extracts. Its published from Madras in 1918.

Title : ***Gānaśāstra***

गानशास्त्र

Author : Anonymous

Size : 11½″ × 4½″

Folios : 9

Language : Sanskrit

Source : Asiatic Society, 1, Park Street, Calcutta-16

Title : ***Gandharvakalāpavyākaraṇa***

गन्धर्वकलापव्याकरण

Author : Śaurīndu Mohan Ṭhākur

Source : British Museum, London

A grammar of musical science in the form of and commentary, following the method of "Kātantra"

Title : ***Gandharvavidyā***

गन्धर्वविद्या

Author : Unknown

Size : 11″ × 4½″

Folios : 10

Language : Sanskrit

Source : Asiatic Society 1, Park Street, Calcutta-16

Title : ***Gandharvavidyā***

गन्धर्वविद्या

Author : Śivaṃ

Source : Venkatesvara Univ., Tirupati

Title : ***Gāyanasaṅgraha***

गायनसंग्रह

Author : Gaṇeṣa Prasāda

Mat. : Paper

Size : 10″ × 6″

Leaves : 16

Lines : 28

Letters : 429

Script : Devanāgarī

Dated : 1879 AD

Source : K M U H H G K S T V, Kashi

Acc. No. : 107 E

Title : ***Gāyanasaṅgraha***

गायनसंग्रह

Author : Rāmakavi

Mat. : Paper

Size : 12″ × 6″

Leaves : 210

Lines : 24

Script : Devanāgarī

Dated : 1870 AD

Source : K M U H H G K S T V, Kashi

Acc. No. : 285

Title : ***Gāyanasaṅgraha***

गायनसंग्रह

Author : Nārāyaṇa

Mat. : Paper

Size : 8″ × 6″

Leaves : 16

Lines : 34

Letters : 388

Script : Devanāgarī

Dated : 1875 AD

Source : K M U H H G K S T V, Kashi

Acc. No. : 247C

Title : ***Gāyanaśāstram***

गायनशास्त्रम्

Author : Unknown

Mat. : Paper

Size : 10.8″ × 4.6″

Folios : 1

Lines : 19

Letters : 45

Script : Devanāgarī

Source : Varanaseya Skt. Visvavidyalaya Lib., Varanasi

S. No. : 45504

Title : ***Ghunyat Al Muyat***

घुन्यत अल मुयत

Language : Persian

Source : Sangeet Natak Academy Lib.

Title : ***Gitābalī***

गीताबली

Author : Sanātana Maṇiratna

Size : 11″ × 1.3″

Pages : 36

Language : Oriya

Source : Utkal Univ. Lib., Bhuvaneswar

Title : *Gītādidoṣavicaraḥ*
गीतादिदोषविचारः
Mat. : Palmleaf
Size : 27 × 4 cm.
Pages : 3
Script : Oriya
Source : G O M L, Triplicane, Madras

Title : *Gītagovinda*
गीतगोविन्द
Author : Jayadeva
Folios : 36 Portraits
Source : Nagpur Univ. Lib., Nagpur

Title : *Gītagovinda*
गीतगोविन्द
Author : Jayadeva
Size : 27 × 9.5 cm.
Folios : 15
Language : Maithilī
Source : Patna Univ. Lib., Bihar

Title : *Gītagovinda*
गीतगोविन्द
Author : Jayadeva
Size : 16 × 8 cm.
Folios : 37
Language : Devanāgarī
Source : Patna Univ. Lib., Bihar

Title : *Gītagovinda*
गीतगोविन्द
Author : Jayadeva
Size : 26 × 10 cm.
Folios : 7
Language : Maithilī
Source : Patna Univ. Lib., Bihar

Title : *Gītagovinda*
गीतगोविन्द
Author : Jayadeva
Size : 32 × 9.7 cm.
Folios : 23
Language : Devanāgarī
Source : Patna Univ. Lib., Bihar

Title : *Gītagovinda*
गीतगोविन्द
Author : Jayadeva
Size : 22 × 9 cm.
Folios : 2
Language : Maithilī
Source : Patna Univ. Lib., Bihar

Title : *Gītālaṅkāra*
गीतालंकार
Author : Bharata
Size : 10½″ × 4⅜″

Folios : 19

Illustration : 12

Source : B O R I, Poona

Acc. No. : 977/1887-91

Title : ***Gītālaṅkāra***

गीतालंकार

Author : Bharata

Leaves : 10

Lines : 52

Letters : 12

Text : Complete

Source : R on the S for S mss in the B P, Bombay

S. No. : 977

Title : ***Gītamālā***

गीतमाला

Language : Nevārī

Source : A C of P & S P mss D L, Nepal, Calcutta,1905

S. No. : 1584 (Ga)

Title : ***Gītamālā***

गीतमाला

Author : Hari Chandana and others

Size : 13″ × 1.2″

Pages : 105

Language : Oriya

Source : Utkal Univ. Lib., Bhuvaneswar

Title : ***Gītamālikā***

गीतमालिका

Author : Unknown

Size : 9.3" × 1.1"

Pages : 69

Language : Oriya

Source : Utkal Univ. Lib., Bhuvaneswar

Title : ***Gītaprakāśa***

गीतप्रकाश

Author : Kṛṣṇadāsa Badajena Mahāpātra

Size : 14″ × 1.3″

Folios : 24

Language : Sanskrit

Source : Bhuvaneswar Museum, Bhuvaneswar

Title : ***Gītaprakāśa***

गीतप्रकाश

Author : Unknown

Leaves : 15

Granths : 400

Source : O I, Baroda

Title	:	***Gītaprakaśa***
		गीतप्रकाश
Author	:	Kṛṣṇadāsa Badajena Mahāpātrā
Size	:	14.5″ × 1.3″
Pages	:	11
Language	:	Oriya
Source	:	Utkal Univ. Lib., Bhuvaneswar

Title	:	***Gītaprakāśa***
		गीतप्रकाश
Author	:	Unknown
Source	:	Venkatesvara Univ., Tirupati

Title	:	***Gītaśaṅkara***
		गीतशंकर
Author	:	Maithila Bhīṣmamiśra
Source	:	T A C C, Wiesbaden, 1962, Pt-I
S. No.	:	7 A

Title	:	***Gītaśāstram***
		गीतशास्त्रम्
Author	:	Unknown
Source	:	Venkatesvara Univ., Tirupati

Title	:	***Gītavādyatāla Nirūpaṇa***
		गीतवाद्यताल निरूपण
Author	:	Unknown
Size	:	12.7″ × 1.1″
Folios	:	13
Language	:	Sanskrit
Source	:	Bhuvaneswar Museum, Bhuvaneswar

Title	:	***Gītāvalī***
		गीतावली
Author	:	Sanātanagosvāmī
Size	:	14.8″ × 1.5″
Folios	:	12
Language	:	Sanskrit
Source	:	Bhuvaneswar Museum, Bhuvaneswar

Title	:	***Gopīnāthaballabha Nāṭaka***
		गोपीनाथवल्लभ नाटक
Author	:	Raghunatha Parīccha
Size	:	12.8" × 1.4"
Folios	:	48
Language	:	Oriya
Source	:	Bhuvaneswar Museum, Bhuvaneswar

H

Title	:	***Hanumadbharataṃ***
		हनुमद्भरतम्
Author	:	Unknown
Folios	:	11
Script	:	Grantha
Source	:	V V R I, Hoshiarpur
Acc. No.	:	5624

Title	:	***Harināmakīrtanam***
		हरिनामकीर्तनम्
Author	:	Tukārāma
Mat.	:	Palmleaf
Size	:	35 × 2.5 c.m.
Pages	:	11
Script	:	Grantha
Source	:	G O M L, Triplicane, Madras

Title	:	***Hastalakṣaṇam***
		हस्तलक्षणम्
Author	:	Unknown
Size	:	8½″ × 4″
Leaves	:	19
Granths	:	200
Script	:	Devanāgarī
Source	:	D C of the S mss in the T M S S M L, Tanjore, Vol XVI
S. No.	:	10702
B. No.	:	6653

Title	:	***Hastalakṣaṇam***
		हस्तलक्षणम्
Author	:	Unknown
Script	:	Devanāgarī
Source	:	D C of the S mss in the T M S S M L, Tanjore, Vol XVI
S. No.	:	10703
B. No.	:	6647

Title	:	***Hastalakṣaṇam***
		हस्तलक्षणम्
Author	:	Unknown
Script	:	Telugu
Source	:	D C of the S mss in the T M S S M L, Tanjore, Vol XVI
S. No.	:	10704
B. No.	:	14179 b

Title	:	***Hastalakṣaṇam***
		हस्तलक्षणम्
Author	:	Unknown
Script	:	Devanāgarī

Source : D C of the S mss in the T M S S M L, Tanjore, Vol XVI

S. No. : 10705

B. No. : 6658

Title : ***Hastalakṣaṇam***

हस्तलक्षणम्

Author : Unknown

Script : Devanāgarī

Source : D C of the S mss in the T M S S M L, Tanjore, Vol XVI

S. No. : 10706

B. No. : 14180

Title : ***Hastalakṣaṇam***

हस्तलक्षणम्

Author : Unknown

Script : Devanāgarī

Source : D C of the S mss in the T M S S M L, Tanjore, Vol XVI

S. No. : 10707

B. No. : 6652

Title : ***Hāsyārṇava***

हास्यार्णव

Author : Jagadīśvara

Size : 16.1″ × 1.3″

Folios : 47

Language : Sanskrit

Source : Bhuvaneswar Museum, Bhuvaneswar

Title : ***Hāsyārṇava Nāṭaka***

हास्यार्णव नाटक

Author : Jagadīśvara Kabirāja

Size : 7.5" × 1"

Folios : 59

Language : Oriya

Source : Utkal Univ. Lib., Bhuvaneswar

Title : ***Hindī Rāgapadasaṅgraha***

हिन्दी रागपदसंग्रह

Author : Unknown

Size : 4⅞″ × 7½″

Folios : 4

Language : Hindi

Source : Nagpur Univ. Lib., Nagpur

Acc. No. : 4461

Title : ***Hindu Musical Scale***

हिन्दू म्यूजिकल स्केल

Author : Kṛṣṇaji Ballāla Deval

Source : British Museum, London

An easy in English with preface.

Title : ***Hiya Hulāsa***

हिय हुलास

Author : Lala Kavi

Size : 8¼″ × 6¼″

Leaves : 8

Lines : 14

Letters : 926

Script : Devanāgarī

Source : K M U H H G K S T V, Kashi

Acc. No. : 243

Title : ***Hiya Hulāsa***

हिय हुलास

Script : Devanāgarī

Source : K M U H H G K S T V, Kashi

Acc. No : 388

Title : ***Hiya Hulāsa***

हिय हुलास

Author : Lāla Kavi

Size : 8¼″ × 6¼″

Leaves : 8

Lines : 14

Script : Devanāgarī & Kaithī

Dated : 1813 AD

Source : K M U H H G K S T V, Kashi

Acc. No. : 243 (K h)

Title : ***Hiya Hulāsa***

हिय हुलास

Size : 10½″ × 5"

Folios : 4

Letters : 17

Script : Devanāgarī

Source : Prachina Sahitya Shodh Sansthana, Udaipur

Title : ***Holī Gajala Ādi***

होली गजल आदि

Author : Prabhu-dayāla

Mat. : Paper

Size : 8" × 6"

Leaves : 16

Lines : 24

Letters : 768

Script : Devanagarī

Source : K M U H H G K S T V, Kashi
There are collection of Rāgarāgiṇī, Holī, Thumarī, Gajal, Dādrī etc. in this book.

Title : ***Hṛdayakautuka***

हृदयकौतुक

Author : Hṛdaya Nārāyana Deva

Edi. by : Bhālacandra Sītārāma Sukthaṅkara

Source : British Museum, London

No. : 14055 e 4(2)

Two metrical tracts on the modes of Indian Music. Its published from Bombay in 1918.

Title : ***Hṛdayaprakāśa***

हृदयप्रकाश

Author : Hṛdaya Nārāyana Deva

Source : British Museum, London

Title : ***Hṛdayaprakāśa***

हृदयप्रकाश

Author : Hṛdayanārāyanadeva

Source : T A C C, Wiesbaden, 1962, Pt-I

S. No. : 85

I

Title	: ***Īlunagar Vaṇigar Peril Kuluvaināṭakam***
	ईलुनगर् वणिगर् पेरिल् कुलुवैनाटकम्
Author	: Unknown
Mat.	: Paper
Size	: 31.7 × 26.7 cm.
Pages	: 4
Language	: Tamil
Script	: Tamil
Source	: G O M L, Triplicane, Madras

Title	: ***Irāgatālaprattāram***
	इरागतालप्रत्तारम्
Author	: Unknown
Mat.	: Paper
Size	: 26.7 × 23.5 cm.
Pages	: 132
Language	: Sanskrit and Tamil
Script	: Tamil and Grantha
Source	: G O M L, Triplicane, Madras

Title	: ***Irāmanāṭakakīrtanāni***
	इरामनाटककीर्तनानि
Author	: Arunacalakkavirayar
Mat.	: Palmleaf
Size	: 36.2 × 3 cm.
Pages	: 80
Language	: Tamil
Script	: Tamil
Source	: G O M L, Triplicane, Madras

Title	: ***Irāmanāṭakam***
	इरामनाटकम्
Author	: Arunacalakkavirayar
Mat.	: Palmleaf
Size	: 34.2 × 3.7 cm.
Pages	: 528
Language	: Tamil
Script	: Tamil
Source	: G O M L, Triplicane, Madras

Title	: ***Irāmāyaṅa ttiruppukal with commentary***
	इरामायण तिरूप्पुकल् व्याख्या के साथ
Author	: Bhāratī
Mat.	: Palmleaf
Size	: 46 × 3 cm.
Pages	: 934

Language : Tamil

Script : Tamil and Bharatī

Source : G O M L, Triplicane, Madras

Title : ***Iraṇyasaṃhāranāṭakam***

इरण्यसंहारनाटकम्

Author : Unknown

Mat. : Paper

Size : 34.2 × 3.7 cm.

Pages : 52

Language : Tamil

Script : Tamil

Source : G O M L, Triplicane, Madras

Title : ***Iśaippadarkoṭṭu***

इशैपाटर्कोट्टु

Author : Bālakari Kṛṣṇan

Mat. : Palmleaf

Size : 38.5 × 3 cm.

Pages : 348

Language : Tamil

Script : Tamil

Source : G O M L, Triplicane, Madras

J

Title	:	***Jagannāthaballabha Nāṭaka***
		जगन्नाथबल्लभ नाटक
Author	:	Unknown
Size	:	13.5″ × 1.1″
Pages	:	113
Language	:	Oriya
Source	:	Utkal Univ. Lib., Bhuvaneswar

Title	:	***Jakkanāṭakam***
		जक्कनाटकम्
Author	:	Unknown
Mat.	:	Paper
Size	:	33 × 22.8 cm.
Pages	:	193
Language	:	Tamil
Script	:	Tamil
Source	:	G O M L, Triplicane, Madras

Title	:	***Jalakrīḍā***
		जलक्रीडा
Mat.	:	Palmleaf
Size	:	47 × 3 cm.
Pages	:	7
Script	:	Grantha
Source	:	G O M L, Triplicane, Madras

Title	:	***Jalwah Nāma***
		जलवह नाम
Size	:	8" × 5"
Folios	:	145-152
Illustration	:	11
Date	:	1796 AD
Source	:	C of P mss in the I O L, London, Vol I, Pt-II
S. No.	:	2764
Acc. No.	:	2420
		Series of nuptial songs celebrating the various stages of wedding feast.

Title	:	***Jamadakninātakam***
		जमदक्निनाटकम्
Author	:	Unknown
Mat.	:	Paper
Size	:	34 × 21.1 cm.
Pages	:	330

Language : Tamil
Script : Tamil
Source : G O M L, Triplicane, Madras

Title : ***Jātiḥ***

जातिः

Author : Unknown
Mat. : Palmleaf
Size : 15½″ × 1⅛″
Leaves : 80
Lines : 4 - 5
Granths : 800
Script : Grantha
Text : Incomplete
Source : D C of the S mss in the T M S S M L, Tanjore, Vol XVI
S. No. : 10851
B. No. : 11608
Copies : 10852-10859
Palmleaf Telugu
Incomplete

K

Title : ***Kalyāṇagāna***

कल्याणगान

Source : British Museum, London

Title : ***Kalyāṇagāna***

कल्याणगान

Pages : 16

Dated : 1896 AD

Source : British Museum, London

No. : 14070

A benedictory song (Sanskrit and English) composed and set to music and sung on the occasion of the presence of Sir Alexander Mackenzie and Lady Mackenzie at an Indian musical party, held at Horocoomar Bhawan.

Title : ***Kamalinī Kalahaṁsinī Nāṭikā***

कमलिनी कलहंसिनी नाटिका

Author : Kavirāja Cūdāmaṇi

Size : 13.3″ × 1.4″

Folios : 39

Language : Sanskrit

Source : Bhuvaneswar Museum, Bhuvaneswar

Title : ***Kanakadāsakīrtanāni***

कनकदासकीर्तनानि

Author : Kanakadāsa

Mat. : Palmleaf

Size : 37 × 3 cm.

Pages : 6

Script : Grantha

Source : G O M L, Triplicane, Madras

Title : ***Kanakadāsakīrtanāni***

कनकदासकीर्तनानि

Author : Kanakadāsa

Mat. : Palmleaf

Size : 37 × 3 cm.

Pages : 70

Script : Grantha

Source : G O M L, Triplicane, Madras

Title : ***Kandāranāṭakam***

कन्दारनाटकम्

Author : Bālasubramaṇyak

Mat. : Palmleaf

Size : 20.3 × 3.8 cm.

Pages : 406

Language : Tamil

Script : Tamil

Source : G O M L, Triplicane, Madras

Title : ***Kanz Altuhaf***

कंज–अलतुहफ

Author : Unknown

Size : 9¼″ × 5½″

Folios : 27

Illustration : 21

Date : 1383 AD

Source : C of P mss in the I O L, London, Vol I, Pt-II

S. No. : 2763

Acc. No. : 2067

An anonymous treatise on music in a Mukand-dimah and four Makālas of 1383 AD

Title : ***Karuppaiyaperil Kuluvaināṭakam***

करुप्पैयपेरिल् कुलुवैनाटकम्

Author : Muttappacettiyā

Mat. : Palmleaf

Size : 36.8 × 3.2 cm.

Pages : 76

Language : Tamil

Script : Tamil

Source : G O M L, Triplicane, Madras

Title : ***Kāttavarāyanāṭakam***

कात्तवरायनाटकम्

Author : Unknown

Mat. : Palmleaf

Size : 37.5 × 2.7 cm.

Pages : 138

Language : Tamil

Script : Tamil

Source : G O M L, Triplicane, Madras

Title : ***Khulastul Aiśa***

खुलस्तुल ऐशा

Author : Raśanud-Daula Zafar Khān

Size : 10″ × 6″

Pages : 62

Language : Persian

Text : Incomplete

Source : Maulana Azad Lib., A M U, Aligarh

Title : ***Khyāla***

ख्याल

Author : Sukhalāla

Mat. : Paper

Size : 9″ × 5″

Leaves : 2

Lines : 13

Letters : 39

Script : Devanāgarī

Source : K M U H H G K S T V, Kashi

Acc. No. : 148B

Title : ***Khyāla***

ख्याल

Author : Rasika

Mat. : Paper

Size : 5 ¾″ × 5½″

Leaf : 1

Lines : 9

Letters : 11

Script : Devanāgarī

Source : K M U H H G K S T V, Kashi

Acc. No. : 124

Title : ***Khyāloṃ kī pustaka***

ख्यालों की पुस्तक

Author : Sukhalāla

Mat. : Paper

Size : 9½″ × 5½″

Leaves : 6

Lines : 23

Letters : 363

Script : Devanāgarī

Source : K M U H H G K S T V, Kashi

Acc. No. : 148a

Title : ***Kīcakanāṭakam***

कीचकनाटकम्

Author : Unknown

Mat. : Palmleaf

Size : 28 × 2.5 cm.

Pages : 70

Language : Tamil

Script : Tamil

Source : G O M L, Triplicane, Madras

Title : ***Kīcakanāṭakam***

कीचकनाटकम्

Author : Unknown

Mat. : Palmleaf

Size : 28 × 2.5 cm.

Pages : 70

Language : Tamil

Script : Tamil

Source : G O M L, Triplicane, Madras

Title : ***Kīrtanani***

कीर्तनानि

Author : Śeṣāyaṇgara

Mat. : Palmleaf

Size : 18.5 × 4 cm.
Pages : 21
Script : Grantha
Source : G O M L, Triplicane, Madras

Title : ***Kīrtanāni***

कीर्तनानि

Mat. : Palmleaf
Size : 23.5 × 4 cm.
Pages : 2
Script : Grantha
Source : G O M L, Triplicane, Madras

Title : ***Kīrtanaṅkal***

कीर्तनन्कल

Author : Unknown
Size : 15 × 1 cm.
Folios : 56
Illustration : 5
Source : D C of T M in M D U V S, I L, Adyar, Madras-26
Acc. No. : 2065 (901)

Title : ***Kīrtanam***

कीर्तनम्

Author : Unknown
Mat. : Palmleaf
Size : 29.2 × 5 cm.
Pages : 30
Language : Sanskrit and Tamil
Script : Tamil and Grantha
Source : G O M L, Triplicane, Madras

Title : ***Kitāb-E-Rāga***

किताब–ए–राग

Author : Unknown
Size : 24.6 × 15.1 cm.
Folios : 45
Illustration : 14
Script : Persian
Source : C of P & A mss in the G O M L, Madras
S. No. : 529
Acc. No. : D 740

Title : ***Kohalarahasyam***

कोहलरहस्यम्

Author : Kohala
Mat. : Paper
Size : 27.7 × 21 cm.
Pages : 8
Script : Devanāgarī
Source : G O M L, Triplicane, Madras

Title : ***Kohalamatam***

कोहलमतम्

Author : Unknown
Size : 8 × 1¾ cm.
Folios : 99

Illustration : 8

Script : Malayalam

Source : A D C of S mss in the C O L, Trivandrum

S. No. : 1221

C.O.L. No. : 1724

Title : ***Kuksāra***

कुक्सार

Mat. : Brittle Paper

Size : 20 × 13 cm.

Pages : 56

Language : Hindi

Script : Urdu

Condition : Old copy, Damaged (Worm eaten)

Source : State Central Lib., Hyderabad, A. P.

Title : ***Kunrakkudi Kumran Peril Kīrttanaikal***

कुन्रकुडिकुमरन पेरिल् कीर्तनैगल्

Author : Alakiyacirrambakavirāy

Mat. : Palmleaf

Size : 36.2 × 2 cm.

Pages : 340

Language : Tamil

Script : Tamil

Source : G O M L, Triplicane, Madras

Title : ***Kurukṣetranāṭakam***

कुरुक्षेत्रनाटकम्

Author : Sāminātḥappul

Mat. : Palmleaf

Size : 38 × 2.5 cm.

Pages : 322

Language : Tamil

Script : Tamil

Source : G O M L, Triplicane, Madras

Title : ***Kuśalavanāṭakam***

कुशलवनाटकम्

Author : Unknown

Mat. : Palmleaf

Size : 43.2 × 2.8 cm.

Pages : 84

Language : Tamil

Script : Tamil

Source : G O M L, Triplicane, Madras.

L

Title	: ***Lahabatasa***
	लहबतस
Author	: Bakṣu Nāyak
Size	: 25.5 × 16 cm.
Pages	: 66
Language	: Persian and Hindi
Script	: Urdu
Date	: 1002 AH
Source	: State Central Lib., Hyderabad, A. P.
	This work deals with Dhurpads of Bakṣu Nāyaka, written 1002 AH. At the instance of captain William Kirk Patric.

Title	: ***Lahjat-E-Sikandar Śāhī***
	लहजत–ए–सिकन्दर शाही
Author	: Ibn-E-Omar Kabuli
Mat.	: Paper
Size	: 24.7 × 15.6 cm.
Pages	: 202
Script	: Nastaliq
Text	: Complete
Source	: GOML, Triplicane, Madras

Title	: ***Lahjat-E-Sikandar Śāhī***
	लहजत–ए–सिकन्दर शाही
Author	: Ibn-E-Omar Kabuli
Size	: 26.9 × 21 cm.
Folios	: 88
Illustration	: 12
Script	: Persian
Dated	: 1908 AD
Source	: C of P & A mss in the G O M L, Madras
S. No.	: 575
Acc. No.	: D 519

Title	: ***Lahjat-E-Sikandar Śāhī***
	लहजत–ए–सिकन्दर शाही
Author	: Ibn-E-Omar Kābulī
Size	: 24.7 × 15.6 cm.
Folios	: 84
Illustration	: 15
Script	: Persian
Source	: C of P & A mss in the G O M L, Madras
S. No.	: 574
Acc. No.	: D 518

Title : ***Lahjat-I-Sikandarī***
लहजत–ए–सिकन्दरी
Language : Persian
Source : Sangeet Natak Academy Lib.

Title : ***Lālīgītam***
लालीगीतम्
Mat. : Palmleaf
Size : 42.5 × 3.5 cm.
Script : Grantha
Source : G O M L, Triplicane, Madras

Title : ***Lalitamādhava Nāṭaka***
ललितमाधव नाटक
Author : Rupagosvāmī
Size : 12.6″ × 1.3″
Folios : 106
Language : Sanskrit
Source : Bhuvaneswar Museum, Bhuvaneswar

Title : ***Lāsyapuṣpāñjaliḥ***
लास्यपुष्पांजलिः
Author : Unknown
Size : $7^{7/8}$″ × $4^{7/8}$″
Leaves : 2
Granths : 20
Script : Devanāgarī
Source : D C of the S mss in the T M S S M L, Tanjore, Vol XVI
S. No. : 10714
B. No. : 14832 c

M

Title	: ***Mādan-Ul-Mūsiqī***
	मादन–उल–मूसिकी
Language	: Persian
Source	: Sangeet Natak Academy Lib.

Title	: ***Madhurāniruddha Nāṭaka***
	मधुरानिरुद्ध नाटक
Author	: Cayani Candra Śekhara Rajaguru
Size	: 14.5 × 9.5 cm.
Pages	: 48
Language	: Sanskrit
Source	: Bhuvaneswar Museum, Bhuvaneswar

Title	: ***Magāmat-I-Hindī-O-Fārasi***
	मगामत–ई–हिन्दी–ओ–फारसी
Author	: Unknown
Line	: 101b -103b
Source	: T M S S M , Tanjore

Title	: ***Mahānāṭaka***
	महानाटक
Author	: Madhusūdana Miśra
Size	: 12.6″ × 1.4″
Folios	: 60
Language	: Sanskrit
Source	: Bhuvaneswar Museum, Bhuvaneswar

Title	: ***Mahānātaka***
	महानाटक
Author	: Madhusūdana Miśra
Size	: 15.2″ × 1.2″
Folios	: 80
Language	: Oriya
Source	: Utkal Univ. Lib., Bhuvaneswar

Title	: ***Mahānāṭaka***
	महानाटक
Author	: Madhusūdana Miśra
Size	: 13" × 1.1"
Folios	: 162
Language	: Oriya
Source	: Utkal Univ. Lib., Bhuvaneswar

Title	: ***Mairavaṇanāṭakam***
	मैरावणनाटकम्
Author	: Unknown

Mat. : Palmleaf
Size : 34.2 × 3.7 cm.
Pages : 128
Language : Tamil
Script : Tamil
Source : G O M L, Triplicane, Madras

Title : ***Majmā-Us-Sima***
मज्मा–उस–सिम
Author : Ulfat Alī
Size : 20 × 12.5 cm.
Pages : 110
Language : Urdu
Time : 1289 AH
Source : State Central Lib., Hyderabad, A. P.
It's divided into 22 parts, dealing with Indian Rāgas and Rāgiṇīs.

Title : ***Mālatīmādhava Nāṭaka***
मालतीमाधव नाटक
Author : Bhavabhūti
Size : 14.1" × 1.4"
Folios : 104
Language : Sanskrit
Source : Bhuvaneswar Museum, Bhuvaneswar

Title : ***Mānamanorañjanam***
मानमनोरंजनम्
Author : Mayāśaṅkara
Leaves : 20
Extent : 121 Śloka
Dated : Śaka 1713
Source : O I, Baroda

Title : ***Maṇimālā Nāṭikā***
मणिमाला नाटिका
Author : Ānadikavi
Size : 15″ × 1.2″
Folios : 102
Language : Sanskrit
Source : Bhuvaneswar Museum, Bhuvaneswar

Title : ***Manmathanāṭakam***
मन्मथनाटकम्
Author : Unknown
Mat. : Palmleaf
Size : 43.2 × 2.8 cm.
Pages : 59
Language : Tamil
Script : Tamil
Source : G O M L, Triplicane, Madras

Title : ***Maqāsid-Ul-Ilhān***
मकासिद–उल–इलहान
Author : Abdul Qādir Bin Gaibi
Size : 18.5 × 16 cm.
Pages : 192

Language : Persian

Source : State Central Lib., Hyderabad, A. P.

It deals with the principles and Greek theory of Music in general and the Arabic music in particular, illustrated with various tables and charts, consist of a Prologue, 12 chapters and an Epilogue.

Title : ***Mārkaṇḍeyanāṭakam***

मार्कण्डेयनाटकम्

Author : Veṅkatācalapati

Mat. : Palmleaf

Size : 33 × 2.5 cm.

Pages : 48

Language : Tamil

Script : Tamil

Source : G O M L, Triplicane, Madras

Title : ***Mārkaṇḍeyanāṭakam***

मार्कण्डेयनाटकम्

Author : Vinaitīrttār

Mat. : Palmleaf

Size : 38.1 × 2.5 cm.

Pages : 50

Language : Tamil

Script : Tamil

Source : G O M L, Triplicane, Madras

Title : ***Mataṅgabharatam***

मतंगभरतम्

Author : Lakṣmaṇārya

Size : 19½″ × 1½″

Leaves : 5

Granths : 600

Script : Telugu

Source : D C of the S mss in the T M S S M L, Tanjore, Vol XVI

S. No. : 10667

B. No. : 11526

Title : ***Mataṅgabharataṃ***

मतंगभरतम्

Author : Lakṣmaṇārya

Script : Telugu

Text : Incomplete

Source : D C of the S mss in the T M S S M L, Tanjore, Vol XVI

S. No. : 10668

B. No. : 11546

Title : ***Mauj-E-Mūsiqī***

मौज–ए–मौशिकी

Author : Hakīma Lal Mohammad

Size : 11″ × 6½″

Pages : 53

Language : Persian

Text : Complete

Source : Maulana Azad Lib., A M U, Aligarh

Title : ***Melādhikāralakṣaṇam***

मेलाधिकारलक्षणम्

Author : Unknown

Mat. : Palmleaf

Size : 12¼" × 1¼"

Leaves : 77

Lines : 6-7

Granths : 2000

Script : Telugu

Text : Complete

Source : D C of the S mss in the T M S S M L, Tanjore, Vol XVI

S. No. : 10846

B. No. : 11603

Copies : 10847

B. No. : 11604

Palmleaf : Telugu Complete

Title : ***Melārāgasarvasaṁgraha***

मेलारागसर्वसंग्रह

Author : Unknown

Ms. W P : T. Rāmarāva of Tanjore

Source : Private Libraries of Southern India, Madras

S. No. : 8327

Title : ***Miftāh-Us-Surud***

मिफताह–उस–सुरुद

Author : Qāzī Hasan Daulatābādī

Size : 21 × 13 cm.

Pages : 70

Language : Persian

Dated : 1074 AH

Source : State Central Lib., Hyderabad, A. P.

Date of transcription 1249 AD, Hyderabad. This small treatise is a translation of 'Bharata Saṅgīta' written in Auraṅgazeb's reign. It gives in four chapters the basic rules of music, the descriptions of vocal rāgas and the instruments. The last chapter deals with "Pakhavaj" and the accompanying dances.

Title : ***Mīnācciyammai Dikkvijayanāṭakaṃ***

मीनाचियम्मै दिग्विजयनाटकम्

Author : Unknown

Mat. : Palmleaf

Size : 30.5 × 3.2 cm.

Pages : 424

Language : Tamil

Script : Tamil

Source : G O M L, Triplicane, Madras

Title : ***Mirāl -I -Āftāb-Numā***

मिराल–ए–आफताब–नुमा

Language : Persian

Source : Sangeet Natak Academy Lib.

Title : ***Miṣbāhu's-Surur***

मिस्बाहुज–सुरुर

Author : Hasana-bin-Khwājā Tāhir-bin-Mohammad

Mat. : Paper

Size : 210 × 120; 180 × 85 mm.

Folios : 24

Illustration : 16

Age : 1074 AH (1664 AD)

Source : Asiatic Society of Bengal, Cal., 1924, Vol I

S. No. : 1629 M. 136

A treatise on Indian music composed in the reign of Auraṅgazeb, by Hasan-bin-Khwājā Tāhil-bin-Muhammad a qādī of Antur, a place in Daulatabad. The work is divided into four bāb's and in the colophon is also Miftāḥu's-Surur transcribed in the 12. AH.

Title : ***Mivatul-Khyāl***

मिवतुल–ख्याल

Language : Persian

Source : Sangeet Natak Academy Lib.

Title : ***Mṛdaṅgalakṣanam with Telugu meaning***

मृदंगलक्षणम् तेलुगू अर्थ के साथ

Mat. : Palmleaf

Size : 37 × 3 cm.

Pages : 5

Script : Telugu

Source : G O M L, Triplicane, Madras

Title : ***Mṛdaṅgalakṣaṇam with Telugu meaning***

मृदंगलक्षणम् तेलुगू अर्थ के साथ

Mat. : Paper

Size : 30 × 20 cm.

Pages : 3

Script : Telugu

Source : G O M L, Triplicane, Madras

Title : ***Mṛdaṅgavādya***

मृदंगवाद्य

Author : Unknown

Size : 5.7″ × 1.4″

Folios : 84

Language : Sanskrit

Source : Bhuvaneswar Museum, Bhuvaneswar

Title : ***Mufarrāh-al-Qulub***

मुफर्राह–अल–कुलुब

Author : Hasan Alī 'Izzat'

Size : 7⅞″ × 5¾″

Folios : 185

Lines : 9

Language : Persian and Urdu

Source : C of the H mss in the I O L, London

S. No : 233

A work on the music of Mysore. Its different tunes and melodies in Persian and Hindustani. The work was commenced in the first year of Tipu Sultan (1197 AH =1783 AD) and was completed two years later in 1785 AD Copies of the above S. No. 234 – 241.

Title : ***Mufarrāh-Ul-Qulub***

मुफर्राह–उल–कुलुब

Author : Hasan Alī 'Izzat'

Size : 20 × 18 cm.

Pages : 90

Language : Persian and Urdu

Source : State Central Lib., Hyderabad, A. P.

This work was composed on the order of Tīpū Sultāna by his court poet 'Izzata'. Instead of usual and popular names of the Rāgas and Rāgiṇīs, here on the instance of the King, new names are adopted for six 'Nagmā, as Abyad, asghar, Ahmar, Zabarjad, Dawood and Abbasi. Under each Nagmā, Persian and Urdu Ghazliyat are given to illustrate it.

Likewise, ghazliyat are to be sung under certain 'Tarz' named as, Sultānī, Sarv Sāhī, Shahinsh Pasandi, Urusi, Ishq Angezi, Mehr Afzal etc.

For the instrument 'Mṛdang', the word 'Suraiya' is work divided into a Muqaddama six chapters.

Title : ***Mukhtasar-Dar-Ilm-E-Mūsiqī***

मुख्तसर–दर–इल्म–ए–मोसिकी

Author : Abdulaqādira Marāghī

Mat. : Paper

Size : 29 × 20.5 cm.

Pages : 114

Script : Nastaliq

Text : Complete

Source : G O M L, Triplicane, Madras

Title : ***Mukhtasar-Dar-Mūsiqī***

मुख्तसर–दर–मौसिकी

Author : Abdul Qadir Marāghī

Size : 29 × 20.5 cm.

Folios : 54

Illustration : 31
Script : Persian
Source : C of P & A mss in the G O M L, Madras
S. No. : 806
Acc. No. : D 520

Title : ***Mūnis-Ul-Ushshaq***
म्यूनिस–उल–उशशाक
Author : Unknown
Leaves : 7a–23a
Source : T M S S M L., Tanjore

Title : ***Muntafa-Ul -Tālibīna***
मुन्तफा–उल–तालिबीन
Author : Unknown
Size : 8″ × 5″
Pages : 6
Language : Persian
Text : Complete
Source : Maulana Azad Lib., A M U, Aligarh

Title : ***Mutaliyār Kirtanaṅkal***
मुदलियार कीर्तनंकल
Author : Kanam Kushnaiyar
Size : 13 × 1 7/8 cm.
Folios : 150
Illustration : 6
Source : D C of T M in M D U V S, I L, Adyar, Madras-26
Acc. No. : 2064 (469)

Title : ***Muttutaṇḍavar-Kīrttanaṅkal***
मुतुतण्डवर कीर्तनंकल
Author : Muttutaṇḍavar
Mat. : Palmleaf
Size : 29.2 × 28 cm.
Pages : 120
Language : Tamil
Script : Tamil
Source : G O M L, Triplicane, Madras

Title : ***Muvvā Gopāla Padamulu***
मुव्वा गोपाल पदमुलु
Author : Kṣetraya
Mat. : Paper
Size : 33 × 21.5 cm.
Pages : 92
Language : Telugu
Script : Telugu
Source : G O M L, Triplicane, Madras

Title : ***Muvvā Gopāla Padamulu***
मुव्वा गोपाल पदमुलु
Author : Kṣetraya
Mat. : Paper
Size : 34.5 × 23 cm.
Pages : 28
Language : Telugu
Script : Telugu

Source : G O M L, Triplicane, Madras

Title : ***Muvvā Gopāla Padamulu***
मुव्वा गोपाल पदमुलु

Author : Kṣetraya

Mat. : Paper

Size : 33 × 20.5 cm.

Pages : 172

Language : Telugu

Script : Telugu

Source : G O M L, Triplicane, Madras

N

Title	: ***Naccuppoykai Nāṭakam***
	नच्चुप्पोय्कै नाटकम्
Author	: Unknown
Mat.	: Palmleaf
Size	: 40 × 17.8 cm.
Pages	: 76
Language	: Tamil
Script	: Tamil
Source	: G O M L, Triplicane, Madras

Title	: ***Nādadīpakam***
	नाददीपकम्
Author	: Bhaṭṭācārya
Folios	: 15
Illustration	: 9
Script	: Bengli
Source	: N of S mss Pub. by G of B, Calcutta, 1871, Vol II
No.	: 538

Title	: ***Nāgendra Saṅgītam***
	नागेन्द्र संगीतम्
Author	: Nāgamalladevī
Source	: Venkatesvara Univ., Tirupati

Title	: ***Nagamāt-Ul-Asrār***
	नगमात–उल–असरार
Author	: Mīr Ahmad Ibn Mirzā Mohammad
Size	: 8½″ × 6″
Pages	: 227
Language	: Persian
Text	: Complete
Source	: Maulana Azad Lib., A M U, Aligarh

Title	: ***Nagamāt-Ul-Asrār***
	नगमात–उल–असरार
Language	: Persian
Source	: Sangeet Natak Academy Lib.

Title	: ***Nagamāt-Ul-Hind***
	नगमात–उल–हिन्द
Language	: Persian
Source	: Sangeet Natak Academy Lib.

Title	: ***Nakṣatrādyabhinayalakṣaṇam***
	नक्षत्राद्यभिनयलक्षणम्
Author	: Unknown

Size : 17½″ × 1⅝″

Leaves : 3

Granths : 65

Script : Telugu

Source : D C of the S mss in the T M S S M L, Tanjore, Vol XVI

S. No. : 10701

B. No. : 11597

Title : ***Nakṣatrādyabhinaya-lakṣaṇam***

नक्षत्राद्यभिनयलक्षणम्

Author : Unknown

Size : 11⅝″ × 1¼″

Leaves : 20

Granths : 225

Script : Telugu

Source : D C of the S mss in the T M S S M L, Tanjore, Vol XVI

S. No. : 10700

B. No. : 11520

Title : ***Nallataṅgal Nāṭakam***

नल्लतंगल् नाटकम्

Author : Jayaraman

Mat. : Palmleaf

Size : 41.2 × 3.2 c.m.

Pages : 128

Language : Tamil

Script : Tamil

Source : G O M L, Triplicane, Madras

Title : ***Nānakkummi***

नानकुम्मि

Author : Vālaidāsa

Mat. : Palmleaf

Size : 35 × 2.5 c.m.

Pages : 30

Language : Tamil

Script : Tamil

Source : G O M L, Triplicane, Madras

Title : ***Nānāvidhagītam***

नानाविधगीतम्

Author : Unknown

Mat. : Palmleaf

Size : 11¼″ × 1″

Leaves : 122

Lines : 3 - 4

Granths : 1200

Script : Telugu

Text : Incomplete

Source : D C of the S mss in the T M S S M L, Tanjore, Vol XVI

S. No. : 10870

B. No. : 11621

Title : ***Nandanārkkīrttanak-Kataivaralāru***

नन्दनार्कीर्तनक्कदैवरलारु

Author : Unknown

Mat. : Palmleaf
Size : 29.8 × 3.2 cm.
Pages : 4
Language : Tamil
Script : Tamil
Source : G O M L, Triplicane, Madras

Title : ***Nandibharatam***

नन्दिभरतम्

Author : Unknown
Folios : 3
Script : Grantha
Source : V V R I, Hoshiarpur
Acc. No. : 562

Title : ***Nāradaśikṣā***

नारदशिक्षा

Extent : 1000
Source : O R I, Mysore

Title : ***Nartananirṇaya***

नर्तननिर्णय

Author : Puṇḍarika Viṭhṭhala
Lines : 9 - 11
Script : Devanāgarī
Dated : 18th century
Source : C of S mss in the I O L, London, Vol II
S. No. : 5197
Acc. No. : 3314 C

A treatise on dancing. Cf. Mitra , Bikaner Catal, pp. 513–14. The summary of contents in Mitra, notices, VIII, 33, show that is only as the Ms. indicates. The fourth and last Prakaraṇa of the work. Prakaraṇa-I is found in Jammu Ms. no. 657 (Stein, Kāśmīra, Cat., p. 40)

Title : ***Nartananirṇaya***

नर्तननिर्णय

Author : Puṇḍarīka Viṭhṭhala
Leaves : 36
Granths : 800
Cond. : Injured
Source : O I, Baroda
Acc. No. : 11620

Title : ***Nartananirṇaya***

नर्तननिर्णय

Author : Puṇḍarīka Viṭhṭhala
Source : T A C C, Wiesbaden, 1962, Pt-I
S. No. : 88

Title : ***Nartananirṇaya***

नर्तननिर्णय

Author : Puṇḍarīka Viṭhṭhala
Source : T A C C, Wiesbaden, 1962, Pt-I
S. No. : 4

Title : ***Nartananirṇayah***

नर्तननिर्णयः

Author : Puṇḍarīka Viṭhṭhala

Size : 4¼" × 6¼"

Leaves : 96

Granths : 170

Script : Devanāgarī

Source : D C of the S mss in the T M S S M L, Tanjore, Vol XVI

S. No. : 10675

B. No. : 6602

Title : ***Nartananirṇayaḥ***

नर्तननिर्णयः

Author : Puṇḍarīka Viṭhṭhala

Mat. : Paper

Size : 10.5" × 4.2"

Folios : 1 - 14

Lines : 9

Letters : 37

Script : Devanāgarī

Source : Varanaseya Skt. Visvavidyalaya Lib., Varanasi

S. No. : 45519

Title : ***Naśāt***

नशात

Author : Unknown

Pages : 46

Size : 20.5 × 15 cm.

Language : Persian

Source : State Central Lib., Hyderabad

Title : ***Nāṭakacandrikā (Alaṅkāra)***

नाटकचन्द्रिका (अलंकार)

Author : Rūpagosvāmin

Source : T A C C, Wiesbaden, 1962, Pt-I

S. No. : 15

Title : ***Nāṭakacandrikā***

नाटकचन्द्रिका

Author : Rūpagosvāmin

Source : T A C C, Wiesbaden, 1962, Pt-I

S. No. : 18

Title : ***Nāṭakadīpa***

नाटकदीप

Author : Tryambaka

Commentary: Nāṭyadīpa नाट्यदीप

Commentator: Rāmkṛṣṇa

Source : T A C C, Wiesbaden, 1962, Pt-I

S. No. : 16 A

Title : ***Nāṭakalakṣaṇa***

नाटकलक्षण

Author : Puṇḍarīka Viṭhṭhala

Size : 9 9/10″ × 4 4/5″

Folios : 15

Illustration : 9

Dated : Śaka 1677

Source : B O R I, Poona

S. No : 43109

Title : ***Nāṭakalakṣaṇa***

नाटकलक्षण

Author : Unknown

Mat. : Paper

Lines : 15

Script : Devanāgarī

Source : Skt. College Banarasa, Allahabad, 1902

No. : 181

G. No. : 3249

Title : ***Nāṭakalakṣaṇa***

नाटकलक्षण

Author : Puṇḍarīka Viṭhṭhala

Source : T A C C, Wiesbaden, 1962, Pt-I

S. No. : 19

Title : ***Nāṭakalakṣaṇa***

नाटकलक्षण

Author : Puṇḍarīka Viṭhṭhala

Source : T A C C, Wiesbaden, 1962, Pt-I

S. No. : 5

Title : ***Nāṭakaparibhāṣā***

नाटकपरिभाषा

Author : Śri Singadharaṇīśa

Size : 13¼″ × 8¾″

Folios : 16

Lines : 21-26

Script : Telugu

Source : C of S mss in the I O L, London, Vol I, Pt-II

S. No. : 1201

Acc. No. : 3029

The Principles of dramaturgy in Śloka by Śri Singdharaṇīśa.

Title : ***Nāṭakaparibhāṣā***

नाटकपरिभाषा

Mat. : European Paper

Size : 9″ × 7¼″

Folios : 11

Lines : 20

Script : Devanāgarī

Dated : 1862 AD

Source : C of S mss in the I O L, London, Vol I, Pt-II

S. No. : 1202

Acc. No. : 3088

Title : ***Nāṭakaparibhāṣā***
नाटकपरिभाषा
Size : 8⅛″ × 12⅞″
Folios : 19
Lines : 31
Script : Devanāgarī
Dated : 1863 AD
Source : C of S mss in the I O L, London, Vol I, Pt-II
S. No. : 5248
Acc. No. : Bubler 123
Another copy of the same work, Transcribed from the preceding mss.

Title : ***Nāṭakaparibhāṣā***
नाटकपरिभाषा
Mat. : Palmyra Leaves
Size : 18⅛″ × 15⅞″
Folios : 11
Lines : 6 - 8 in 308 verses
Script : Telugu
Dated : 18th century
Source : C of S mss in the I O L, London, Vol I, Pt-II
S. No. : 7913
Acc. No. : 3781

Title : ***Nāṭakaparibhāṣā***
नाटकपरिभाषा
Author : Śṛṅgadharaṇīśa
Size : 8½″ × 12⅛″
Lines : 31
Script : Devanāgarī
Source : C of S mss in the I O L, London, Vol II
S. No. : 5248
Acc. No. : Bubler 123

Title : ***Nāṭakaparibhāṣā***
नाटकपरिभाषा
Author : Śṛṅgadharaṇīśa
Size : 18½″ × 15⅞″
Folios : 11
Script : Telugu
Source : C of S mss in the I O L, London, Vol II
S. No. : 7913
Acc. No. : 3781

Title : ***Nāṭakaparibhāṣā***
नाटकपरिभाषा
Author : Śṛṅgadharaṇisena
Source : T A C C, Wiesbaden, 1962, Pt-I
S. No. : 17

Title : ***Nāṭakaparibhāṣā***
नाटकपरिभाषा
Author : Śṛṅgadharaṇīśa
Source : T A C C, Wiesbaden, 1962, Pt-I
S. No. : 3

Title : ***Nāṭakaśāra***

नाटकसार

Author : Unknown

Folios : 204

Script : Malayalam

Source : V V R I, Hoshiarpur

Acc. No. : 3848

Title : ***Nātakāvatāra***

नाटकावतार

Author : Mohanadāsa

Source : T A C C, Wiesbaden, 1962, Pt-I

S. No. : 20

Oxf. No. : 143 a

Title : ***Naṭāṅkuśaḥ***

नटांकुषः

Author : Unknown

Source : Venkatesvara Univ., Tirupati

Title : ***Naṭāṅkuśam***

नटांकुशम्

Author : Unknown

Mat. : Paper

Size : 27.2 × 24.1 cm.

Script : Devanagarī

Source : G O M L, Triplicane, Madras

Title : ***Nāṭyacūḍāmaṇiḥ***

नाट्यचूडामणिः

Author : Unknown

Mat. : Paper

Size : 31.5 × 25 cm.

Script : Devanāgarī

Source : G O M L, Triplicane, Madras

Title : ***Nāṭyacūḍāmaṇiḥ with Telugu meaning***

नाट्यचूडामणिः तेलुगू अर्थ के साथ

Author : Somanārya

Mat. : Paper

Size : 27 × 20 cm.

Script : Telugu

Source : G O M L, Triplicane, Madras

Title : ***Nāṭyadarpaṇaḥ***

नाट्यदर्पणः

Author : Unknown

Source : Venkatesvara Univ., Tirupati

Title : ***Nāṭyadarpaṇasūtra***

नाट्यदर्पणसूत्र

Author : Rāmacandra and Gunacandra

Size : 10¾″ × 4¾″

Folios : 10

Illustration : 9

Dated : 12th century

Source : B O R I, Poona
Acc. No. : 352/1892-95

Title : ***Nāṭyalakṣaṇam***
नाट्यलक्षणम्
Author : Unknown
Mat. : Palmleaf
Size : 24 × 3.2 cm.
Script : Grantha
Source : G O M L, Triplicane, Madras

Title : ***Nāṭyalakṣaṇam***
नाट्यलक्षणम्
Author : Śṛṅgabhūpa
Leaves : 5
Extent : 83 Śloka
Cond. : Injured
Source : O I, Baroda
Acc. No. : 13044

Title : ***Nāṭyalakṣaṇam***
नाट्यलक्षणम्
Author : Bharataśāstra
Ms. W P : H. H. the Mahārājā of Travancore
Source : L of S mss in P L of S I, Madras, 1880, Vol I
S. No. : 6018

Title : ***Nāṭyalakṣaṇam***
नाट्यलक्षणम्
Author : Siṅgabhūpāla
Folios : 16
Script : Malayalam
Source : V V R I, Hoshiarpur
Acc. No. : 5860

Title : ***Nāṭyalocana***
नाट्यलोचन
Author : Trilocanāditya
Size : $10^{1/5}$″ × $4^{3/5}$″
Folios : 1-7, 14 -37
Illustration : 8
Script : Devanāgarī
Dated : 1933 AD
Source : B O R I, Poona
S. No. : 42936

Title : ***Nāṭyalocana***
नाट्यलोचन
Author : Trilocanāditya
Source : T A C C, Wiesbaden, 1962, Pt-I
S. No. : 24

Title : ***Nāṭyaprabhā***
नाट्यप्रभा
Author : Unknown

Source : B O R I, Poona
S. No : 42296

Title : ***Nāṭyapradīpa***
नाट्यप्रदीप
Author : Sundara Miśra Aujāgarī
Size : 9″ × 4″
Folios : 52
Lines : 10
Script : Devanāgarī
Dated : 1613 AD
Source : C of S mss in the I O L, London, Vol I, Pt-II
S. No. : 1199
Acc. No. : 1148 d

A manual of the scenic art, composed in 1613 AD by Sundara Miśra Aujāgarī. Perhaps the author's original manuscript.

Title : ***Nāṭyapradīpa***
नाट्यप्रदीप
Size : 12″ × 4¼″
Folios : 35
Lines : 11
Script : Devanāgarī
Source : C of S mss in the I O L, London, Vol I, Pt-II
S. No. : 1200
Acc. No. : 843 A

Copy of the above is incorrect.

Title : ***Nāṭyapradīpa***
नाट्यप्रदीप
Author : Sundara Miśra
Size : 9 1/5″ × 4 1/5″
Folios : 52
Illustration : 8
Script : Devanāgarī
Source : B O R I, Poona
S. No. : 41618

Title : ***Nāṭyapradīpa***
नाट्यप्रदीप
Author : Sundara Miśra
Source : T A C C, Wiesbaden, 1962, Pt-I
S. No. : 22

Title : ***Nāṭyapradīpaḥ***
नाट्यप्रदीपः
Author : Sundara Miśra
Source : Venkatesvara Univ., Tirupati

Title : ***Nāṭyapraśaṁsā***
नाट्यप्रशंसा
Author : Unknown
Size : 16″ × 1″
Leaves : 6
Granths : 100
Script : Grantha

Source : D C of the S mss in the T M S S M L, Tanjore, Vol XVI

S. No. : 10709

B. No. : 11517 d

Title : ***Nāṭyapraśaṁsā***

नाट्यप्रशंसा

Author : Unknown

Script : Grantha

Source : D C of the S mss in the T M S S M L, Tanjore, Vol XVI

S. No. : 10710

B. No. : 11521 c

Title : ***Nāṭyapraśaṁsā***

नाट्यप्रशंसा

Author : Unknown

Script : Telugu

Source : D C of the S mss in the T M S S M L, Tanjore, Vol XVI

S. No. : 10711

B. No. : 11521 b

Title : ***Nāṭyapraśaṁsā***

नाट्यप्रशंसा

Author : Unknown

Script : Grantha

Source : D C of the S mss in the T M S S M L, Tanjore, Vol XVI

S. No. : 10712

B. No. : 14181 d

Title : ***Nāṭyasarvasvadīpikā***

नाट्यसर्वस्वदीपिका

Author : Unknown

Folios : 64

Size : 10″ × 5⅞″

Illustration : 10

Source : B O R I, Poona

Acc. No. : 41/1916-18

Title : ***Nāṭyaśāstra***

नाट्यशास्त्र

Author : Bharata

Folios : 237

Size : 11½″ × 5⅜″

Illustration : 11

Dated : Sam. 1931

Source : B O R I, Poona

Acc. No. : 69/1873-74

Title : ***Nāṭyaśāstra***

नाट्यशास्त्र

Author : Bharata

Size : 13⅜″ × 8⅜″

Folios : 209

Illustration : 20

Cond. : Old Ms.

Source : B O R I, Poona

Acc. No. : 39/1916-18

Title : ***Nāṭyaśāstra***

नाट्यशास्त्र

Author : Bharata

Size : 3½" × 8¼"

Folios : 116

Illustration : 20

Cond. : Not old Ms

Source : B O R I, Poona

Acc. No. : 36/1916-18

Title : ***Nāṭyaśāstra***

नाट्यशास्त्र

Author : Bharata

Size : 13 3/8" × 8 3/8"

Folios : 105

Illustration : 19

Dated : Copy of 1916-18

Source : B O R I, Poona

Acc. No. : 37/1916-18

Title : ***Nāṭyaśāstra***

नाट्यशास्त्र

Author : Bharata

Size : 11½" × 5½"

Folios : 260

Illustration : 10

Dated : Sam. 1930

Source : B O R I, Poona

Acc. No. : 68/1873-74

Title : ***Nāṭyaśāstra***

नाट्यशास्त्र

Author : Bharatamuni

Source : British Museum, London

No. : 42

Title : ***Nāṭyaśāstra***

नाट्यशास्त्र

Author : Unknown

Size : 7 × 2 cm.

Folios : 57

Illustration : 10

Script : Malayalam

Source : A D C of the S mss in the H H M P L, Trivandrum

S. No. : 1411

On different Rāgas and origin of Natya-śastra.

Title : ***Nāṭyaśāstra***

नाट्यशास्त्र

Author : Unknown

Size : 7 × 2 cm.

Folios : 80

Illustration : 6

Script : Malayalam

Source : A D C of the S mss in the H H M P L, Trivandrum

S. No. : 1410

A criticism on Abhinaya in Kerala

Title : ***Nāṭyaśāstra***

नाट्यशास्त्र

Author : Bharata

Size : 8 3/8″ × 13″

Lines : 17-18

Script : Devanāgarī

Dated : 1880 AD

Source : C of S mss in the I O L, London, Vol II

S. No. : 5200

Acc. No. : Bubler 124

A treatise on the poetise of the drama and kindred topics as expounded by Bharata, the eponymous founder of the art.

Title : ***Nāṭyaśāstra***

नाट्यशास्त्र

Author : Bharata

Size : 13½″ × 8 1/5″

Folios : 545

Illustration : 23

Script : Devanāgarī

Source : B O R I, Poona

S. No. : 42727

Title : ***Nāṭyaśāstra***

नाट्यशास्त्र

Author : Bharata

Size : 8 3/5″ × 12½″

Folios : 90

Illustration : 18

Script : Devanāgarī

Source : B O R I, Poona

S. No. : 40767

Title : ***Nāṭyaśāstra***

नाट्यशास्त्र

Author : Bharataśāstra

Ms. W P : H. H the Mahārājā of Travancore

Source : L of S mss in P L of S I, Madras, 1880, Vol I

S. No. : 6019

Title : ***Nāṭyaśāstra***

नाट्यशास्त्र

Author : Bharata

Source : T A C C, Wiesbaden, 1962, Pt-I

S. No. : 25

Title : ***Nāṭyaśāstram***

नाट्यशास्त्रम्

Author : Bharata

Mat. : Paper

Size : 22 × 7 cm.

Script : Telugu

Source : G O M L, Triplicane, Madras

Title : ***Nāṭyaśāstram***

नाट्यशास्त्रम्

Author : Bharata

Mat. : Paper

Size : 19 × 15 cm.

Script : Telugu

Source : G O M L, Triplicane, Madras

Title : ***Nāṭyaśāstram***

नाट्यशास्त्रम्

Author : Bharata

Mat. : Paper

Size : 19 × 15 cm.

Script : Telugu

Source : G O M L, Triplicane, Madras

Title : ***Nāṭyaśāstraṃ***

नाट्यशास्त्रम्

Author : Bharata

Mat. : Paper

Size : 27.2 × 24.5 cm.

Script : Devanagarī

Source : G O M L, Triplicane, Madras

Title : ***Nāṭyaśāstram***

नाट्यशास्त्रम्

Author : Bharata

Mat. : Paper

Size : 27.2 × 24.5 cm.

Script : Devanagarī

Source : G O M L, Triplicane, Madras

Title : ***Nāṭyaśāstram***

नाट्यशास्त्रम्

Author : Bharata

Mat. : Paper

Size : 27 × 24.4 cm.

Script : Devanagarī

Source : G O M L, Triplicane, Madras

Title : ***Nāṭyaśāstram***

नाट्यशास्त्रम्

Author : Bharata

Mat. : Paper

Size : 27 × 24.4 cm.

Script : Devanagarī

Source : G O M L, Triplicane, Madras

Title : ***Nāṭyaśāstram with commentary Abhinavabhāratī Volume I***

नाट्यशास्त्रम् अभिनवभारती टीका के साथ वाल्यूम I

Author : Bharata Maheśvara Abhinavaguptacarya

Mat. : Paper

Size : 27 × 24 cm.
Script : Devanāgarī
Source : G O M L, Triplicane, Madras

Title : ***Nāṭyaśāstram with commentary Abhinavabhāratī Volume II***
नाट्यशास्त्रम् अभिनवभारती टीका के साथ वाल्यूम–*II*
Author : Bharata Maheśvara Abhinavaguptācārya
Mat. : Paper
Size : 27 × 24.4 cm.
Script : Devanāgarī
Source : G O M L, Triplicane, Madras

Title : ***Nāṭyaśāstram***
नाट्यशास्त्रम्
Source : O R I, Mysore
No. : 2555

Title : ***Nāṭyaśāstram***
नाट्यशास्त्रम्
Source : O R I, Mysore
No. : 4472

Title : ***Nāṭyaśāstram***
नाट्यशास्त्रम्
Author : Bharataḥ
Source : Venkatesvara Univ., Tirupati

Title : ***Nāṭyaśāstram***
नाट्यशास्त्रम्
Author : Unknown
Source : Venkatesvara Univ., Tirupati

Title : ***Nāṭyaśāstram***
नाट्यशास्त्रम्
Author : Bharata
Folios : 85
Script : Malayalam
Source : V V R I, Hoshiarpur
Acc. No. : 6280

Title : ***Nāṭyaśāstravartikam***
नाट्यशास्त्रवर्तिकम्
Author : Mānyapati
Mat. : Paper
Size : 27.1 × 24.3 cm.
Script : Devanāgarī
Source : G O M L, Triplicane, Madras

Title : ***Nāṭyaśāstravartikam***
नाट्यशास्त्रवर्तिकम्
Author : Mānyapati
Mat. : Paper
Size : 27 × 24 cm.
Script : Devanāgarī
Source : G O M L, Triplicane, Madras

Title : ***Nāṭyaśāstravartikam***

नाट्यशास्त्रवर्तिकम्

Author : Mānyapati

Mat. : Paper

Size : 27.7 × 24.8 cm.

Script : Devanagarī

Source : G O M L, Triplicane, Madras

Title : ***Nāṭyaśāstravartikam***

नाट्यशास्त्रवर्तिकम्

Author : Mānyapatiḥ

Source : Venkatesvara Univ., Tirupati

Title : ***Nāṭyaśāstravivṛtti (Abhinavabharatī)***

नाट्यशास्त्रविवृत्ति (अभिनवभारती)

Author : Abhinavagupta

Size : 8 3/8" × 13 3/8"

Folios : 531

Illustration : 28

Dated : 1925 AD

Source : B O R I, Poona

Acc. No. : 41/1925 - 26

Title : ***Nāṭyaśikṣārambhaḥ***

नाट्यशिक्षारम्भः

Author : Unknown

Size : 17¼" × 1 7/8"

Leaves : 8

Granths : 75

Script : Telugu

Source : D C of the S mss in the T M S S M L, Tanjore, Vol XVI

S. No. : 10708

B. No. : 1532

Title : ***Nāṭyaveda with Vyākhyā***

नाट्यवेद व्याख्या के साथ

Author : Bharatamuni & Abhinavagupta

Size : 13½ × 8¼ cm.

Folios : 530

Illustration : 20

Script : Devanāgrī

Source : A D C of S mss in the C O L, Trivandrum

S. No. : 1216 A+B

C.O.L. No. : 566 A+B

Title : ***Nāṭyaveda***

नाट्यवेद

Author : Bharata

Size : 24 × 2 cm.

Folios : 154

Illustration : 8

Script : Malayalam

Source : A D C of the S mss in the H H M P L, Trivandrum

S. No. : 1406

Title	:	***Nāṭyaveda***
		नाट्यवेद
Author	:	Bharata
Size	:	13 × 2 cm.
Folios	:	118
Illustration	:	10
Script	:	Malayalam
Source	:	A D C of the S mss in the H H M P L, Trivandrum
S. No.	:	1408

Title	:	***Nāṭyaveda***
		नाट्यवेद
Author	:	Bharata
Size	:	18 × 2 cm.
Folios	:	135
Illustration	:	10
Script	:	Malayalam
Source	:	A D C of the S mss in the H H M P L, Trivandrum
S. No.	:	1407

Title	:	***Nāṭyaveda***
		नाट्यवेद
Author	:	Bharata
Size	:	17 × 2 cm.
Folios	:	46
Illustration	:	13
Script	:	Malayalam
Source	:	A D C of the S mss in the H H M P L, Trivandrum
S. No.	:	1409

Title	:	***Nāṭyavedāgamaḥ***
		नाट्यवेदागमः
Author	:	Tulārāja
Size	:	17″ × 1½″
Leaves	:	3
Granths	:	55
Script	:	Telugu
Source	:	D C of the S mss in the T M S S M L, Tanjore, Vol XVI
S. No.	:	10671
B. No.	:	11532 a

Title	:	***Nāṭyavedavivṛtti (Abhinavabhāratī)***
		नाट्यवेदविवृत्ति (अभिनवभारती)
Author	:	Abhinavagupta
Size	:	9½″ × 13¼″
Folios	:	73
Illustration	:	20
Dated	:	Copy made in 1916 -18 AD
Source	:	B O R I, Poona
Acc. No.	:	38/1916 -18

Title	:	***Nāṭyavedavivṛtti***
		नाट्यवेदविवृत्ति
Author	:	Abhinavagupta

Size : 8$^{3/}$″ × 13½″
Folios : 180
Illustration : 14
Script : Devanāgarī
Source : B O R I, Poona
S. No. : 40765

Title : ***Nāṭyavedavivṛtti***
नाट्यवेदविवृत्ति
Author : Abhinavagupta
Size : 8½″ × 13$^{1\backslash 5}$″
Folios : 189
Illustration : 24
Script : Devanāgarī
Source : B O R I, Poona
S. No. : 40766

Title : ***Nāṭyavedavivṛtti***
नाट्यवेदविवृत्ति
Author : Abhinavagupta
Size : 8$^{1/3}$″ × 13$^{1\backslash 5}$″
Folios : 620
Illustration : 19
Script : Devanāgarī
Source : B O R I, Poona
S. No. : 40768

Title : ***Nāṭyavedavivṛtiḥ***
नाट्यवेदविवृत्तिः
Author : Abhinavagupta
Size : 13½ × 8 ½ cm.
Folios : 447
Illustration : 16
Script : Devanāgrī
Source : A D C of S mss in the C O L, Trivandrum
S. No. : 1217
C.O.L. No. : 551A+B

Title : ***Nāṭyavedavivṛtiḥ***
नाट्यवेदविवृत्तिः
Author : Abhinavagupta
Size : 11 × 2 cm.
Folios : 128
Illustration : 8
Script : Malayalam
Source : A D C of S mss in the C O L, Trivandrum
S. No. : 1218
C.O.L. No. : 1854

Title : ***Nāṭyavedavivṛtiḥ***
नाट्यवेदविवृत्तिः
Author : Abhinavagupta
Size : 13½ × 8 ½ cm.
Folios : 161
Illustration : 15
Script : Devanāgrī
Source : A D C of S mss in the C O L, Trivandrum

S. No. : 1219
C.O.L. No. : 259 A

Title : ***Nāṭyavedavyākhyā***
नाट्यवेदव्याख्या
Author : Abhinavagupta
Size : 13½ × 8½ cm.
Folios : 232
Illustration : 24
Script : Devanāgrī
Source : A D C of S mss in the C O L, Trivandrum
S. No. : 1216 C
C.O.L. No. : 566 C

Title : ***Nāṭyaviṣayamu***
नाट्यविषयमु
Author : Unknown
Size : 14″ × 1¼″
Lines : 37
Illustration : 6
Granths : 750
Source : A D C of the T mss in the T M S S M L, Waltair, 1933, A U S-11
No. : 722 - 723
B. No. : M. 693

Title : ***Nāṭyaviṣayamu***
नाट्यविषयमु
Author : Unknown
Pages : 60
Language : Sanskrit transliterated in Telugu with a commentary
Source : Andhra Univ. Lib., A. P.

Title : ***Niśat Āra Dār Ilm E Mūśiqī***
निषत आर दार इल्म ए मौषिकी
Author : Unknown
Size : 12″ × 8″
Pages : 7
Language : Persian
Text : Complete
Dated : 19th century
Source : Maulana Azad Lib., A M U, Aligarh

Title : ***Nītikkīrttanaikal***
नीतिकीर्तनैकल
Author : Unknown
Mat. : Paper
Size : 31.7 × 25.5 cm.
Pages : 364
Language : Tamil
Script : Tamil
Source : G O M L, Triplicane, Madras

Title : ***Nivāta Kavaca Kāla Keyarnāṭakam***
निवाट कवच काल केयरनाटकम्
Author : Unknown

Mat. : Palmleaf
Size : 47 × 2.5 cm.
Pages : 388
Language : Tamil
Script : Tamil
Source : G O M L, Triplicane, Madras

Title : ***Nṛttādhyāyaḥ***
नृत्ताध्याय:
Author : Aśokamallaḥ
Source : Venkatesvara Univ., Tirupati

Title : ***Nṛttalakṣaṇaṃ with Telugu commentary***
नृत्तलक्षणम् तेलुगू व्याख्या के साथ
Author : Unknown
Mat. : Palmleaf
Size : 24 × 3 cm.
Script : Grantha
Source : G O M L, Triplicane, Madras

Title : ***Nṛttaraṅga Navīkaraṇam***
नृत्तरंग नवीकरणम्
Author : Unknown
Source : Venkatesvara Univ., Tirupati

Title : ***Nṛttaprayoga***
नृत्तप्रयोग
Author : Bharata Śāśtra
Ms. W P : H. H. Mahārājā of Travancor
Source : L of S mss in P L of S I, Madras, 1880, Vol I
S. No. : 6026

Title : ***Nṛttaprayoga***
नृत्तप्रयोग
Author : Unknown
Source : T A C C, Wiesbaden, 1962, Pt-I
S. No. : 7 c

Title : ***Nṛttaratnākara***
नृत्तरत्नाकर
Author : Unknown
Size : 14½ × 2 cm.
Folios : 34
Illustration : 9
Script : Malayalam
Source : A D C of the S mss in the H H M P L, Trivandrum
S. No. : 1412

Title : ***Nṛttaratnāvalī***
नृत्तरत्नावली
Author : Jayasenāpati

Size : 9″ × 4″

Folios : 1 - 30

Language : Sanskrit

Source : Asiatic Society, 1, Park Street, Calcutta-16

Title : ***Nṛttaratnāvalī***
नृत्तरत्नावली

Author : Gaṇapatideva gajasādhanikā Jayaśenāpati

Mat. : Paper

Size : 21.2 × 17.1 cm.

Script : Devanāgarī

Source : G O M L, Triplicane, Madras

Title : ***Nṛttaratnāvalī***
नृत्तरत्नावली

Author : Jayasenāpati

Size : 15¾″ × 1 3/8″

Leaves : 100

Granths : 1900

Script : Telugu

Source : D C of the S mss in the T M S S M L, Tanjore, Vol XVI

S. No. : 10672

B. No. : 11540

Title : ***Nṛttaratnāvalī***
नृत्तरत्नावली

Author : Unknown

Script : Grantha

Text : Complete

Source : D C of the S mss in the T M S S M L, Tanjore, Vol XVI

S. No. : 10673

B. No. : 11541

Title : ***Nṛttaratnāvalī***
नृत्तरत्नावली

Author : Jayasenāpati

Source : Venkatesvara Univ., Tirupati

Title : ***Nṛttaśāstra***
नृत्तशास्त्र

Author : Unknown

Mat. : Paper

Size : 30 × 14 cm.

Folios : 7

Lines : 14

Letters : 51 - 53

Script : Devanāgarī

Text : Complete

Dated : 50 Years old

Source : Gujrat Vidya Sabha, Ahmedabad

S. No : 2639

Acc. No. : 867

Title	: ***Nṛttaśāstra***
	नृत्तशास्त्र
Author	: Unknown
Mat.	: Paper
Size	: 23.5 × 11.5 cm.
Folios	: 2 - 13
Lines	: 10
Letters	: 36 - 40
Script	: Devanāgarī
Text	: Incomplete
Dated	: 300 Years old
Source	: Gujrat Vidyā Sabhā, Ahmedabad
S. No.	: 2640
Acc. No.	: 868

Title	: ***Nṛttatālalakṣaṇam***
	नृत्तताललक्षणम्
Author	: Unknown
Mat.	: Palmleaf
Size	: 43.5 × 3.5 cm.
Script	: Telugu
Source	: G O M L, Triplicane, Madras

Title	: ***Nṛttatālalakṣaṇam with Telugu meaning***
	नृत्तताललक्षणम् तेलुगू अर्थ के साथ
Author	: Unknown
Mat.	: Paper
Size	: 33 × 21 cm.
Script	: Telugu
Source	: G O M L, Triplicane, Madras

Title	: ***Nṛttatālalakṣaṇam with Telugu meaning***
	नृत्तताललक्षणम् तेलुगू अर्थ के साथ
Author	: Unknown
Mat.	: Paper
Size	: 24 × 17.5 cm.
Script	: Telugu
Source	: G O M L, Triplicane, Madras

Title	: ***Nṛttatālalakṣaṇam with Telugu Padyās***
	नृत्तताललक्षणम् तेलुगू पद्यों के साथ
Author	: Unknown
Mat.	: Paper
Size	: 20 × 16 cm.
Script	: Telugu
Source	: G O M L, Triplicane, Madras

Title	: ***Nṛttaprayoga***
	नृत्तप्रयोग
Author	: Bharataśāstra
Ms. W P	: H. H. the Mahārājā of Travancore

Source : L of S mss in P L of S I, Madras, 1880, Vol I

S. No. : 6026

Title : ***Nṛtyādhyāya***

नृत्याध्याय

Author : Aśokamalla

Leaves : 81

Granths : 2000

Dated : 1936 AD

Source : O I, Baroda

Acc. No. : 13798

Title : ***Nṛtyanirūpaṇam***

नृत्यनिरूपणम्

Author : Unknown

Size : 9½″ × 5½″

Leaves : 20

Granths : 3

Script : Devanāgarī

Source : D C of the S mss in the T M S S M L, Tanjore, Vol XVI

S. No. : 10674

B. No. : 6616

Title : ***Nṛtyasarvasva***

नृत्यसर्वस्व

Author : Unknown

Source : T A C C, Wiesbaden, 1962, Pt-I

S. No. : 10

Oxf. No. : 126 a

Title : ***Nṛtyaśāstra***

नृत्यशास्त्र

Author : Unknown

Source : T A C C, Wiesbaden, 1962, Pt-I

S. No. : 9

P

Title	:	***Pālaiyanūrnāṭakam***
		पालैयनूरनाटकम्
Author	:	Unknown
Mat.	:	Palmleaf
Size	:	36.9 × 2 cm.
Pages	:	136
Language	:	Tamil
Script	:	Tamil
Source	:	G O M L, Triplicane, Madras

Title	:	***Palaminoṇḍināṭakam***
		पलमिनोण्डिनाटकम्
Author	:	Unknown
Mat.	:	Palmleaf
Size	:	38.8 × 3.2 cm.
Pages	:	134
Language	:	Tamil
Script	:	Tamil
Source	:	G O M L, Triplicane, Madras

Title	:	***Palatirappāḍārriraṭṭu***
		पलत्तिरपाडारिरट्टु
Author	:	Unknown
Mat.	:	Palmleaf
Size	:	26.7 × 3.2 cm.
Pages	:	40
Language	:	Tamil
Script	:	Tamil
Source	:	G O M L, Triplicane, Madras

Title	:	***Palavakaik-Kirtanaṅkal***
		पलवकैक्कीर्तनंगल
Author	:	Unknown
Size	:	$18^{5/8} \times 1^{1/8}$ cm.
Folios	:	79
Illustration	:	5
Source	:	D C of T M in M D U V S, I L, Adyar, Madras-26
Acc. No.	:	2071 (840)

Title	:	***Palavidakkīrttanaṅkal***
		पलविदकीर्तनंगल्
Author	:	Unknown
Mat.	:	Palmleaf
Size	:	46.2 × 3.8 cm.
Pages	:	27

Language : Tamil

Script : Tamil

Source : G O M L, Triplicane, Madras

Title : ***Pañcamasaṃhitā***

पंचमसंहिता

Author : Nārada

Size : 14″ × 3″

Folios : 5

Language : Sanskrit

Source : Asiatic Society, 1, Park Street, Calcutta-16

Title : ***Pañcamasārasaṃhitā***

पंचमसारसंहिता

Author : Nārada

Folios : 11

Illustration : 3

Script : Bengali

Source : N of S mss Pub. by G of B, Calcutta, 1871, Vol I

No. : 322

Title : ***Pañcavarṇagalu***

पंचवर्णगलु

Author : Govinda Sāmi

Pages : 14

Dated : 1908 AD

Source : British Museum, London

No. : 14055 b f

Musical notation of 5 tunes.

Title : ***Pāṇḍavaśūdāṭṭanāṭakam***

पाण्डवशूदाट्टनाटकम्

Author : Śeṣkavi

Mat. : Palmleaf

Size : 45.2 × 1.5 cm.

Pages : 83

Language : Tamil

Script : Tamil

Source : G O M L, Triplicane, Madras

Title : ***Parāṅkuśanāṭakam***

परांकुशनाटकम्

Author : Unknown

Mat. : Palmleaf

Size : 35.6 × 3.8 cm.

Pages : 40

Language : Tamil

Script : Tamil

Source : G O M L, Triplicane, Madras

Title : ***Perūrandanāṭakam***

पेरूरन्दनाटकम्

Author : Unknown

Mat. : Palmleaf

Size : 43.2 × 3.2 cm.

Pages : 46

Language : Tamil

Script : Tamil

Source : G O M L, Triplicane, Madras

Title : ***Piṅgal***

पिंगल

Size : 27.5 × 18 cm.

Pages : 64

Language : Hindi

Script : Urdu

Dated : 1270 AH

Source : State Central Lib., Hyderabad

On the instance of Nawāba Samasul-Mulk Hyderabad, this treatise was transcribed into Urdu script from Devanāgarī by Gulāma Alī Qawwāl.

Title : ***Pirakalādanāṭakam***

पिरगलादनाटकम्

Author : Unknown

Mat. : Palmleaf

Size : 35 × 2.8 cm.

Pages : 180

Language : Tamil

Script : Tamil

Source : G O M L, Triplicane, Madras

Title : ***Prabodhacandrodaya Nāṭaka***

प्रबोधचन्द्रोदय नाटक

Author : Kṛṣṇa Miśra

Size : 14.8" × 1.3"

Folios : 49

Language : Sanskrit

Source : Bhuvaneswar Museum, Bhuvaneswar

Title : ***Prahlādacaritam***

प्रह्लादचरितम्

Author : Tukārāma-Svāmī

Mat. : Palmleaf

Size : 35 × 8.5 cm.

Pages : 4

Script : Grantha

Source : G O M L, Triplicane, Madras

Title : ***Prahlāda Nāṭaka***

प्रह्लाद नाटक

Author : Rājā Rāmakṛṣṇa

Size : 10.2" × 9.5"

Pages : 113

Language : Oriya

Source : Bhuvaneswar Museum, Bhuvaneswar

Title : ***Pramudita Govinda Nāṭaka***

प्रमुदित गोविन्द नाटक

Author : Kaviratna Purohita Udgātā

Size : 8" × 6.5"

Pages : 93

Language : Sanskrit

Source : Bhuvaneswar Museum, Bhuvaneswar

Title : ***Pūjā Viṭayaṅkalum***

पूजा विटयंकलुम्

Author : Cankita Viṭayankalum

Size : 9½ × 1¼ cm.

Folios : 98

Illustration : 5

Source : D C of T M in M D U V S, I L, Adyar, Madras-26

Accession No. : 2066 (1274)

Title : ***Pullānipperūmāl Katavutiranttar Pāṭṭu***

पुल्लाणिपेरूमाल् कदवुतिरन्तर पाट्टु

Author : Unknown

Mat. : Palmleaf

Size : 46.2 × 3.8 cm.

Pages : 5

Language : Tamil

Script : Tamil

Source : G O M L, Triplicane, Madras

Title : ***Pullaṇi emberūmān nalaṅku***

पुल्लाणि एम्पेरूमान् नलंगु

Author : Vedānta Kavi

Mat. : Palmleaf

Size : 46.2 × 3.8 cm.

Pages : 6

Language : Tamil

Script : Tamil

Source : G O M L, Triplicane, Madras

Title : ***Purandaradāsakīrtanāni***

पुरन्दरदासकीर्तनानि

Author : Purandara Dāsa

Mat. : Palmleaf

Size : 37 × 3 cm.

Pages : 16

Script : Grantha

Source : G O M L, Triplicane, Madras

Title : ***Purandaradāsakīrtanāni***

पुरन्दरदासकीर्तनानि

Author : Purandara Dāsa

Mat. : Palmleaf

Size : 41 × 3 cm.

Pages : 4

Script : Grantha

Source : G O M L, Triplicane, Madras

Title : ***Purandara Viṭhṭhalakīrtanāni***

पुरन्दर विठ्ठलकीर्तनानि

Author : Purandara Dāsa

Mat. : Palmleaf

Size : 37 × 2.5 cm.

Pages : 45

Script : Grantha

Source : G O M L, Triplicane, Madras

Title : ***Pūrvaraṅgaḥ***

पूर्वरङ्गः

Author : Unknown

Size : 17½" × 1¼"

Leaves : 4

Granths : 200

Script : Telugu

Source : D C of the S mss in the T M S S M L, Tanjore, Vol XVI

S. No. : 10713

B. No. : 11538 c

Q

Title	: ***Qār-Ul-Asmā***		Bankipore, Patna
	क्वार–उल–अस्मा	No.	: 2235
Author	: Ṣhayakh 'Abdul-Haq Dihlag		A legal discussion on the difference of opinion in respect of song and music among Sūfis and Dar Uṛ Ṣhes.
Folios	: 60 b – 75 a		
Dated	: 1052 AH (1642 AD)		
Source	: Oriental Public Lib.,		

R

Title	: *Rādhāpremamālā Nāṭaka*
	राधाप्रेममाला नाटक
Author	: Kiśora Candra Rājendra
Size	: 9.2″ × 1.4″
Folios	: 112
Language	: Sanskrit
Source	: Bhuvaneswar Museum, Bhuvaneswar

Title	: *Rāga*
	राग
Author	: Unknown
Leaves	: 13
Granths	: 250
Source	: O I, Baroda
Acc. No.	: 10010 (e)

Title	: *Rāgacandrodaya*
	रागचन्द्रोदय
Author	: Puṇḍarīka Viṭhṭhala
Mat.	: Paper
Size	: 23 × 13 cm.
Folios	: 53
Lines	: 10
Letters	: 25 - 27
Script	: Devanāgarī
Text	: Incomplete
Dated	: Sam. 1627
Source	: Gujrat Vidya Sabha, Ahmedabad
S. No.	: 2641
Acc. No.	: 697

Title	: *Rāgacandrodaya*
	रागचन्द्रोदय
Author	: Unknown
Leaves	: 24
Granths	: 300
Text	: Complete
Cond.	: Injured
Source	: O I, Baroda
Acc. No.	: 12873

Title	: *Rāgacandrodaya*
	रागचन्द्रोदय
Author	: Vimal

Source : T A C C, Wiesbaden, 1962, Pt-I

S. No. : 26

Title : ***Rāgadarasa***

रागदरस

Author : Khuśalāl Khān

Size : 29.5 × 16.5 cm.

Pages : 121

Language : Persian

Cond. : Worm eaten, Old & Damaged copy

D O C : 1230 AH

D O T : 1242 AH

Source : State Central Lib., Hyderabad

This work was composed in the reign of Nawāb Sikandar Jah, third Nizāma of Hyderabad, dedicated to Mahārājā candu Lāl, the diwān of the state. It is divided into seven chapters, in which describes rāgas and rāgiṇīs in Hindi Dohās. This work ends at page 121. The pages 122 to 132 comprises another short treatise on general and Arabic music by Mīr Sadruddin Mohammad.

Title : ***Rāgadarpaṇa***

रागदर्पण

Author : Faqīra or Faqīrullāha

Size : 8.5 × 5.25; 6.5 × 3.25 cm.

Folios : 56

Letters : 14

Dated : 1070 AH (1666 AD)

Source : Asiatic Society of Bengal, Calcutta

S. No. : 639

It is composed in 1070 AH (1666 AD) by Faqīra or Faqīru'l-lah, divided into 10 bab's and based on a Hindi work of Māna Siṅga of Gwalior. There are many marginal notes and glosses.

Title : ***Rāgadarpaṇa***

रागदर्पण

Author : Faqīrullāh Alāmagir Śāha

Size : 9″ × 6½″

Pages : 56

Language : Persian

Text : Complete

Dated : 1665 AD

Source : Maulana Azad Lib., A M U, Aligarh

Title : ***Rāgadarpaṇa***

रागदर्पण

Language : Persian

Source : Sangeet Natak Academy Lib.

Title : ***Rāgadarpaṇa***

रागदर्पण

Author : Faqīrullāh

Size : 22.5 × 14 cm.

Pages : 42

Language : Persian

Source : State Central Lib., Hyderabad

This work composed in 1073 AH. in the reign of Rājā Māna Siṁha Gwalior. It is a transcription of Manak Tomal, divided into eight chapters and deals with rāgas, rāginīs, their timing and instrument etc.

Title : ***Rāgadarpaṇa***

रागदर्पण

Author : Faqīrullāha

Size : 25.5 × 15 cm.

Pages : 68

Language : Persian

Dated : 1219 AH

Scribe : Bilāsa Rāya alias Manohara Dāsa

Source : State Central Lib., Hyderabad

Title : ***Ragadarśana***

रागदर्शन

Author : Khuśahāl Khān

Mat. : Paper

Size : 20.7 × 12.7 cm.

Pages : 160

Script : Nastaliq

Text : Complete

Source : G O M L, Triplicane, Madras

Title : ***Rāgadarśana***

रागदर्शन

Author : Khuśahāl Khān

Size : 20.7 × 12.7 cm.

Folios : 80

Illustration : 9

Script : Persian

Source : C of P & A mss in the G O M L, Madras

S. No. : 958

Acc. No. : D 515

Title : ***Rāgadarśana***

रागदर्शन

Author : Khuśahāl Khān

Size : 30.6 × 24 cm.

Folios : 29

Illustration : 23

Script : Persian

Source : C of P & A mss in the G O M L, Madras

S. No. : 959

Acc. No. : D 1024

Title : ***Rāgadhyānāni***

रागध्यानानि

Author : Unknown

Size : 8¼″ × 4⅞″

Folios : 2

Language : Sanskrit

Text : Incomplete

Source : Nagpur Univ. Lib., Nagpur

S. No : 4

Acc. No. : 4456

Title : ***Rāgagaṇanāmādhyāya***

रागगणनामाध्याय

Author : Unknown

Size : 28.1 × 14.4 cm.

Folios : 1

Illustration : 10

Script : Devanāgarī

Cond. : Old

Scurce : A C of mss in the A B S P, Lucknow

No. : 1151

Title : ***Rāgagauḍā***

रागगौड़ा

Author : Haridāsa

Dated : Sam.1520 – 40

P. Year : 1922 AD

Source : Nagari Pracharini Sabha, Varanasi,Vol II

S. No. : 37 F

Title : ***Rāgagyānasaṅgraha***

रागज्ञानसंग्रह

Author : Harivilāsa

Mat. : Paper

Size : 8″ × 6″

Leaves : 24

Lines : 30

Letters : 328

Script : Devanāgarā

Dated : 1875 AD

Source : K M U H H G K S T V, Kashi

Acc. No. : 149C

Title . ***Rāga-I-Hind or Sahas Ras***

राग–ए–हिन्द और सहस रस

Language : Persian

Source : Sangeet Natak Academy Lib.

Title	: ***Rāgakalpadruma***
	रागकल्पद्रुम
Author	: Kṛṣṇananda Vyāsa
Dated	: Sam. 1899
P. Year	: 1923 AD
Source	: Nagari Pracharini Sabha, Varanasi, Vol II
S. No.	: 223

Title	: ***Rāgakalpadruma Nityakīrtanasaṅgraha***
	रागकल्पद्रुम नित्यकीर्तनसंग्रह
Author	: Śrī Kṛṣṇānanda
Size	: 16 × 8 cm.
Folios	: 84
Letters	: 56
Dated	: 1842 AD
Source	: T T R on the S of H Ms, Allahabad
No.	: 223

Here is the Bhajans of Suradasa etc. or set in the different Ragas

Title	: ***Rāgakutūhala***
	रागकुतूहल
Author	: Harivallabha
Dated	: V. S. 1816
Source	: A C of mss in the L of H H the M of U, Udaipur, 1943, S B L
No.	: 185

Title	: ***Rāgalakṣamaṇi***
	रागलक्षमणि
Size	: 10¾″ × 4⅝″
Folios	: 22
Lines	: 9-11
Script	: Devanāgarī
Dated	: 18th century
Source	: C of S mss in the I O L, London, Vol II
S. No.	: 5192
Acc. No.	: 3314 a

A treatise on the characteristics of the difficult musical Rāgas. The Ms. is not at all correct. It may be noted that this accords in context in some couriduable measure with Prakaraṇa III of the nartana-nirṇaya of Puṇdarīka Viṭhthal and conceivably – as he is the author of their parts of mss is really part of their work.

Title	: ***Rāgalakṣaṇa***
	रागलक्षण
Author	: Unknown
Source	: British Museum, London
No.	: 14055 e 3 (5)

A treatise on the modes of music in verses. Edited by Dattātreya Keśava Jośī pp. VII. 68 Bombay, Poona, 1914.

Title : ***Rāgalakṣaṇa***

रागलक्षण

Author : Unknown

Ms. W P : H. H. the Mahārājā of Travancore

Source : L of S mss in P L of S I, Madras, 1880, Vol I

S. No. : 6166

Title : ***Rāgalakṣaṇa***

रागलक्षण

Author : Unknown

Source : T A C C, Wiesbaden, 1962, Pt-I

S. No. : 34

Title : ***Rāgamālā***

रागमाला

Author : Kṣemakaraṇa

Size : 25 × 10.5 cm.

Folios : 1 - 6, 8 - 15

Illustration : 9

Script : Devanāgarī

Dated : V. S.-1682

Source : A C of mss in the A B S P, Lucknow

No. : 24

Title : ***Rāgamālā***

रागमाला

Author : Kṣemakaraṇa

Size : 10″ × 4½″

Folios : 15

Language : Sanskrit

Source : Asiatic Society, 1, Park Street, Calcutta-16

Title : ***Rāgamālā***

रागमाला

Author : Puṇḍrīka Viṭṭhal

Size : 9¼″ × 4½″

Folios : 25

Illustration : 10

Dated : Sam. 1671

Source : B O R I, Poona

Acc. No. : 1026/1884 - 87

Title : ***Rāgamālā***

रागमाला

Author : Puṇḍrīka Viṭṭhal

Size : 5¼″ × 9½″

Folios : 3

Illustration : 24

Cond. : Old mss

Source : B O R I, Poona

Acc. No. : 646(b)/1899-1915

Title	:	***Rāgamālā***
		रागमाला
Author	:	Jīvarāja Dīksita
Size	:	8¾″ × 4¾″
Folios	:	9
Illustration	:	9
Cond.	:	New mss
Source	:	B O R I, Poona
Acc. No.	:	349/1895 - 98

Title	:	***Rāgamālā***
		रागमाला
Author	:	Unknown
Source	:	B I S M H G C, Poona
No.	:	7269

Title	:	***Rāgamālā***
		रागमाला
Author	:	Puṇḍarīka Viṭhṭhala
Source	:	British Museum, London
No.	:	14055 e 3 (4)

A metrical treatise on Indian music. It is edited by Nārāyaṇa Govinda Rātāñjankara, Gaṇapati Rāva & Gopāla Rāva, p. 26, Bombay, 1914.

Title	:	***Rāgamālā***
		रागमाला
Author	:	Bharata
Size	:	10″ × 4″
Folios	:	14
Lines	:	7
Ślokas	:	233
Language	:	Nevārī
Source	:	A C of P & S P mss D L, Nepal, Calcutta,1905
S. No.	:	1478

Title	:	***Rāgamālā***
		रागमाला
Author	:	Viṭhṭhala
Mat.	:	Paper
Size	:	24.5 × 10.5 cm.
Folios	:	16
Lines	:	9
Letters	:	31
Script	:	Devanāgarī
Text	:	Complete
Dated	:	Sam. 1680
Source	:	Gujrat Vidya Sabha, Ahmedabad
S. No.	:	2642

Acc. No. : 2073

Title : ***Rāgamālā***

रागमाला

Author : Unknown

Mat. : Paper

Size : 24.5 × 11.5 cm.

Folios : 11

Lines : 13

Letters : 33

Script : Devanāgarī

Text : Complete

Dated : Sam. 1616

Source : Gujrat Vidya Sabha, Ahmedabad

S. No. : 2643

Acc. No. : 2535

Title : ***Rāgamālā***

रागमाला

Author : Kṣemakṛṣṇa Pāṭhaka

Size : 9½″ × 4¼″

Lines : 8

Script : Modern Bengālī

Dated : 1492 Śaka (1570 AD)

Source : C of S mss in the I O L, London, Vol I, Pt-II

No. : 1516 b

A description of various musical modes composed for Jāṭava (Yātavā) Bhūpati in Śaka 1492 (1570 AD) by Kṣemarkṛṣṇa Pāṭhaka, son of Maheśa Pāṭhaka in the chapter. The treatise has an introductory chapter called 'Rāga-Sūcana' seems to the wanting in the Oxford mss (Aufrecht, Cat. No. 48).

The copyist allusion to Akabar 1556–1605 AD, seems to have come either from the author's own mss, or from an early copy. For another treatise of the 'Same Title' by 'Jīva-Rāja', see Raj Mitr, Notices, VII, p. 21.

Title : ***Rāgamālā***

रागमाला

Author : Unknown

Mat. : Paper

Size : 6″ × 5½″

Leaves : 3

Lines : 10

Letters : 34

Script : Devanāgarī

Source : K M U H H G K S T V, Kashi

Acc. No. : 192

36 Rāgiṇīs are described in this book in Sanskrit and Hindi language.

Title	: ***Rāgamālā***
	रागमाला
Author	: Unknown
Mat.	: Paper
Size	: 9¼″ × 6″
Leaves	: 27
Lines	: 19
Letters	: 577
Script	: Devanāgarī
Source	: K M U H H G K S T V, Kashi
Acc. No.	: 193

Title	: ***Rāgamālā***
	रागमाला
Author	: Unknown
Size	: 7″ × 6″
Leaves	: 8
Lines	: 8
Letters	: 55
Script	: Devanāgarī
Source	: K M U H H G K S T V, Kashi
Acc. No.	: 403

Title	: ***Rāgamālā***
	रागमाला
Author	: Unknown
Size	: 3.5″ × 5″
Leaves	: 36
Lines	: 6
Letters	: 216
Script	: Devanāgarī
Source	: K M U H H G K S T V, Kashi
Acc. No.	: 404

Title	: ***Rāgamālā***
	रागमाला
Author	: Garati-jana
Mat.	: Paper
Size	: 8″ × 6″
Leaves	: 6
Lines	: 20
Letters	: 175
Script	: Devanāgarī
Dated	: 1855 Sam.
Source	: K M U H H G K S T V, Kashi
Acc. No.	: 131

Title	: ***Rāgamālā***
	रागमाला
Author	: Kudura-Tulla
Mat.	: Paper
Size	: 10″ × 6″
Leaves	: 120
Lines	: 32
Letters	: 1400
Script	: Devanāgarā
Dated	: 1880 AD

Source : K M U H H G K S T V, Kashi

Acc. No. : 206 C

Title : ***Rāgamālā***

रागमाला

Author : Unknown

Size : 8″ × 5½″

Leaves : 5

Lines : 11

Letters : 198

Script : Devanāgarī

Dated : 1880 AD

Source : K M U H H G K S T V, Kashi

Acc. No. : 276

Title : ***Rāgamālā***

रागमाला

Author : Unknown

Mat. : Paper

Size : 26 × 11 cm.

Pages : 7

Lines : 15

Extent : 40

Script : Devanāgarī

Text : Complete

Dated : V. S. 1750

Source : C of S & P mss in M S P C, L D B S V, Ahmedabad

S. No. : 6357

Acc. No : 8927

Title : ***Rāgamālā***

रागमाला

Author : V. Puṇḍarīka

Mat. : Paper

Size : 21.4 × 12.3 cm.

Pages : 14

Lines : 9

Extent : 35

Script : Devanāgarī

Text : Complete

Dated : V. S. 1887

Source : C of S & P mss in M S P C, L D B S V, Ahmedabad

S. No. : 6358E

Acc. No : 508

Title : ***Rāgamālā***

रागमाला

Author : Kṣemakaraṇa

Source : A C of mss in the L of H H the M of U, Udaipur, 1943, S B L

No. : 815

Title : ***Rāgamālā***

रागमाला

Author : Kṣemakaraṇa

Dated : V. S. 1823

Source : A C of mss in the L of H H

the M of U, Udaipur, 1943, S B L

S. No. : 1654

Title : ***Rāgamālā***

रागमाला

Author : Ghanaśyāma

Dated : Sam. 1700

P. Year : 1901

Source : Nagari Pracharini Sabha, Varanasi

S. No. : 102

Title : ***Rāgamālā***

रागमाला

Author : Tānasena

P. Year : 1902 AD

Source : Nagari Pracharini Sabha, Varanasi, Vol II

S. No. : 40

Title : ***Rāgamālā***

रागमाला

Author : Tārānātha

P. Year : 1904 AD

Source : Nagari Pracharini Sabha, Varanasi, Vol II

S. No. : 138

Title : ***Rāgamālā***

रागमाला

Author : Vyāsa jī

Dated : Sam.1855

P. Year : 1906 AD

Source : Nagari Pracharini Sabha, Varanasi, Vol II

S. No. : 118 A

Title : ***Rāgamālā***

रागमाला

Author : Durjanadāsa

P. Year : 1906 AD

Source : Nagari Pracharini Sabha, Varanasi, Vol II

S. No. : 163

Title : ***Rāgamālā***

रागमाला

Author : Deva

Dated : Sam. 1869

P. Year : 1906 AD

Source : Nagari Pracharini Sabha, Varanasi, Vol II

S. No. : 155

Title : ***Rāgamālā***

रागमाला

Author : Navalakiśora

P. Year : 1922 AD

Source : Nagari Pracharini Sabha, Varanasi, Vol II

S. No. : 76

Title : ***Rāgamālā***
रागमाला
Author : Yaśodānanda
Dated : Sam. 1815
P. Year : 1909 AD
Source : Nagari Pracharini Sabha, Varanasi, Vol II
S. No. : 334

Title : ***Rāgamālā***
रागमाला
Author : Unknown
P. Year : 1904 AD
Source : Nagari Pracharini Sabha, Varanasi, Vol II
S. No. : 486

Title : ***Rāgamālā***
रागमाला
Author : Jīvarāja Dīkṣita
Size : 17 × 11 cm.
Folios : 10
Language : Sanskrit
Source : National Lib., Belvedere, Calcutta-27
S. No. : 5

Title : ***Rāgamālā***
रागमाला
Author : Jīvarāja Dīkṣita
Leaves : 20
Granths : 160
Dated : 1921 AD
Source : O I, Baroda
Acc. No. : 11238

Title : ***Rāgamālā***
रागमाला
Author : Meṣakarṇa
Leaves : 24
Granths : 190
Text : Incomplete
Source : O I, Baroda
Acc. No. : 4553

Title : ***Rāgamālā***
रागमाला
Author : Viṭhṭhala
Leaves : 11
Granths : 200
Dated : Śaka 1498
Source : O I, Baroda
Accession No : 1985

Title : ***Rāgamālā***
रागमाला
Author : Unknown
Leaves : 12
Granths : 200

Source : O I, Baroda
Acc. No. : 11457

Title : ***Rāgamālā***
रागमाला
Author : Vṛajanātha Dīkṣita
Folios : 10
Dated : 1894 AD
Source : R P G Vol II, O R I, Jodhpur
No. : 4199

Title : ***Rāgamālā***
रागमाला
Author : Unknown
Folios : 2
Dated : 19th century
Source : R P G Vol II, O R I, Jodhpur
No. : 5094

Title : ***Rāgamālā***
रागमाला
Author : Unknown
Size : 24 × 10 cm.
Folios : 3
Language : Lans/Maithilī
Text : Incomplete
Cond. : Old
Source : Patna Univ. Lib., Bihar

Title : ***Rāgamālā***
रागमाला
Author : Unknown
Size : 10″ × 4¼″
Folios : 11
Illustration : 17
Script : Devanāgarī
Dated : Sam. 1758 (18th century)
Source : Prachina Sahitya Shodh Sansthana, Udaipur
Acc. No. : 1 (संगीतग्रन्थ)

Title : ***Rāgamālā***
रागमाला
Author : Hīrachanda
Size : 4¼″ × 7″
Folios : 3
Illustration : 27
Script : Devanāgarī
Dated : Sam. 1691
Source : Prachina Sahitya Shodh Sansthana, Udaipur
Acc. No. : 2 (संगीतग्रन्थ)

Title : ***Rāgamālā***
रागमाला
Author : Unknown
Size : 10″ × 4¼″
Folios : 2
Illustration : 20

Script : Devanāgarī

Dated : Sam. 1746

Source : Prachina Sahitya Shodh Sansthana, Udaipur

Acc. No. : 3 (संगीतग्रन्थ)

Title : ***Rāgamālā***

रागमाला

Size : 4¾″ × 16″

Folio : 1

Illustration : 45

Script : Devanāgarī

Dated : 19th century

Source : Prachina Sahitya Shodh Sansthana, Udaipur

Acc. No. : 5 (संगीतग्रन्थ)

Six Rāgas & thirty six Rāganis in this book.

Title : ***Rāgamālā***

रागमाला

Size : 10″ × 4″

Folio : 1

Illustration : 13

Script : Devanāgarī

Text : Incomplete

Dated : 19th century

Source : Prachina Sahitya Shodh Sansthana, Udaipur

Acc. No. : 6 (संगीतग्रन्थ)

Title : ***Rāgamālā***

रागमाला

Author : Lakṣmīprabhu

Size : 4¼″ × 7″

Folios : 2

Illustration : 27

Script : Devanāgarī

Dated : 18th century

Source : Prachina Sahitya Shodh Sansthana, Udaipur

Acc. No. : 7 (संगीतग्रन्थ)

Title : ***Rāgamālā***

रागमाला

Author : Abdul Walī 'Uzalat'

Size : 23 × 11 cm.

Pages : 126

Language : Urdu

Source : State Central Lib., Hyderabad This work is in Mathnavi (epic) form of Urdu poetry, composed by a famous urdu poet.

Title : ***Rāgamālā***

रागमाला

Author : Kṣemakarṇa

Source : T A C C, Wiesbaden, 1962, Pt-I

S. No. : 31

Title	:	***Rāgamālā***
		रागमाला
Author	:	Puṇdarīka Viṭhṭhala
Source	:	T A C C, Wiesbaden, 1962, Pt-I
S. No.	:	7

Title	:	***Rāgamālā***
		रागमाला
Author	:	Kṣemakaraṇa
Source	:	T A C C, Wiesbaden, 1962, Pt-III
S. No.	:	1

Title	:	***Rāgamālā***
		रागमाला
Author	:	Unknown
Mat.	:	Paper
Size	:	7.8″ × 4.2″
Folios	:	1-5
Lines	:	9
Letters	:	19
Script	:	Devanāgarī
Source	:	Varanaseya Skt. Visvavidyalaya Lib., Varanasi
S. No.	:	45514

Title	:	***Rāgamālā***
		रागमाला
Author	:	Unknown
Mat.	:	Paper
Size	:	6.5″ × 4.6″
Folios	:	9-43
Lines	:	5
Letters	:	13
Script	:	Devanāgarī
Source	:	Varanaseya Skt. Visvavidyalaya Lib., Varanasi
S. No.	:	45980

Title	:	***Rāgamālā***
		रागमाला
Author	:	Unknown
Mat.	:	Paper
Size	:	10.3″ × 5.4″
Folios	:	1
Lines	:	18
Letters	:	45
Script	:	Devanāgarī
Source	:	Varanaseya Skt. Visvavidyalaya Lib., Varanasi
S. No.	:	46143

Title	:	***Rāgamālā***
		रागमाला
Author	:	Unknown
Mat.	:	Paper
Size	:	7.8″ × 5.6″
Folios	:	1, 1, 1-51, +1
Lines	:	15
Letters	:	12
Script	:	Devanāgarī
Source	:	Varanaseya Skt. Visvavidyalaya Lib., Varanasi
S. No.	:	46249

Title	: ***Rāgamālā Cintāmaṇi***
	रागमाला चिन्तामणि
Author	: Poluri Govindakavi
Mat.	: Paper
Size	: 22 × 16.5 cm.
Pages	: 44
Language	: Telugu
Script	: Telugu
Source	: G O M L, Triplicane, Madras

Title	: ***Rāgamālikā***
	रागमालिका
Author	: Saṅgītadāmodara
Mat.	: Palmleaf
Size	: 27 × 4 cm.
Pages	: 7
Script	: Oriya
Source	: G O M L, Triplicane, Madras

Title	: ***Rāgamālikā***
	रागमालिका
Author	: Kaviratna
Mat.	: Palmleaf
Size	: 27 × 4 cm.
Pages	: 3
Script	: Oriya
Source	: G O M L, Triplicane, Madras

Title	: ***Rāgamālikā***
	रागमालिका
Mat.	: Paper
Size	: 28.5 × 24 cm.
Pages	: 5
Script	: Devanāgarā
Source	: G O M L, Triplicane, Madras

Title	: ***Rāgamālikā***
	रागमालिका
Mat.	: Paper
Size	: 28.5 × 24 cm.
Pages	: 5
Script	: Devanāgarī
Source	: G O M L, Triplicane, Madras

Title	: ***Rāgamañjarī***
	रागमंजरी
Author	: Puṇḍarīka Viṭhṭhala
Source	: British Museum, London
No.	: 14055 e 4(3)
	A metrical tract on modes of music.

Title	: ***Rāgamañjarī***
	रागमंजरी
Author	: Śākdṛpi Bhūdhara Miśra
Folios	: 27
Illustration	: 8
Script	: Devanāgarī
Dated	: 18th century
Source	: Prachina Sahitya Shodh Sansthana, Udaipur

Title	: ***Rāgamañjarī***
	रागमंजरी
Author	: Viṭhṭhala puṇḍarīka
Mat.	: Paper

Size : 17.2 × 21.6 cm.
Folios : 5
Lines : 9
Illustration : 36
Script : Devanāgarī
Text : Complete
Dated : V. S. 1908
Source : R O I, Jodhpur, Pt.-II
S. No. : 537 E
Acc. No. : 209

Title : ***Rāgamañjarī***
रागमंजरी
Author : Puṇḍarīka Viṭhṭhala
Source : T A C C, Wiesbaden, 1962, Pt-I
S. No. : 30

Title : ***Rāgamanohara***
रागमनोहर
Author : Gaṇeśa Prasada
Mat. : Paper
Size : 8″ × 6″
Leaves : 34
Lines : 32
Letters : 854
Script : Devanāgarī
Dated : 1865 AD
Source : K M U H H G K S T V, Kashi
Acc. No. : 107 I

Title : ***Rāgamanohara***
रागमनोहर
Author : Gaṅeśa Prasada
Dated : Sam. 1922
P. Year : 1929 AD
Source : Nagari Pracharini Sabha, Varanasi, Vol II
S. No. : 109 I

Title : ***Rāganāmamālāmūrtiḥ***
रागनाममालामूर्तिः
Author : Unknown
Mat. : Paper
Size : 7.6″ × 4.3″
Folios : 1-6, 1-47, 49-51
Lines : 15
Letters : 11
Script : Devanāgarī
Source : Varanaseya Skt. Visvavidyalaya Lib., Varanasi
S. No. : 45502

Title : ***Rāganirṇaya***
रागनिर्णय
Author : Dasa
Dated : Sam. 1835
P. Year : 1901 AD
Source : Nagari Pracharini Sabha, Varanasi, Vol II
S. No. : 154

Title : ***Rāganirūpaṇa***

रागनिरूपण

Author : Puran Miśra

P. Year : 1902 AD

Source : Nagari Pracharini Sabha, Varanasi, Vol II

S. No. : 42

Title : ***Rāganirūpaṇam***

रागनिरूपणम्

Author : Nārada

Mat. : Paper

Sheets : 14

Lines : 11

Size : 8 5/8″ × 4″

Script : Devanāgarī

Granths : 286

Text : Complete

Source : D C of the S mss in the T M S S M L, Tanjore, Vol XVI

S. No. : 10814

B. No. : 6651

There are description of 140 Rāgas. It is Published by D. K. Joshi in 1914 AD from Poona.

Title : ***Rāgaprabodha***

रागप्रबोध

Author : Nandalāla

Mat. : Paper

Size : 9″ × 6″

Leaves : 52

Lines : 19

Letters : 618

Script : Devanāgarī

Dated : 1787 AD

Source : K M U H H G K S T V, Kashi

Acc. No. : 319

Title : ***Rāgapradīpaḥ***

रागप्रदीपः

Mat. : Paper

Size : 28 × 24 cm.

Pages : 13

Script : Telugu

Source : G O M L, Triplicane, Madras

Title : ***Ragaprakāśa***

रागप्रकाश

Author : Madhava Siṅha

Dated : Sam. 1915

P. Year : 1901 AD

Source : Nagari Pracharini Sabha, Varanasi, Vol II

S. No. : 290 K

Title : ***Rāgarāginī***

रागरागिनी

Author : Unknown

Source : O I, Baroda

Acc. No. : 12710

Title : ***Rāgarāginī***

रागरागिनी

Author : Unknown

Source : O I, Baroda

Acc. No. : 13265

Title : ***Rāgarāginībheda***

रागरागिनीभेद

Author : Unknown

Size : 9¾″ × 6½″

Leaves : 2

Lines : 18

Letters : 108

Script : Devanāgarī

Source : K M U H H G K S T V, Kashi

Acc. No. : 277

Title : ***Rāgarāginīsvarūpa***

रागरागिनीस्वरूप

Author : Unknown

Size : 8″ × 5″

Leaves : 3

Lines : 11

Letters : 99

Script : Devanāgarī

Source : K M U H H G K S T V, Kashi

Acc. No. : 194

Title : ***Rāgarāgiṇīsvarūpāṇi***

रागरागिणीस्वरूपाणि

Author : Unknown

Size : 9¼″ × 3⅝″

Folios : 6

Illustration : 6

Cond. : Old mss.

Source : B O R I, Poona

Acc. No. : 978/1887-91

Title : ***Rāgarāgiṇīsvarūpāṇi***

रागरागिणीस्वरूपाणि

Author : Unknown

Leaves : 6

Lines : 26

Letters : 7

Text : Complete

Source : R on the S for S mss in the B P, Bombay

S. No. : 978

Title : ***Rāgarāgiṇīsvarūpasūcī***

रागरागिणीस्वरूपसूची

Author : Unknown

Mat. : Paper

Size : 10.8″ × 4.5″

Folio : 1

Lines : 16

Letters : 27

Script : Devanāgarī

Source : Varanaseya Skt. Visvavidyalaya Lib., Varanasi

S. No. : 45505

Title : ***Rāga Rāgiṇiyon Ka Varṇana***

राग रागिणियों का वर्णन

Author : Unknown

P. Year : 1901 AD

Source : Nagari Pracharini Sabha, Varanasi, Vol II

S. No. : 553

Title : ***Rāgaratna***

रागरत्न

Author : Māṇikya

Size : 9" × 5"

Folios : 1-4, less 1 folio

Language : Sanskrit

Source : Asiatic Society, 1, Park Street, Calcutta-16

Title : ***Rāgaratnākara***

रागरत्नाकर

Author : Devadatta

P. Year : 1912 AD

Source : Nagari Pracharini Sabha, Varanasi, Vol II

S. No. : 50 A

Title : ***Rāgaratnākara***

रागरत्नाकर

Author : Rādhākṛṣṇa

P. Year : 1901 AD

Source : Nagari Pracharini Sabha, Varanasi, Vol II

S. No. : 335

Title : ***Rāgaratnākara***

रागरत्नाकर

Author : Rādhākṛṣṇa

Dated : Sam. 1853

Source : Nagari Pracharini Sabha, Varanasi, Vol II

Title : ***Rāgaratnākara***

रागरत्नाकर

Author : Kavikṛṣṇa

Size : 8¾" × 5"

Folios : 26

Script : Devanāgarī

Dated : Sam. 1895

Source : Nagpur Univ. Lib., 1957

S. No. : 1768

Acc. No. : 2608

Title : ***Rāgaratnākara***
रागरत्नाकर
Author : Kavikṛṣṇa
Size : 8¾″ × 4¾″
Folios : 26
Language : Hindi
Dated : Sam. 1895
Source : Nagpur Univ. Lib., Nagpur
Acc. No. : 2608

Title : ***Rāgaratnākara***
रागरत्नाकर
Author : Śaṅkarṣaṇa
Leaves : 7
Granths : 49 Śloka
Source : O I, Baroda
Acc. No. : 11027

Title : ***Rāgaratnākara***
रागरत्नाकर
Author : Unknown
Size : 20 × 16 cm.
Folios : 62
Language : Devanāgarī
Text : Complete
Source : Patna Univ. Lib., Bihar

Title : ***Rāgaratnākara***
रागरत्नाकर
Author : Gandharvarāja
Mat. : Paper
Size : 8¼″ × 4½″
Sheets : 19
Lines : 10
Granths : 222
Script : Devanāgarī
Text : Complete
Source : D C of the S mss in the T M S S M L, Tanjore, Vol XVI
S. No. : 10811
B. No. : 6642
Copies : 10812 B. No. 6644 Paper Devanāgarī Complete 10813 B. No. 6645 Paper Devanāgarī Complete

Title : ***Rāgaratnaprakāśa***
रागरत्नप्रकाश
Author : Devadatta
Dated : Sam. 1893
P. Year : 1920 AD
Source : Nagari Pracharini Sabha, Varanasi, Vol II
S. No. : 39 C

Title : ***Rāgaratnāvalī***
रागरत्नावली
Author : Gopala Siṅha
Dated : Sam. 1758
P. Year : 1906 AD

Source : Nagari Pracharini Sabha, Varanasi

S. No. : 42

Title : ***Rāgārohāvarohaṇa Paṭṭiāk***

रागारोहावरोहण पट्‌टैक

Author : Unknown

Leaves : One long Sheet

Script : Devanāgarī

Source : D C of the S mss in the T M S S M L, Tanjore, Vol XVI

S. No. : 10956

B. No. : 13961

Showing the Rāgās and their ascending and descending processes.

Title : ***Rāgarūpamālā***

रागरूपमाला

Author : Bālakṛṣṇa

Mat. : Paper

Size : 8" × 6"

Leaves : 27

Lines : 15

Letters : 405

Script : Devanāgarī

Dated : 1705 BC

Source : K M U H H G K S T V, Kashi

Acc. No. : 16

Title : ***Rāgasāgara***

रागसागर

Author : Parasarāma

Size : 12″ × 10″

Leaves : 79

Lines : 25

Letters : 3500

Script : Devanāgarī

Source : K M U H H G K S T V, Kashi

Acc. No. : 163 C

Title : ***Rāgasāgara***

रागसागर

Author : Unknown

Size : 9" × 6"

Leaves : 126

Lines : 9

Letters : 1564

Script : Devanāgarī

Source : K M U H H G K S T V, Kashi

Acc. No. : 278

Title : ***Rāgasāgara or Saṅgītakalpadruma***

रागसागर और संगीतकल्पद्रुम

Author : Kṛṣṇānanda

Mat. : Paper

Size : 8″ × 6″

Leaves : 23

Lines : 12
Letters : 345
Script : Devanāgarī
Source : K M U H H G K S T V, Kashi
Acc. No. : 125

Title : ***Rāgasāgara***
रागसागर
Author : Manasiṅha
P. Year : 1902 AD
Source : Nagari Pracharini Sabha, Varanasi, Vol II
S. No. : 77

Title : ***Rāgasāgara***
रागसागर
Author : Visvanāthasiṅha
P. Year : 1920 AD
Source : Nagari Pracharini Sabha, Varanasi
S. No. : 205

Title : ***Rāgasāgaram Nāradīyam***
रागसागरम् नारदीयम्
Author : Nārada
Mat. : Paper
Size : 28 × 25 cm.
Pages : 27
Script : Devanāgarī
Source : G O M L, Triplicane, Madras

Title : ***Rāgasamūha***
रागसमूह
Author : Kṛṣṇa
Dated : Sam. 1846
P. Year : 1917 AD
Source : Nagari Pracharini Sabha, Varanasi, Vol II
S. No. : 100

Title : ***Rāgasāgaraḥ***
रागसागरः
Mat. : Paper
Size : 19 × 16 cm.
Pages : 23
Script : Telugu
Source : G O M L, Triplicane, Madras

Title : ***Rāgasāgaraḥ***
रागसागरः
Mat. : Paper
Size : 26 × 20 cm.
Pages : 12
Script : Telugu
Source : G O M L, Triplicane, Madras

Title	:	***Rāgasāgaraḥ***
		रागसागरः
Mat.	:	Paper
Size	:	19.5 × 15 cm.
Pages	:	24
Script	:	Telugu
Source	:	G O M L, Triplicane, Madras

Title	:	***Rāgasaṅgraha***
		रागसंग्रह
Author	:	Devakīnandana
Mat.	:	Papaer
Size	:	10″ × 6″
Leaves	:	50
Lines	:	24
Letters	:	720
Script	:	Devanāgarī
Dated	:	1870 AD
Source	:	K M U H H G K S T V, Kashi
Acc. No.	:	96

Title	:	***Rāgasaṅgraha***
		रागसंग्रह
Author	:	Mannā Lāla
Size	:	8″ × 6″
Leaves	:	84
Lines	:	36
Letters	:	1624
Script	:	Devanāgarī
Dated	:	1874 A.D.
Source	:	K M U H H G K S T V, Kashi
Acc. No.	:	229B

Title	:	***Rāgasaṅgraha***
		रागसंग्रह
Author	:	Garībadāsa
Mat.	:	Paper
Size	:	5″ × 4″
Leaves	:	6
Lines	:	13
Letters	:	78
Script	:	Devanāgarī
Source	:	K M U H H G K S T V, Kashi
Acc. No.	:	64

Title	:	***Rāgasaṅgrahaḥ***
		रागसंग्रहः
Author	:	Unknown
Mat.	:	Paper
Size	:	6.5″ × 4.3″
Folios	:	1 - 42
Lines	:	13
Letters	:	12
Script	:	Devanāgarī
Source	:	Varanaseya Skt. Visvavidyalaya Lib., Varanasi
S. No.	:	45848

Title	:	***Rāgasaṅgraham***
		रागसंग्रहम्
Author	:	Datīlaṃ
Source	:	Venkatesvara Univ., Tirupati

Title	:	***Rāgasaṅkīrṇa***
		रागसंकीर्ण
Author	:	Svamīkārtika
P. Year	:	1901 AD
Source	:	Nagari Pracharini Sabha, Varanasi, Vol II
S. No.	:	473

Title	:	***Rāgasaṅkhyāvelā***
		रागसंख्यावेला
Author	:	Unknown
Size	:	6¼" × 3½"
Folios	:	2
Language	:	Sanskrit
Source	:	Nagpur Univ. Lib., Nagpur
Acc. No.	:	5647

Title	:	***Rāgasāra***
		रागसार
Author	:	Harivilāsa
Size	:	8" × 6"
Leaves	:	36
Lines	:	34
Letters	:	972
Script	:	Devanāgarī
Source	:	K M U H H G K S T V, Kashi
Acc. No.	:	149 A

Title	:	***Rāgasāra***
		रागसार
Author	:	Harivilāsa
Mat.	:	Paper
Size	:	8″ × 6″
Leaves	:	48
Lines	:	32
Letters	:	1211
Script	:	Devanāgarī
Dated	:	1883 AD
Source	:	K M U H H G K S T V, Kashi
Acc. No.	:	149B

Title	:	***Rāgasaragama Nāradīyam***
		रागसरगम नारदीयम्
Author	:	Nārada
Mat.	:	Paper
Size	:	28 × 25 cm.
Pages	:	27
Script	:	Devanāgarī
Source	:	G O M L, Triplicane, Madras

Title	:	***Rāgasāraḥ***
		रागसारः
Author	:	Dattilaḥ
Source	:	Venkatesvara Univ., Tirupati

Title	:	***Rāgasārasaṅgraha***
		रागसारसंग्रह
Author	:	Mannā lāla
Mat.	:	Paper
Size	:	8″ × 6″
Leaves	:	72
Lines	:	36
Letters	:	1309
Script	:	Devanāgarā
Dated	:	1884 AD
Source	:	K M U H H G K S T V, Kashi
Acc. No.	:	229 A

Title	:	***Rāgasvarūpalakṣaṇam***
		रागस्वरूपलक्षणम्
Author	:	Unknown
Source	:	B I S M H G C, Poona
No.	:	22675

Title	:	***Rāgasvarūpavarṇana (Saṅgītaratnākare)***
		रागस्वरूपवर्णन (संगीतरत्नाकरे)
Author	:	Unknown
Mat.	:	Paper
Size	:	16.5 × 10 cm.
Folios	:	24
Lines	:	6
Letters	:	15
Script	:	Devanāgarī
Text	:	Complete
Dated	:	Sam. 1840
Source	:	Gujrat Vidya Sabha, Ahmedabad
S. No.	:	2644
Acc. No.	:	2661

Title	:	***Rāgatālacintāmaṇi***
		रागतालचिन्तामणि
Author	:	Poluri Govinḍ Kavi
Mat.	:	Paper
Size	:	22 × 16.5 cm.
Pages	:	44
Language	:	Telugu
Script	:	Telugu
Source	:	G O M L, Triplicane, Madras

Title	:	***Rāgataraṅgiṇī***
		रागतरंगिणी
Author	:	Locana Paṇḍita
Source	:	British Museum, London
No.	:	14055 e 4(3)
		A metrical tract on musical modes.

Title	:	***Rāgatattvavibodha***
		रागतत्त्वविबोध
Author	:	Śrīnivāsa Paṇḍita
Dated	:	1918 AD

Source : British Museum, London

No. : 14055 e 4 (3)

A metrical tracts on musical modes.

Title : ***Rāgatattvavibodha***

रागतत्त्वविबोध

Author : Śrīnivāsa

Source : B I S M H G C, Poona

No. : 22676

Title : ***Rāgatattvavibodha***

रागतत्त्वविबोध

Author : Śrīnivāsa

Leaves : 36

Granths : 700

Source : O I, Baroda

Acc. No. : 10818

Title : ***Rāgatattvavibodha***

रागतत्त्वविबोध

Author : Śrīnivāsa

Source : T A C C, Wiesbaden, 1962, Pt-II

S. No. : 19

Title : ***Rāgatattvavibodha***

रागतत्त्वविबोध

Author : Śrīnivāsa

Source : T A C C, Wiesbaden, 1962, Pt-I

S. No. : 27 B

Title : ***Rāgavarṇanirūpaṇam***

रागवर्णनिरूपणम्

Author : Unknown

Mat. : Palmleaf

Size : 43 × 4 cm.

Pages : 15

Script : Telugu

Source : G O M L, Triplicane, Madras

Title : ***Rāgavarṇanirūpaṇam***

रागवर्णनिरूपणम्

Author : Unknown

Mat. : Paper

Size : 32.5 × 25.5 cm.

Pages : 13

Script : Devanāgarī

Source : G O M L, Triplicane, Madras

Title : ***Rāgavartmacandrikā***

रागवर्त्मचन्द्रिका

Author : Viśvanātha Cakravartī

Pages : 188

Source : British Museum, London

No. : 14060 b b 11(1)

Being part of Bhaktivartma-pradarśakagrantha. It is

published from Calcutta in 1915.

Title : ***Rāgavibodha***

रागविबोध

Author : Soma

Size : 10″ × 4½″

Folios : 15

Language : Sanskrit

Source : Asiatic Society, 1, Park Street, Calcutta-16

Title : ***Rāgavibodha***

रागविबोध

Author : Somanātha

Edi. by : Richard Simon

Source : British Museum, London

It is a musical composition of Somanātha. He was a son of Mudgala. The verses 37-166 in the 5th chapter of this book.

Title : ***Rāgavibodha***

रागविबोध

Author : Somanātha

Source : British Museum, London

Title : ***Rāgavibodha***

रागविबोध

Author : Soma

Leaves : 33

Granths : 500

Source : O I, Baroda

Acc. No. : 2045

Title : ***Rāgavibodha***

रागविबोध

Author : Unknown

Leaves : 7, 8, 10, 14, 18

Granths : 200

Source : O I, Baroda

Acc. No. : 10891

Title : ***Rāgavibodha***

रागविबोध

Author : Soma (Son of Mudgala)

Source : T A C C, Wiesbaden, 1962, Pt-I

S. No. : 35

O × f. No. : 200 a

Title : ***Rāgavibodhaḥ***

रागविबोधः

Author : Somanāthaḥ

Source : Venkatesvara Univ., Tirupati

Title : ***Rāgavibodhaviveka with Ṭīkā***

रागविबोधविवेक टीका के साथ

Author : Unknown

Size : 10⅝″ × 5 ¾″

Folios : 161

Illustration : 15

Dated : 1609 AD

Source : B O R I, Poona

Acc. No. : 276/ Viṣrama I

Title : ***Rāgavicāra***

रागविचार

Author : Lacchīrāma

Size : 10″ × 4″

Folios : 2

Illustration : 11

Script : Devanāgarī

Dated : 18th century

Source : Prachina Sahitya Shodh Sansthana, Udaipur

Acc. No. : 9 (संगीतग्रन्थ)

Title : ***Rāgavicāraḥ***

रागविचारः

Author : Unknown

Mat. : Paper

Size : 13 × 2.7 cm.

Pages : 205

Script : Grantha

Source : G O M L, Triplicane, Madras

Title : ***Rāgavijñāna***

रागविज्ञान

Author : Unknown

Source : Venkateśvara Univ., Tirupati

Title : ***Rāgavilāsa***

रागविलास

Author : Devīprasada

Mat. : Paper

Size : 8" × 6"

Leaves : 120

Lines : 34

Letters : 2190

Script : Devanāgarī

Dated : 1839 AD

Source : K M U H H G K S T V, Kashi

Acc. No. : 84 C

Title : ***Rāgaviveka***

रागविवेक

Author : Puruṣottama

Dated : Sam. 1715

P. Year : 1903 AD

Source : Nagari Pracharini Sabha, Varanasi, Vol II

S. No. : 48

Title : ***Rāgotpaṭti***

रागोत्पत्ति

Author : Unknown

Ms. W P : H H the Mahārājā of

Travancore
Source : L of S mss in P L of S I, Madras, 1880, Vol I
S. No. : 6167

Title : ***Rājavijayaḥ***
राजविजयः
Author : Unknown
Source : Venkatesvara Univ., Tirupati

Title : ***Rāmaṣodaśataraṅgamālā***
रामषोडशतरंगमाला
Author : Upaniṣad Brahmendra
Mat. : Paper
Size : 32.2 × 25
Pages : 33
Script : Devanāgarī
Source : G O M L, Triplicane, Madras

Title : ***Rāmaṣodaśataraṅgamālā***
रामषोडशतरंगमाला
Author : Upaniṣad Brahmendra
Mat. : Paper
Size : 34.2 × 21.5 cm.
Pages : 16
Script : Devanāgarī
Source : G O M L, Triplicane, Madras

Title : ***Rasagoṣṭhi Rūpaka***
रसगोष्ठी रूपक
Author : Ānandī
Size : 15.2″ × 1″
Folios : 16
Language : Sanskrit
Source : Bhuvaneswar Museum, Bhuvneswar

Title : ***Rasakaumudī***
रसकौमुदी
Author : Śrīkaṇṭhakavi
Size : 9¾″ × 4″
Folios : 45
Illustration : 9
Dated : Sam. 1652
Source : B O R I, Poona
Acc. No. : 303/1880 - 81

Title : ***Rasakaumudī***
रसकौमुदी
Author : Śrīkaṇṭha
Leaves : 75
Granths : 2000
Dated : 1936 AD
Source : O I, Baroda
Acc. No. : 13799

Title : ***Rasakaumudī***
रसकौमुदी
Author : Śrīkaṇṭha
Leaves : 75

Granths : 2000
Cond. : Injured
Dated : 1936 AD
Source : O I, Baroda
Acc. No. : 11840

Title : ***Rasakaumudī (Volume II)***
रसकौमुदी (वोल्यूम II)
Author : Śrīkaṇṭhaḥ
Source : Venkatesvara Univ., Tirupati

Title : ***Rasa Mūratha, Aṅga Śobhā, Madan Mūratha etc.***
रस मूरथ, अंग शोभा, मदन मूरथ आदि
Author : Mohammad Ārif 'Jān' Bilgrāmī
Size : 23.5 × 16 cm.
Pages : 100
Language : Hindi
Script : Urdu
Dated : 1182 A.H.
Source : State Central Lib., Hyderabad
All in one; by famous Hindi poet of Bilgrāma. Ārif was the famous nephew of famous scholar writer Gulām Alī Āzāda Bilgrāmī. Rāsa mūratha work consist of 306 Dohās and Kavittas.

Title : ***Rasaprabodha***
रसप्रबोध
Author : Gulām Nabī 'Raslīn' Bilgrāmī
Size : 21.5 × 17cm.
Pages : 42
Language : Hindi
Script : Urdu
Source : State Central Lib., Hyderabad
This consists of 530 Hindi Dohās.

Title : ***Rasarahasa***
रसरहस
Author : Gulām Alī
Size : 28 × 18 cm.
Pages : 56
Language : Hindi
Script : Urdu
Dated : 1272 AH
Source : State Central Lib., Hyderabad

Title : ***Rasarāja***
रसराज
Author : Math Rāma
Size : 20 × 11 cm.
Pages : 66
Language : Hindi
Script : Urdu
Source : State Central Lib., Hyderabad
It was written in fine Nastaliq script, illuminated opening, gold ruled margins throughout. Urdu meanings

of certain Hindi words between the lines.

Title : ***Rasarāja***

रसराज

Author : Math Rām

Size : 24 × 15 cm.

Pages : 186

Language : Hindi

Script : Urdu

Dated : 1236 AH (1816 AD)

Source : State Central Lib., Hyderabad

Title : ***Rasikajanamanollāsinī***

रसिकजनमनोल्लासिनी

Author : Veṅkata Sundarasāmi

Edi. by : M. N. Subha, Narasimhā

Source : British Museum, London

No. : 14055 b f

A metrical compilation treating of in Dramatology, Histrotic, Art, Music and Dancing.

Title : ***Rasikapriya***

रसिकप्रिय

Author : Keśava Dāsa

Size : 17.5 × 11.5 cm.

Pages : 228

Language : Hindi

Script : Urdu

Source : State Central Lib., Hyderabad Headings and Persian explanatory notes on margins in red. Under sixteen prabhav, it gives Dohās and kavittas.

Title : ***Risalah-E-Mūsiqī***

रिसाला–ए–मौशिकी

Author : Unknown

Mat. : Paper

Size : 24.4 × 14.7 cm.

Pages : 107

Script : Nastaliq

Cond. : Wants Beginning

Source : G O M L, Triplicane, Madras

Title : ***Risalah-E-Mūsiqī***

रिसाला–ए–मौशिकी

Author : Unknown

Size : 24.4 × 14.7 cm

Folios : 55

Illustration : 11

Script : Persian

Source : C of P & A mss in the G O M L, Madras

S. No. : 1069

Acc. No. : D 517

Title : ***Risalah-E-Mūsiqī***

रिसाला–ए–मौशिकी

Author : Unknown

Size : 27 × 23.3 cm

Folios : 44

Illustration : 20

Script : Persian

Source : C of P & A mss in the G O M L, Madras

S. No. : 1070

Acc. No. : D 766

Title : ***Risalah-E-Mūsiqī***

रिसाला–ए–मौशिकी

Author : Mohammad Alī

Folios : 35 b – 39 a

Language : Nasṭaliq

Dated : 19th century

Source : Oriental Public Lib., Bankipore, Patna

No. : 2241

Title : ***Risalah-I-Mūsiqī***

रिसाला–ए–मौशिकी

Author : Jānā Begum

Size : 10" × 12½

Folios : 54

Dated : 1078 A.H. 1668 AD.

Source : Bodleian Lib., Oxford, U.K.

S. No. : (39) 2346

A metrical treatise in Hindustani based on Rāgas and Rāginis. Corresponding to the number of the Rāgas there are six Rāgmalas, showing their relationship to the Rāginis.

In Part-I Nos. 184 onwards – various Persian works on Rāgas and Rāginis.

In Part–II Fifty three pictures, representing Hindi Rāgas Harem or Zenāna scenes.

Title : ***Risalah-I-Mūsiqī***

रिसाला–ए–मौशिकी

Language : Persian

Source : Sangeet Natak Academy Lib.

Title : ***Risālah-E-Rāgamālā***

रिसाला–ए–रागमाला

Author : Md. Hasan Alī

Mat. : Paper

Size : 29.6 × 17.5 cm.

Pages : 9

Script : Nastaliq

Text : Complete

Source : G O M L, Triplicane, Madras

Title : ***Risālah-E-Rāgamālā***

रिसाला–ए–रागमाला

Author : Md. Husain Alī

Size : 29.6 × 17.5 cm.

Folios : 5

Illustration : 17

Script : Persian

Source : C of P & A mss in the G O M L, Madras

S. No. : 1094

Acc. No. : D507 b

Title : ***Risālah-E-Rāgamālā***

रिसाला–ए–रागमाला

Author : Md. Husain Alī

Size : 26 × 23.7 cm.

Folios : 3

Illustration : 20

Script : Persian

Source : C of P & A mss in the G O M L, Madras

S. No. : 1095

Acc. No. : D516

Title : ***Risālah-E-Rāga-E-Hindī***

रिसाला–ए–राग–ए–हिन्दी

Author : Unknown

Folios : 41b – 47 b

Dated : 1107 AH

Source : A D C of the O mss in the D L, Bahawalpur

No. : 266 (4)

Title : ***Risalah-E-Sima-E-Nagma***

रिसाला–ए–सिम–ए–नग्मा

Author : Unknown

Folios : 103 b – 125 b

Dated : 1157 AH

Source : A D C of the O mss in the D L, Bahawalpur

No. : 266 (8)

Title : ***Risālah-fī-'Ilm al-Mūsiqī***

रिसाला–फी–इल्म–अल–मौशिकी

Author : Abū Nasr Farebī

Size : 20.5 × 13 cm.

Pages : 170

Language : Arabic

Source : State Central Lib., Hyderabad This work by the famous Arab philosopher Al- Farebī deals with the theory and philosophy of Music. It consists of five Maqāla.

Title : ***Risālah-fī-'Ilm al-Nagmā***

रिसाला–फी–इल्म–अल–नगमा

Author : Saifuddīn Abdul Azīz Hillī

Size : 22 × 16 cm.

Pages : 128

Language : Arabic

Text : Incomplete at end

Source : State Central Lib., Hyderabad
It deals, in the beginning, with the Greek theory of music and its philosophy. Afterwards Arabic music and songs are given.

Title : ***Risālah Karamiyah***
रिसाला करमियह

Author : Nīmat Khān Alī

Size : 7″ × 3½″

Pages : 6

Lang : Persian

Text : Complete

Source : Maulana Azad Lib., A M U, Aligarh

Title : ***Risālah Rāgamālā***
रिसाला रागमाला

Language : Persian

Source : Sangeet Natak Academy Lib.

Title : ***Risālah Rāga O Rāgiṇī***
रिसाला राग ओ रागिणी

Author : Manakthohil

Size : 9″ × 6″

Pages : 27

Language : Persian

Text : Complete

Dated : 1662 AD

Source : Maulana Azad Lib., A M U, Aligarh

Title : ***Risālah Yār Jātaka***
रिसाला यार जातक

Author : Ahobala

Size : 12″ × 6½″

Pages : 111

Language : Persian

Text : Complete

Dated : 1828 AD

Source : Maulana Azad Lib., A M U, Aligarh

Title : ***Riyād Mānā***
रियाद माना

Author : Mohammad Badrūddīna Khāna 'Laiq'

Size : 21 × 14 cm.

Pages : 312

Language : Persian

Text : Incomplete at end

Source : State Central Lib., Hyderabad
This work is a Persian translation of 'Singhāra' and specially deals with the portion of 'Nāyaka Bhed'. It is divided into five chapters.

Title : ***Rūpakaparibhāṣā***
रूपकपरिभाषा

Author : Raṅgarāja

Source : T A C C, Wiesbaden, 1962, Pt-I

S. No. : 41 A

Title : ***Rūpamañjarī***

रूपमंजरी

Author : Unknown

Dated : Sam. 1949

P. Year : 1917 AD

Source : Nagari Pracharini Sabha, Varanasi, Vol II

S. No. : 66

Title : ***Rūpamañjarī***

रूपमंजरी

Author : Unknown

P. Year : 1917 AD

Source : Nagari Pracharini Sabha, Varanasi, Vol II

S. No. : 67

S

Title : *Sabhālakṣaṇaṃ with Kannaḍa meaning*

सभालक्षणम् कन्नड अर्थ के साथ

Author : Unknown

Mat. : Palmleaf

Size : 28.2 × 3 cm.

Pages : 6

Script : Nandināgarī

Source : G O M L, Triplicane, Madras

Title : *Sabhāyāṃ Nāṭaka Paṭhana Śravaṇarīti*

सभायाम् नाटक पठन श्रवणरीति

Author : Unknown

Source : O I, Baroda

Acc. No. : 5871

Title : *Sadāśivabharataṃ*

सदाशिवभरतम्

Source : O R I, Mysore

No. : V 941

Title : *Ṣaḍjādisvararāgādi-lakṣaṇa*

षड्जादिस्वररागादिलक्षण

Author : Unknown

Mat. : Paper

Size : 26.7 × 11.5 cm.

Pages : 3

Lines : 11

Extent : 32

Script : Devanāgarī

Text : Complete

Dated : V. S. 1750

Source : C of S & P mss in M S P C, L D B S V, Ahmedabad

S. No. : 6359

Acc. No : 692

Title : *Ṣaḍrāgacandrodaya*

षड्रागचन्द्रोदय

Author : Puṇḍrīkaviṭhṭhala

Size : 10½″ × 5″

Folios : 14

Language : Sanskrit

Source : Asiatic Society, 1, Park Street, Calcutta-16

Title : ***Ṣaḍrāgacandrodaya***

षड्रागचन्द्रोदय

Author : Pundrīka Viṭṭhal

Folios : 13

Size : 5¼″ × 9½″

Illustration : 24

Cond. : Old MS.

Source : B O R I, Poona

Acc. No. : 646(a)/1899-1902

Title : ***Ṣaḍrāgacandrodaya***

षड्रागचन्द्रोदय

Author : Puṇḍarīka Viṭhṭhala

Source : British Museum, London

No. : 14055 e 3 (2)

A metrical work on the modes of music composed under the patronage of Būrhāna Khāna Fārkī. Its edited by Gaṇeśa Vajra Taṅka, pp 28, Bombay, 1912.

Title : ***Ṣadrāgacandrodaya***

षड्रागचन्द्रोदय

Author : Puṇḍarīka Viṭhṭhala

Size : 10⅝″ × 4⅜″

Folios : 28 (Folio 1 is lost)

Lines : 12

Script : Devanāgarī

Dated : 18th century

Source : C of S mss in the I O L, London, Vol II

S. No. : 5193

Acc. No. : 3314 b

A treatise on music, in three Prasāda by Puṇḍarīka Viṭhṭhala. This work is under the style 'Ṣaḍ-Rāga-Candrodaya' is mentioned by Mitra Bikaner Cat. p. 529. It seems clear that this is quite a distinct work of the Nartana-Nirṇaya, S.N. 5197 of the mss.

Title : ***Ṣaḍrāgacandrodaya***

षड्रागचन्द्रोदय

Author : Unknown

Size : 24 × 17 cm.

Folios : 5

Language : Sanskrit

Source : National Lib., Belvedere, Calcutta 27

Title : ***Ṣaḍrāgacandrodaya***

षड्रागचन्द्रोदय

Author : Puṇḍarīka Viṭhṭhala

Source : T A C C, Wiesbaden, 1962, Pt-I

S. No. : 41 B

Title : ***Ṣaḍrāgavarṇanaṃ***

षड्रागवर्णनम्

Author : Nāradaḥ

Mat. : Paper

Size : 12.8″ × 4.1″

Folios : 1 - 2,+2

Lines : 6

Letters : 42

Script : Bengali

Source : Varanaseya Skt. Visvavidyalaya Lib., Varanasi

S. No. : 45506

Title : ***Śāhajīrājāṣṭapadī***

शाहजीराजाष्टपदी

Author : Unknown

Leaves : 35

Granths : 175

Script : Telugu

Source : D C of the S mss in the T M S S M L, Tanjore, Vol XVI

S. No. : 10959

B. No. : 10303

Title : ***Śāhavilāsagītam***

शाहविलासगीतम्

Author : Unknown

Leaves : 56

Granths : 500

Script : Devanāgarī

Source : D C of the S mss in the T M S S M L, Tanjore, Vol XVI

S. No. : 10957

B. No. : 6662

On the model of Gīta-Govindaṃ

Title : ***Śaiyakkaḍi perilnoṇḍi-nāṭakam with commentary***

शैयक्कडि पेरिल्नोण्डि–नाटकम् व्याख्या के साथ

Author : Unknown

Mat. : Palmleaf

Size : 37.4 × 2.5 cm.

Pages : 53

Lang : Tamil

Script : Tamil

Source : G O M L, Triplicane, Madras

Title : ***Sakalabharatasārasaṅ-grahaḥ***

सकलभरतसारसंग्रहः

Author : Unknown

Mat. : Paper

Size : 20.5 × 16 cm.

Pages : 54

Script : Telugu

Source : G O M L, Triplicane, Madras

Title : ***Śakuntalaivilāsam***

शकुन्तलैविलासम्

Author : Candiran

Mat. : Palmleaf
Size : 35 × 3.8 cm.
Pages : 98
Language : Tamil
Script : Tamil
Source : G O M L, Triplicane, Madras

Title* : *Śakuntalā Nāṭaka
शकुन्तला नाटक
Author : Kālidāsa
Size : 12.5" × 1.3"
Pages : 108
Language : Oriya
Source : Utkal Univ. Lib., Bhuvaneswar

Title* : *Saṁkīrṇarāgāḥ
संकीर्णरागाः
Author : Unknown
Folios : 10
Size : 7 3/8" × 4½"
Illustration : 8
Cond. : Old Ms.
Source : B O R I, Poona
Acc. No. : 440/1892-95

Title* : *Saṁkīrṇarāgalakṣaṇa
संकीर्णरागलक्षण
Author : Unknown
Size : 5½" × 4"
Folios : 6
Language : Sanskrit
Source : Asiatic Society, 1, Park Street, Calcutta-16

Title* : *Sandeśahastādilakṣaṇam
सन्देशहस्तादिलक्षणम्
Source : O R I, Mysore
No. : 4798

Title* : *Saṅgānasāgara
संगानसागर
Author : Śubhaṅkara
Size : 12" × 2"
Folios : 15 - 67, Less 24
Language : Sanskrit
Source : Asiatic Society, 1, Park Street, Calcutta-16

Title* : *Śāṅkarīsaṅgītam
शांकरीसंगीतम्
Author : Jayanārāyaṇa
Mat. : Paper
Size : 27.5 × 24.5 cm.
Pages : 18
Script : Telugu
Source : G O M L, Triplicane, Madras

Title	:	***Saṅgītabolī***
		संगीतबोली
Mat.	:	Palmleaf
Size	:	27 × 4 cm.
Pages	:	17
Language	:	Sanskrit
Script	:	Oriya
Source	:	G O M L, Triplicane, Madras

Title	:	***Saṅgītabhāskara***
		संगीतभास्कर
Author	:	Jagajjyotimalla
Size	:	14″ × 4″
Folios	:	192
Lines	:	8
Ślokas	:	538
Language	:	Nevārī
Source	:	A C of P & S P mss D L, Nepal, Calcutta,1905
S. No.	:	222

Title	:	***Saṅgītacandra***
		संगीतचन्द्र
Author	:	Vipradāsa
Leaves	:	180
Granths	:	1500
Dated	:	Sam. 1994
Source	:	O I, Baroda
Acc. No.	:	13930

Title	:	***Saṅgītacandra***
		संगीतचन्द्र
Author	:	Unknown
Size	:	14" × 4"
Folios	:	215
Lines	:	8
Śloka	:	5805
Language	:	Nevārī
Source	:	A C of P & S P mss D L, Nepal, Calcutta,1905
S. No.	:	222

Title	:	***Saṅgītacandrikā***
		संगीतचन्द्रिका
Author	:	Mādhava Bhaṭṭaḥ
Source	:	Venkatesvara Univ., Tirupati

Title	:	***Saṅgītacaupadī***
		संगीतचौपदी
Author	:	Upendra Bhañja & Dīnabandhu
Size	:	9″ × 1.4″
Pages	:	162
Language	:	Oriya
Source	:	Utkal Univ. Lib., Bhuvaneswar

Title	:	***Saṅgītacaupadī***
		संगीतचौपदी
Author	:	Kabi Sūrya

Size : 11.3″ × 1.4″

Pages : 153

Language : Oriya

Source : Utkal Univ. Lib., Bhuvaneswar

Title : ***Saṅgītacintāmaṇi***

संगीतचिन्तामणि

Author : Anonymous

Size : 8″ × 4″

Folios : 1-2 & 1-3

Language : Sanskrit

Source : Asiatic Society, 1, Park Street, Calcutta-16

Title : ***Saṅgītacintāmaṇi***

संगीतचिन्तामणि

Author : Śrī Vīranārāyaṇa Bhūpāla

Size : 21½ × 2 cm.

Folios : 144

Illustration : 8

Source : A D C of the S mss in the H H M P L, Trivandrum

S. No. : 1417

Title : ***Saṅgītacintāmaṇi***

संगीतचिन्तामणि

Author : Śrī Vīranārayaṇa Bhūpāla

Size : 21 × 1½ cm.

Folios : 224

Illustration : 6

Script : Malayalam

Source : A D C of the S mss in the H H M P L, Trivandrum

S. No. : 1418

Title : ***Saṅgītacintāmaṇi***

संगीतचिन्तामणि

Author : Vīranārāyaṇa Vembhūpāla

Mat. : Palmleaf

Language : Sanskrit

Script : Malayalam

Source : Kerala Univ. Lib., Trivandrum

Ms. No. : 1417

Title : ***Saṅgītacintāmaṇi***

संगीतचिन्तामणि

Author : Vīranārāyaṇa Vembhūpāla

Mat. : Palmleaf

Language : Sanskrit

Script : Malayalam

Source : Kerala Univ. Lib., Trivandrum

Ms. No. : 1418

Title : ***Saṅgītacintāmaṇi***

संगीतचिन्तामणि

Author : Cintāmaṇi

Mat. : Paper

Size : 8″ × 6″

Leaves : 32

Lines : 24

Letters : 672

Script : Devanāgarī

Dated : 1839 AD

Source : K M U H H G K S T V, Kashi

Acc. No. : 71 B

Title : ***Saṅgītacintamaṇi***

संगीतचिन्तामणि

Author : Unknown

Dated : Sam. 1866

P. Year : 1929 AD

Source : Nagari Pracharini Sabha, Varanasi, Vol II

S. No. : 71 B

Title : ***Saṅgītacintamaṇi***

संगीतचिन्तामणि

Author : Harivallabha

P. Year : 1929 AD

Source : Nagari Pracharini Sabha, Varanasi, Vol II

Title : ***Saṅgītaciṅtāmaṇi***

संगीतचिन्तामणि

Author : Unknown

Mat : Palmleaf

Size : 19″ × 1½″

Pages : 61

Leaves : 6

Lines : 5

Granths : 100

Script : Devanāgarī

Text : Incomplete and not printed

Source : D C of the S mss in the T M S S M L, Tanjore, Vol XVI

S. No. : 10715

B. No. : 11569 A

The work is written as if the music is taught by Shaṅkara to Pārvatī, Nārada and others. The bibliography at the end of the Saṅgītá-Ratnākara (Ānanda Śarma Ed.) contains a work of this name by Kāmalocana. It is not possible to say if this is part of that. This manuscript contains the first chapter only.

Title : ***Saṅgītacintāmaṇi***

संगीतचिन्तामणि

Author : Kāmalocana

Source : T A C C, Wiesbaden, 1962, Pt-I

S. No. : 48

Title : ***Saṅgītacintāmaṇiḥ***

संगीतचिन्तामणिः

Author : Vemabhūpālaḥ

Source : Venkatesvara Univ., Tirupati

Title : ***Saṅgītacūḍāmaṇi***
संगीतचूड़ामणि

Author : Unknown

Size : 14½ × 1¾ cm.

Folios : 70

Illustration : 9

Script : Malayalam

Source : A D C of S mss in the C O L, Trivandrum

S. No. : 1226

C.O.L. No. : 147

Title : ***Saṅgītacūḍāmaṇi***
संगीतचूड़ामणि

Author : Pratāpacakravartī

Size : 11 × 8½ cm.

Folios : 83

Illustration : 20

Script : Devanāgarī

Source : A D C of S mss in the C O L, Trivandrum

S. No. : 1227

C.O.L. No. : 581

Title : ***Saṅgītacūḍāmaṇiḥ***
संगीतचूड़ामणिः

Author : Kavicakravartī

Leaves : 69

Granths : 900

Source : O I, Baroda

Acc. No. : 9892

Title : ***Saṅgītacūḍāmaṇiḥ***
संगीतचूड़ामणिः

Source : O R I, Mysore

No. : 5081

Title : ***Saṅgītacūḍāmaṇiṭīkā***
संगीतचूड़ामणिटीका

Source : O R I, Mysore

No. : 1298

Title : ***Saṅgītadāmodara***
संगीतदामोदर

Author : Dāmodarācārya

Size : 7.1″ × 1.3″

Folios : 32

Language : Sanskrit

Source : Bhuvaneswar Museum, Bhuvaneswar

Title : ***Saṅgītadāmodara***
संगीतदामोदर

Author : Śubhaṅkara

Size : 15¾″ × 4″

Folios : 52

Lines : 6

Script : Modern Bengālī

Dated : Sam. 1644

Source : C of S mss in the I O L, London, Vol I, Pt-II

No. : 1486

A treatise on music and dancing, by Śubhaṅkara. Apparently on abstract of the preceding work.

Title : ***Saṅgītadāmodara***

संगीतदामोदर

Author : Śubhaṅkara

Source : T A C C, Wiesbaden, 1962, Pt-I

S. No. : 51

Title : ***Saṅgītadāmodaraḥ***

संगीतदामोदरः

Author : Unknown

Source : Venkatesvara Univ., Tirupati

Title : ***Saṅgītadāmodaro***

संगीतदामोदरो

Author : Śubhaṅkara

Folios : 121

Illustration : 4

Script : Bengali

Age : Śaka 1643

Source : N of S mss Pub. by G of B, Calcutta, 1871, Vol I

No. : 318

Title : ***Saṅgītadarpaṇa***

संगीतदर्पण

Author : Catura Dāmodara

Size : 13¼″ × 7⅝″

Folios : 30

Illustration : 16

Dated : 15th century

Source : B O R I, Poona

Acc. No. : 837/1886 - 92

Title : ***Saṅgītadarpaṇa***

संगीतदर्पण

Author : Catura Dāmodara

Size : 13″ × 4¾″

Folios : 54

Illustration : 9

Cond. : Old Ms.

Source : B O R I, Poona

Acc. No. : 441/1892-95

Title : ***Saṅgītadarpaṇa***

संगीतदर्पण

Author : Catura Dāmodara

Size : 9″ × 4¼″

Folios : 86

Illustration : 10

Dated : Sam. 1719

Source : B O R I, Poona

Acc. No. : 1027/1884-87

Title : ***Saṅgītadarpaṇa (Rāgādhyāya)***

संगीतदर्पण (रागाध्याय)

Author : Catura Dāmodara

Size : 10½″ × 5″

Folios : 5

Illustration : 13

Cond. : Old mss.

Source : B O R I, Poona

Acc. No. : 644/1899-1915

Title : ***Saṅgītadarpaṇa***

संगीतदर्पण

Author : Dāmodara

Dated : 1902 AD

Source : British Museum, London

Acc. No. : 8815/2

Title : ***Saṅgītadarpaṇa***

संगीतदर्पण

Author : Dāmodara

Edited by : Ratnajī Līlādhara Ṭhakkara

Source : British Museum, London

No. : 14055 e 1

Chapter I-2 edited with Gujrati translation and commentary by Ratnajī Līlādhara Ṭhakkara, pp. i, 112, Bombay, 1910.

Title : ***Saṅgītadarpaṇa***

संगीतदर्पण

Author : Dāmodara Bhaṭṭa

Mat. : Paper

Size : 26.5 × 11.5 cm.

Folios : 71

Lines : 13

Letters : 30

Script : Devanāgarī

Text : Complete

Dated : Sam. 1933

Source : Gujarat Vidya Sabha, Ahmedabad

S. No. : 2645

Acc. No. : 2691

Title : ***Saṅgītadarpaṇa***

संगीतदर्पण

Author : Dāmodara

Size : 8½″ × 4 ¾″

Folios : 73

Lines : 20 – 25

Volume : 8

Script : Devanāgarī

Dated : Sam. 1839, Śaka 1704

Source : C of S mss in the I O L, London, Vol I, Pt-II

No. : 2231

A manual of instrumental music, singing and dancing

in seven chapters, by Dāmodara, son of Lakṣmīdhara.

1. Svaragatādhyāya Śloka – 1-162
2. Rāgavivekādhyāya Śloka – 163-305
3. Prakīrṇakādhyāya Śloka – 63 by folios 16b
4. Prabandhādhyāya Śloka – 188, by folios 19b
5. Vādyādhyāya Śloka – 94, by folios 29
6. Tālādhyāya by folios 34
7. Nṛtyādhyāya by folios 34

Title : ***Saṅgītadarpaṇa***

संगीतदर्पण

Author : Maganirāma

Size : 9" × 6¼"

Folios : 55

Lines : 17

Volume : 8

Script : Devanāgarī

Dated : Sam. 1964

Source : C of S mss in the I O L, London, Vol I, Pt-II

No. : 1709 b

There are six chapters in this book.

Title : ***Saṅgītadarpaṇa***

संगीतदर्पण

Size : 8¾ " × 7¾"

Folios : 82

Lines : 15

Script : Devanāgarī

Source : C of S mss in the I O L, London, Vol I, Pt-II

No. : 2399

The Rāgādhyāya and Tālādhyāya of the Saṅgītadarpaṇa with the same commentary.

Title : ***Saṅgītadarpaṇa***

संगीतदर्पण

Size : 9" × 4"

Folios : 107

Lines : 8

Script : Devanāgarī

Source : C of S mss in the I O L, London, Vol I, Pt-II

No. : 2410

A portion of the Saṅgīta-Darpaṇa (chapter I and beginning of II) with a commentary in Bhāṣā.

The letter begins ; दोहा प्रथम करत कर जोरि कै नमस्कारसुमरूप.

The Rāgādhyāya begins on folios 107 a; but the manuscripts breaks off abruptly at the bottom of folios 107 b.

Title	:	***Saṅgītadarpaṇa***
		संगीतदर्पण
Author	:	Dāmodara
Source	:	A C of mss in the L of H H the M of U, Udaipur, 1943, S B L
S. No.	:	816

Title	:	***Saṅgītadarpaṇa***
		संगीतदर्पण
Author	:	Cintāmaṇi
Dated	:	Sam. 1880
P. Year	:	1923 AD
Source	:	Nagari Pracharini Sabha, Varanasi, Vol II
S. No.	:	150 E

Title	:	***Saṅgītadarpaṇa***
		संगीतदर्पण
Author	:	Dāmodara
Size	:	9¼″ × 5¼″
Folios	:	1-2, 17-26
Language	:	Sanskrit
Source	:	Nagpur Univ. Lib., Nagpur
Acc. No.	:	3016

Title	:	***Saṅgītadarpaṇa***
		संगीतदर्पण
Author	:	Dāmodara
Leaves	:	22
Granths	:	400
Text	:	Incomplete
Source	:	O I, Baroda
Acc. No.	:	1631

Title	:	***Saṅgītadarpaṇa***
		संगीतदर्पण
Author	:	Dāmodara
Leaves	:	42
Granths	:	1500
Dated	:	Sam. 1922
Source	:	O I, Baroda
Acc. No.	:	11515

Title	:	***Saṅgītadarpaṇa***
		संगीतदर्पण
Author	:	Unknown
Leaves	:	2 - 23
Granths	:	400
Text	:	Incomplete
Cond.	:	Injured
Source	:	O I, Baroda
Acc. No.	:	12874

Title	:	***Saṅgītadarpaṇa***
		संगीतदर्पण
Language	:	Hindi

Source : Sangeet Natak Academy Lib.

Title : ***Saṅgītadarpaṇa***

संगीतदर्पण

Author : Dāmodara

Source : T A C C, Wiesbaden, 1962, Pt-I

S. No. : 48

Title : ***Saṅgītadarpaṇa***

संगीतदर्पण

Author : Dāmodara(Son of Lakṣmīdhara)

Source : T A C C, Wiesbaden, 1962, Pt-II

S. No. : 10

Title : ***Saṅgītadarpaṇa***

संगीतदर्पण

Author : Dāmodara

Source : T A C C, Wiesbaden, 1962, Pt-II

S. No. : 20

Title : ***Saṅgītadarpaṇa***

संगीतदर्पण

Author : Harivallabha

Size : 8½ × 5½ cm.

Folios : 69

Letters : 20

Dated : 1802 AD

Source : T T R on the S of H Ms, Allahabad

No. : 150(e)

Title : ***Saṅgītadarpaṇa***

संगीतदर्पण

Author : Harivallabha

Size : 8 × 6 cm.

Folios : 150

Letters : 36

Dated : 1823 AD

Source : T T R on the S of H Ms, Allahabad

No. : 150(f)

Title : ***Saṅgītadarpaṇa***

संगीतदर्पण

Author : Cuturadāmodara

Mat. : Paper

Size : 10¾″ × 4¾″

Sheets : 135

Lines : 9

Script : Devanāgarī

Text : Complete 1-7 Chapters

Source : D C of the S mss in the T M S S M L, Tanjore, Vol XVI

S. No. : 10716

B. No. : 6599

The author is called Hari Bhaṭṭa and is the son of Lakṣaṇamārya. Copies
10717 B. No. 6619 Paper Devanāgarī Complete
10718 B. No. 11499 Pamleaf Telugu Complete
10719 B. No. 6621 Paper Devanāgarī Complete
10720 B. No. 11500 Pamleaf Telugu Incomplete I-V
10721 B. No. 11501 Pamleaf Telugu Incomplete
10722 B. No. 11502 Pamleaf Telugu Incomplete II
10723 B. No. 6320 Pamleaf Telugu Incomplete VI

Title : ***Saṅgītadarpaṇa***

संगीतदर्पण

Author : Dāmodara

Source : T A C C, Wifesbaden, 1962, Part-III

S. No. : 4

Title : ***Saṅgītadarpaṇa***

संगीतदर्पण

Author : Dāmodara

Mat. : Paper

Size : 9.6″ × 4.1″

Folios : 2 - 11

Lines : 9

Letters : 43

Script : Devanāgarī

Source : Varanaseya Sanskrit Visvavidyalaya Lib., Varanasi

S. No. : 45515

Title : ***Saṅgītadarpaṇaḥ***

संगीतदर्पण:

Author : Dāmodaraḥ

Mat. : Paper

Size : 9.8″ × 4.2″

Folios : 1 - 60

Lines : 10

Letter : 38

Script : Devanāgarī

Source : Varanaseya Skt. Visvavidyalaya Lib., Varanasi

Title : ***Saṅgītadarpaṇaḥ***

संगीतदर्पण:

Author : Dāmodara Bhaṭṭaḥ

Mat. : Paper

Size : 11.2″ × 4.9″

Folios : 1-35

Lines : 9

Letters : 43

Script : Devanāgarī
Source : Varanaseya Skt. Visvavidyalaya Lib., Varanasi
S. No. : 45517

Title : ***Saṅgītadarpaṇaḥ***
संगीतदर्पणः
Author : Haribhaṭṭa
Mat. : Paper
Size : 11.3″ × 8″
Folios : 1, 2
Lines : 22
Letters : 9
Script : Devanāgarī
Source : Varanaseya Skt. Visvavidyalaya Lib., Varanasi
S. No. : 45518

Title : ***Saṅgītadarpaṇaḥ***
संगीतदर्पणः
Author : Dāmodara
Source : Venkatesvara Univ., Tirupati

Title : ***Saṅgītadarpaṇam***
संगीतदर्पणम्
Author : Caturadāmodara
Mat. : Palmleaf
Size : 34 × 3.5 cm.
Pages : 40
Script : Nandināgarī
Source : G O M L, Triplicane, Madras

Title : ***Saṅgītadarpaṇam with Telugu meaning***
संगीतदर्पणम् तेलुगू अर्थ के साथ
Author : Caturadāmodara and Haribhaṭṭa
Mat. : Paper
Size : 21.5 × 17 cm.
Pages : 207
Script : Devanāgarī and Telugu
Source : G O M L, Triplicane, Madras

Title : ***Saṅgītadarpaṇam with Telugu commentary***
संगीतदर्पणम् तेलुगू व्याख्या के साथ
Author : Caturadāmodara and Haribhaṭṭa
Mat. : Paper
Size : 33.5 × 20 cm.
Pages : 33
Script : Telugu
Source : G O M L, Triplicane, Madras

Title : ***Saṅgītadarpaṇam***
संगीतदर्पणम्
Author : Dāmodara
Mat. : Paper
Folios : 14
Language : Sanskrit
Script : Devanāgarī
Source : Kerala Univ. Lib., Trivandrum
Ms. No. : 7276

Title	:	***Saṅgītadarpaṇam***
		संगीतदर्पणम्
Source	:	O R I, Mysore
No.	:	2847

Title	:	***Saṅgītādhyāyaḥ***
		संगीताध्याय:
Mat.	:	Palmleaf
Size	:	40.8 × 3.7 cm.
Pages	:	3
Language	:	Sanskrit
Script	:	Telugu
Source	:	G O M L, Triplicane, Madras

Title	:	***Saṅgītādhyāyaḥ***
		संगीताध्याय:
Mat.	:	Paper
Size	:	31.5 × 25 cm.
Pages	:	4
Language	:	Sanskrit
Script	:	Devanāgarī
Source	:	G O M L, Triplicane, Madras

Title	:	***Saṅgītadīpikā***
		संगीतदीपिका
Author	:	Śārngadhara
P. Year	:	1901 AD
Source	:	Nagari Pracharini Sabha, Varanasi, Vol II
S. No.	:	410

Title	:	***Saṅgītagaṅgādhara with Śravaṇanandinī***
		संगीतगंगाधर श्रवणनन्दिनी के साथ
Author	:	Nanjarāja Kāśīpati Paṇḍita
Mat.	:	Palmleaf
Size	:	42.4 × 4.2 cm.
Pages	:	64
Language	:	Sanskrit
Script	:	Grantha
Source	:	G O M L, Triplicane, Madras

Title	:	***Saṅgītagaṅgādhara with Śravaṇanandinī***
		संगीतगंगाधर श्रवणनन्दिनी के साथ
Author	:	Nanjarājā Kāśīpati Paṇḍita
Mat.	:	Paper
Size	:	27.2 × 24.1 cm.
Pages	:	10
Script	:	Devanāgarī
Source	:	G O M L, Triplicane, Madras

Title	:	***Saṅgītagaṅgādhara with Śravaṇanandinī***
		संगीतगंगाधर श्रवणनन्दिनी के साथ
Author	:	Nanjarāja Kāśīpati Paṇḍita
Mat.	:	Paper
Size	:	28.3 × 24.2 cm.

Pages : 23

Script : Devanāgarī

Source : G O M L, Triplicane, Madras

Title : ***Saṅgītagaṅgādharaḥ***

संगीतगंगाधरः

Source : O R I, Mysore

No. : 5114

Title : ***Saṅgītagaṅgādharaḥ***

संगीतगंगाधरः

Source : O R I, Mysore

No. : 4422

Title : ***Saṇgītagaṅgādhara-vyākhyā Śravaṇanandinī***

संगीतगंगाधरव्याख्या श्रवणनन्दिनी

Author : Kāśīpati

Source : T A C C, Wiesbaden, 1962, Pt-I

S. No. : 47

Title : ***Saṅgītagranthaḥ***

संगीतग्रन्थः

Author : Unknown

Size : 11½ × 9 cm.

Folios : 68

Illustration : 20

Script : Malayalam

Source : A D C of S mss in the C O L, Trivandrum

S. No. : 1225

C.O.L. No. : 886

Title : ***Saṅgītagrantha***

संगीतग्रन्थ

Author : Harivallabha

Dated : Sam. 1894

P. Year : 1901 AD

Source : Nagari Pracharini Sabha, Varanasi, Vol II

S. No. : 568

Title : ***Saṅgītagulaśana***

संगीतगुलशन

Author : Jasavantaraya

Dated : Sam. 1918

P. Year : 1929 AD

Source : Nagari Pracharini Sabha, Varanasi, Vol II

S. No. : 169

Title : ***Saṅgītagulaśana***

संगीतगुलशन

Author : Unknown

Mat. : Paper

Size : 10″ × 6″

Leaves : 40

Lines : 28
Letters : 1308
Script : Devanāgarī
Dated : 1842 AD
Source : K M U H H G K S T V, Kashi
Acc. No. : 169

Title : ***Saṅgītakalānidhi***
संगीतकलानिधि
Author : Haribhaṭṭa
Source : Nagari Pracharini Sabha, Varanasi
S. No. : 42

Title : ***Saṅgītakalpalatā***
संगीतकल्पलता
Author : Haladhara Miśra
Size : 14″ × 1.3″
Folios : 64
Language : Sanskrit
Source : Bhuvaneswar Museum, Bhuvaneswar

Title : ***Saṅgītakalpataruṭīkā***
संगीतकल्पलतरुटीका
Author : Gaṇeśadevaḥ
Source : Venkatesvara Univ., Tirupati

Title : ***Saṅgītakalpataruṭīkā Subodhinī***
संगीतकल्पतरुटीका सुबोधिनी
Author : Gaṇeśadeva
Source : T A C C, Wiesbaden, 1962, Pt-I
S. No. : 44

Title : ***Saṅgītakaumadī***
संगीतकौमुदी
Author : Unknown
Size : 14″ × 1.3″
Folios : 14
Language : Sanskrit
Source : Bhuvaneswar Museum, Bhuvaneswar

Title : ***Saṅgītakaumudī***
संगीतकौमुदी
Mat. : Paper
Size : 27.5 × 24.6 cm.
Pages : 13
Script : Devanāgarī
Source : G O M L, Triplicane, Madras

Title : ***Saṅgītakaumudī***
संगीतकौमुदी
Author : Gadādhara Dāsa
Size : 14.4″ × 1.3″
Pages : 113
Language : Oriya
Source : Utkal Univ. Lib., Bhuvaneswar

Title	: ***Saṅgītakaumudī***
	संगीतकौमुदी
Author	: Gadādhara Dāsa
Size	: 15″ × 1.3″
Pages	: 14
Language	: Oriya
Source	: Utkal Univ. Lib., Bhuvaneswar

Title	: ***Saṅgītakaumudī***
	संगीतकौमुदी
Author	: Unknown
Size	: 13.1″ × 1.1″
Pages	: 76
Language	: Oriya
Source	: Utkal Univ. Lib., Bhuvaneswar

Title	: ***Saṅgītakaumudī Nṛtyakhaṇḍa***
	संगीतकौमुदी नृत्यखण्ड
Author	: Unknown
Size	: 14.5" × 1.3"
Pages	: 85
Language	: Oriya
Source	: Utkal Univ. Lib., Bhuvaneswar

Title	: ***Saṅgītakautuka***
	संगीतकौतुक
Author	: Anonymous
Size	: 8″ × 5″
Folios	: 6
Language	: Sanskrit
Source	: Asiatic Society, 1, Park Street, Calcutta-16

Title	: ***Saṅgīta kī Pustaka***
	संगीत की पुस्तक
Author	: Gaurīśaṅkara Bhaṭṭa
Mat.	: Paper
Size	: 6″ × 6″
Leaves	: 44
Lines	: 20
Letters	: 660
Script	: Devanāgarī
Dated	: 1883 AD
Source	: K M U H H G K S T V, Kashi
Acc. No.	: 101 D

Title	: ***Sangīta kī Pustaka or Sangītaratnākara***
	संगीत की पुस्तक और संगीतरत्नाकर
Author	: Gaurīśaṅkara
Dated	: Sam. 1940
P. Year	: 1929 AD
Source	: Nagari Pracharini Sabha, Varanasi, Vol II
S. No.	: 101 D & E

Title	:	***Saṅgītakkoṭṭu***
		संगीतकोट्टु
Author	:	Tyāgarāja and others
Mat.	:	Palmleaf
Size	:	40.1 × 3.2 cm.
Pages	:	268
Language	:	Tamil, Sanskrit and Telugu
Script	:	Tamil, Grantha and Telugu
Source	:	G O M L, Triplicane, Madras

Title	:	***Saṅgītalaharī***
		संगीतलहरी
Author	:	Jagadeva
Size	:	13.9″ × 1.3″
Pages	:	86
Language	:	Oriya
Source	:	Utkal Univ. Lib., Bhuvaneswar

Title	:	***Saṅgītalakṣaṇadīpikā***
		संगीतलक्षणदीपिका
Source	:	O R I, Mysore
No.	:	832

Title	:	***Saṅgītalakṣaṇam***
		संगीतलक्षणम्
Source	:	O R I, Mysore
No.	:	1102

Title	:	***Saṅgītamakaranda***
		संगीतमकरन्द
Author	:	Nārada
Source	:	British Museum, London
No.	:	14090 b 48 A manual of music in four pāda's purporting to the work of Nārada edited with introduction and appendices Edited by Bhaṅgeśa Rāmakṛṣṇa Telaṅga, pp. XI, IV 64, Baroda, Bombay, 1920

Title	:	***Saṅgītamakaranda***
		संगीतमकरन्द
Author	:	Nārada
Leaves	:	32
Granths	:	5200
Dated	:	Śaka 1599
Source	:	O I, Baroda
Acc. No.	:	11228

Title	:	***Saṅgītamakaranda***
		संगीतमकरन्द
Author	:	Veda
Mat.	:	Paper
Size	:	9¾″ × 5½″
Pages	:	60
Lines	:	9 - 10
Granths	:	1380
Script	:	Devanāgarī

Text : Complete

Dated : 1650 AD

Source : D C of the S mss in the T M S S M L, Tanjore, Vol XVI

S. No. : 10724

B. No. : 6623

Calophon : इति श्रीसंगीतमकरन्दे वेदकृतौ नृत्याध्यायः समाप्तः ।

शके १५७२ विकृतिनामसंवत्सरे भाद्रपदशुद्धषष्ठी लिखितमिदं पुस्तकम् ।

The author is patron seems to be Śāhji, father of Śivāji.

Copies : 10725 B.No 664 Paper Devanāgarī Complete 10726 B. No 11511 Pamleaf Telugu Incomplete

Title : ***Saṅgītamakaranda***

संगीतमकरन्द

Author : Vedā

Source : T A C C, Wiesbaden, 1962, Pt-I

S. No. : 57

B. No. : 60 a

Title : ***Saṅgītamakarandaḥ***

संगीतमकरन्दः

Source : O R I, Mysore

No. : A 141

Title : ***Saṅgītamakarandaḥ***

संगीतमकरन्दः

Author : Vedakaviḥ

Source : Venkatesvara Univ., Tirupati

Title : ***Saṅgītamālā***

संगीतमाला

Author : Priyādāsa

Mat. : Paper

Size : 8″ × 6″

Leaves : 24

Lines : 28

Letters : 316

Script : Devanāgarī

Dated : 1867 AD

Source : K M U H H G K S T V, Kashi

Acc. No. : 273F

Title : ***Saṅgītamālā***

संगीतमाला

Author : Kabisūrya Rāyaguru

Size : 13.3″ × 1.5″

Pages : 85

Language : Oriya

Source : Utkal Univ. Lib., Bhuvaneswar

Title : ***Saṅgītamālā***

संगीतमाला

Author : Hari Candana and others

Size : 8.2″ × 1.1″

Pages : 120

Language : Oriya

Source : Utkal Univ. Lib., Bhuvaneswar

Title : ***Saṅgītamālikā***

संगीतमालिका

Author : Mohammad Sābī

Folios : 11 - 53

Letters : 20

Script : Devanāgarī

Dated : 18th century

Place : Prachina Sahitya Shodh Sansthana, Udaipur

Title : ***Saṅgītamanīṣa***

संगीतमनीष

Author : Sudhā Kalaśa

Source : Venkatesvara Univ., Tirupati

Title : ***Saṅgītamanohara***

संगीतमनोहर

Author : Rāmacarana

Mat. : Paper

Size : 10" × 8"

Leaves : 64

Lines : 26

Letters : 1352

Script : Devanāgarī

Dated : 1916 AD

Source : K M U H H G K S T V, Kashi

Acc. No. : 282

Title : ***Saṅgītamanoramā or Nāṭyamanoramā***

संगीतमनोरमा और नाट्यमनोरमा

Author : Raghunātha Ratha

Size : 12.9″ × 1.4″

Folios : 62

Language : Sanskrit

Source : Bhuvaneswar Museum, Bhuvaneswar

Title : ***Saṅgītamīmāṁsā***

संगीतमीमांसा

Author : Kumbhakarṇamahimendu

Source : T A C C, Wiesbaden, 1962, Pt-I

S. No. : 58

Title : ***Saṅgītāmṛta***

संगीतामृत

Author : Kamalalocana

Source : T A C C, Wiesbaden, 1962, Pt-I

S. No. : 81

Title : ***Saṅgītamuktāvalī***

संगीतमुक्तावली

Author : Devendra

Mat. : Palmleaf

Size : 17¼″ × 1¼″

Pages : 60

Leaves : 75

Lines : 5

Granths : 1600

Script : Telugu

Text : Complete

Source : D C of the S mss in the T M S S M L, Tanjore, Vol XVI

S. No. : 10728

B. No. : 11513

The Manuscript is in a fairly good condition. The author mention a list of great authors on singing and-Pravartaka among whom there are the names of 'Udbhaṭa', Lollata, Abhinavagupta, Bhojaraja.

Copies : 10728 Paper Incomplete — B. No. 6646 Devanāgarī
10729 Paper Incomplete — B. No. 6655 Devanāgarī
10730 Pamleaf Fragment — B. No. 11514a Telugu

Title : ***Saṅgītamuktāvalī***

संगीतमुक्तावली

Author : Devendra

Source : T A C C, Wiesbaden, 1962, Pt-I

S. No. : 59

B. No. : 60 a

Title : ***Saṅgītamuktāvalī***

संगीतमुक्तावली

Author : Devendrācārya

Source : Venkatesvara Univ., Tirupati

Title : ***Saṅgītanārāyaṇa***

संगीतनारायण

Author : Puruṣottama Miśra

Size : 15½″ × 5½″

Folios : 69

Language : Sanskrit

Source : Asiatic Society, 1, Park Street, Calcutta-16

Title : ***Saṅgītanarayaṇa with Oriyā translation***

संगीतनारायण उड़िया अनुवाद के साथ

Author : Jagannātha Nārāyaṇa Deva

Size : 14.2″ × 1.6″

Folios : 186

Language : Sanskrit

Source : Bhuvaneswar Museum, Bhuvaneswar

Title : *Saṅgītanārāyaṇa*

संगीतनारायण

Author : Puruṣottama Miśra

Folios : 80

Illustration : 5

Script : Bengali

Source : N of S mss Pub. by G of B, Calcutta, 1871, Vol I

No. : 389

Title : *Saṅgītanārāyaṇa*

संगीतनारायण

Author : Nārāyaṇa

Source : T A C C, Wiesbaden, 1962, Pt-II

S. No. : 11

Title : *Saṅgītanārāyaṇa*

संगीतनारायण

Author : Gajapati Nārāyaṇa Deba

Size : 11.5″ × 1.1″

Pages : 140

Language : Oriya

Source : Utkal Univ. Lib., Bhuvaneswar

Title : *Saṅgītanārāyaṇa*

संगीतनारायण

Author : Unknown

Size : 13.6″ × 1.6″

Pages : 14

Language : Oriya

Source : Utkal Univ. Lib., Bhuvaneswar

Title : *Saṅgītanārāyaṇa*

संगीतनारायण

Author : Gadādhar Dāsa

Size : 14.5″ × 1.2″

Pages : 37

Language : Oriya

Source : Utkal Univ. Lib., Bhuvaneswar

Title : *Saṅgītanārāyaṇa*

संगीतनारायण

Author : Nārāyaṇa

Source : T A C C, Wiesbaden, 1962, Pt-I

S. No. : 52

Title : *Saṅgītanārāyaṇaḥ*

संगीतनारायणः

Author : Unknown

Source : Venkatesvara Univ., Tirupati

Title	: ***Saṅgītanārāyaṇam***
	संगीतनारायणम्
Author	: Nārāyaṇa-Bhūpāla
Mat.	: Paper
Size	: 27.5 × 24 cm.
Pages	: 56
Language	: Sanskrit
Script	: Devanāgarī
Source	: G O M L, Triplicane, Madras

Title	: ***Saṅgītanarāyaṇam***
	संगीतनारायणम्
Author	: Nārāyaṇa-Bhūpāla
Mat.	: Paper
Size	: 27.5 × 24.5 cm.
Pages	: 64
Script	: Devanāgarī
Source	: G O M L, Triplicane, Madras

Title	: ***Saṅgītanṛttaratnākara***
	संगीतनृत्तरत्नाकर
Author	: Viṭhṭhala
Source	: T A C C, Wiesbaden, 1962, Pt-I
S. No.	: 53
B. No.	: 60 b

Title	: ***Saṅgītanṛtyākara***
	संगीतनृत्याकर
Author	: Bhaṭṭācārya
Source	: T A C C, Wiesbaden, 1962, Pt-I
S. No.	: 54

Title	: ***Saṅgītanūpāṅkuśa***
	संगीतनूपांकुश
Author	: Anūpa Siṁha
Source	: T A C C, Wiesbaden, 1962, Pt-II
S. No.	: 15

Title	: ***Saṅgītapadyāni***
	संगीतपद्यानि
Source	: O R I, Mysore
No.	: 4236

Title	: ***Saṅgītapadyāvalī***
	संगीतपद्यावली
Source	: O R I, Mysore
No.	: 1936

Title	: ***Saṅgītapārijāta***
	संगीतपारिजात
Author	: Ahobala
Size	: 10½″ × 4½″
Folios	: 31
Language	: Sanskrit
Source	: Asiatic Society, 1, Park Street, Calcutta-16

Title : ***Saṅgītapārijāta***
संगीतपारिजात
Author : Ahobala
Folios : 20
Size : 10⅝″ × 4¾″
Illustration : 20
Dated : 17th century
Source : B O R I, Poona
Acc. No. : 1028/1884 - 87

Title : ***Saṅgītapārijāta-I***
संगीतपारिजात-*I*
Author : Ahobala
Pages : 18
Dated : 1891 AD
Source : British Museum, London
No. : 24
A treatise on music.

Title : ***Saṅgītapārijāta-II***
संगीतपारिजात-*II*
Author : Ahobala
Pages : 134
Dated : 1897 AD
Pub. from : Poona
Source : British Museum, London

Title : ***Saṅgītapārijāta***
संगीतपारिजात
Author : Ahobala
Pages : 134
Source : British Museum, London
S. No. : 32

Title : ***Saṅgītapārijāta***
संगीतपारिजात
Author : Ahobala
Leaves : 267
Granths : 2000
Dated : 1870 AD
Source : O I, Baroda
Acc. No. : 13006

Title : ***Saṅgītapārijāta***
संगीतपारिजात
Author : Ahobala
Source : T A C C, Wiesbaden, 1962, Pt-I
S. No. : 55

Title : ***Saṅgītapārijāta***
संगीतपारिजात
Author : Ahobala
Source : T A C C, Wiesbaden, 1962, Pt-II
S. No. : 12

Title : ***Saṅgītapārijāta***
संगीतपारिजात
Author : Ahobala Paṇḍita

Folios : 5

Script : Devanāgarī

Source : V V R I, Hoshiarpur

Acc. No. : 5723

Title : ***Saṅgītapirattāram***

संगीतपिरत्तारम्

Author : Unknown

Mat. : Paper

Size : 28 × 24.8 cm.

Pages : 56

Language : Tamil

Script : Tamil

Source : G O M L, Triplicane, Madras

Title : ***Saṅgītaprakaraṇam with Ṭīkā***

संगीतप्रकरणम् टीका के साथ

Author : Unknown

Source : B I S M H G C, Poona

No. : 36858

Title : ***Saṅgītaprakaraṇam with Ṭīkā***

संगीतप्रकरणम् टीका के साथ

Author : Unknown

Source : B I S M H G C, Poona

No. : 25203

Title : ***Saṅgītaprakāśaḥ***

संगीतप्रकाशः

Mat. : Palmleaf

Size : 27 × 4 cm.

Pages : 30

Language : Sanskrit

Script : Oriya

Source : G O M L, Triplicane, Madras

Title : ***Saṅgītapuṣpāñjali***

संगीतपुष्पांजलि

Author : Vedā

Source : T A C C, Wiesbaden, 1962, Pt-I

S. No. : 56

Title : ***Saṅgītarāgakalpadruma***

संगीतरागकल्पद्रुम

Author : Unknown

Leaves : 200

Language : Sanskrit

Script : Devanāgarī

Source : B H U, Varanasi

S. No. : 1141

Title : ***Sangītarāgakalpadruma***

संगीतरागकल्पद्रुम

Author : Kṛṣṇananda Vedavyāsa

Folios : 31

Size : 10¼″ × $5^{3/8}$″

Illustration : 12

Cond. : Copy of old Ms.

Source : B O R I, Poona

Acc. No. : 980/1887-91

Title : ***Saṅgītarāgakalpadruma***

संगीतरागकल्पद्रुम

Author : Kṛṣṇānand Vyāsadeva Rāgasāgara

Source : British Museum, London

No. : 14055 eee Encyclopedia of Indian music. Comprising popular songs in various languages: Sanskrit, Hindi, Gujrati, Karnatic, Telugu, Tamil, Bengali, Oriya, Arabic, Persian, Pegnan,dialectic of Rajasthan. It is edited by Nagendranātha Vasu.

In 3 volumes from Bangiya Sahitya Parishad, Calcutta in 1914-16

Title : ***Saṅgītarāgakalpadruma Prakīrṇakādhyāya***

संगीतरागकल्पद्रुम प्रकीर्णकाध्याय

Author : Unknown

Leaves : 31

Letters : 12

Lines : 38

Text : Complete

Source : R on the S for S mss in the B P, Bombay

S. No. : 978

Title : ***Saṅgītarāghava***

संगीतराघव

Author : Cinabūmabhūpāla

Mat. : Paper

Size : 10″ × 4¾″

Sheets : 27

Lines : 8

Script : Devanāgarī

Granths : 450

Text : Complete 1-6 chapters

Source : D C of the S mss in the T M S S M L, Tanjore, Vol XVI

S. No. : 10783

B. No. : 6659

This is a work like Gitagovinda written by Cinabūmabhūpāla. The story of the Rāmāyaṇā is depicted. It is doubtful if this author is the same as Cinaboma, the patron of the famous Appaya Dīkṣita.

Copies : 10785 B. No. 11512 Palmleaf Telugu Complete

Title : ***Saṅgītarāghava***

संगीतराघव

Author : Cinnabūma Bhūpāla

Source : T A C C, Wiesbaden, 1962, Pt-I

S. No. : 66

Title : ***Saṅgītaraghunandana***

संगीतरघुनन्दन

Author : Viśvanātha Śinhā

Leaves : 58

Granths : 1500

Dated : Sam. 1892

Source : O I, Baroda

Acc. No. : 13116

Title : ***Saṅgītaraghunandana***

संगीतरघुनन्दन

Author : Viśvanātha

Source : T A C C, Wiesbaden, 1962, Pt-I

S. No. : 60

Title : ***Saṅgītaraghunandanam with Vyangyārtha-candrikā***

संगीतरघुनन्दनम् व्यंग्यार्थ चन्द्रिका के साथ

Author : Viśvanātha

Mat. : Paper

Folios : 74

Language : Sanskrit

Script : Devanāgarī

Source : Kerala Univ. Lib., Trivandrum

Ms. No. : 10029

Title : ***Saṅgītaraghunandana saṭīkam***

संगीतरघुनन्दन सटीकम्

Author : Unknown

Mat. : Paper

Size : 12.2″ × 4″

Folios : 1 - 67

Lines : 11

Letters : 37

Script : Devanāgarī

Source : Varanaseya Skt. Visvavidyalaya Lib., Varanasi

S. No. : 45511

Title : ***Saṅgītarāja***

संगीतराज

Author : Kumbhakarṇa Mahimendra

Size : 10⅝″ × 5¾″

Folios : 17

Illustration : 9

Dated : 1440 AD

Source : B O R I, Poona

Acc. No. : 365/1879-80

Title : ***Saṅgītarāja***

संगीतराज

Author : Kumbhakarṇarājā

Leaves : 100
Granths : 1500
Source : O I, Baroda
Acc. No. : 11545

Title : ***Saṅgītarāja***
संगीतराज
Author : Kumbhakarṇamahimendu
Source : T A C C, Wiesbaden, 1962, Pt-I
S. No. : 67

Title : ***Saṅgītarāja***
संगीतराज
Author : Kumbhakarṇa
Source : Venkatesvara Univ., Tirupati

Title : ***Saṅgītarāja***
संगीतराज
Author : Kālasena
Source : Venkatesvara Univ., Tirupati

Title : ***Saṅgītarāja (Nṛtyaratnakoṣa)***
संगीतराज (नृत्यरत्नकोष)
Author : Kumbhakarṇarājā
Leaves : 144
Granths : 3000
Source : O I, Baroda
Acc. No. : 2046

Title : ***Saṅgītarāja (Pāṭhyaratnakoṣa)***
संगीतराज (पाठ्यरत्नकोष)
Author : Kumbhakarṇarājā
Leaves : 87
Granths : 1800
Source : O I, Baroda
Acc. No. : 2046

Title : ***Saṅgītarāja (Rasaratnakoṣa)***
संगीतराज (रसरत्नकोष)
Author : Mahārānā Kumbhakarṇa
Source : A C of mss in the L of H H the M of U, Udaipur, 1943, S B L
No. : 1742

Title : ***Saṅgītarāja (Rasaratnakoṣa)***
संगीतराज (रसरत्नकोष)
Author : Mahārānā Kumbhakarṇa
Dated : V. S. 2000
Source : A C of mss in the L of H H the M of U, Udaipur, 1943, S B L
No. : 1805

Title	:	***Saṅgītarāja (Vādyaratnakoṣa)*** संगीतराज (वाद्यरत्नकोष)
Author	:	Kumbhakarṇarājā
Leaves	:	63
Granths	:	1500
Source	:	O I, Baroda
Acc. No.	:	9934

Title	:	***Saṅgītarasakalā*** संगीतरसकला
Author	:	Dīnabandhu Hari Candana
Size	:	8.1″ × 1.1″
Pages	:	99
Language	:	Oriya
Source	:	Utkal Univ. Lib., Bhuvaneswar

Title	:	***Saṅgītaratnākara*** संगीतरत्नाकर
Author	:	Śārṅgadeva
Size	:	9″ × 4″
Folios	:	40
Language	:	Sanskrit
Source	:	Asiatic Society, 1, Park Street, Calcutta-16

Title	:	***Sangītaratnākara*** संगीतरत्नाकर
Author	:	Śarṇgadeva
Size	:	11½″ × 5″
Folios	:	298
Illustration	:	10
Dated	:	1633 AD
Source	:	B O R I, Poona
Acc. No.	:	979/1887-91

Title	:	***Sangītaratnākara*** संगीतरत्नाकर
Author	:	Viṭhṭhala
Size	:	5¼″ × 9½″
Folios	:	20
Illustration	:	24
Cond.	:	Old mss
Source	:	B O R I, Poona
Acc. No.	:	646(c)/1899-1915

Title	:	***Saṅgītaratnākara*** संगीतरत्नाकर
Author	:	Śārṅgadeva
Com.	:	Sinha Bhūpāla
Pages	:	47
Dated	:	1891 AD
Source	:	British Museum, London
S. No.	:	17

Title	:	***Saṅgītaratnākara*** संगीतरत्नाकर
Author	:	Niśāṅka Śārṅgadeva

Comm. : Kalānidhi

Com. : Catura Kallinātha

Source : British Museum, London

No. : 35

Published from Poona in 1896 -97.

Title : ***Saṅgītaratnākara***

संगीतरत्नाकर

Author : Unknown

Size : 11¾″ × 4″

Folios : 82

Lines : 9 & 11

Script : Devanāgarī

Source : C of S mss in the I O L, London, Vol I, Pt-II

No. : 1503 a

Nrttādhyāya

Title : ***Saṅgītaratnākara***

संगीतरत्नाकर

Author : Śārṅgadeva

Size : 14¼″ × 5½″

Folios : 229

Lines : 9

Script : Devanāgarī

Source : C of S mss in the I O L, London, Vol I, Pt-II

No. : 3000

A compendium of the musical science, in seven Adhyāyas, by Śārṅgadeva, son of Soṭhala or Soḍhala and grandson of Bhāskara, a Kāśmīrian.

1. Svaragatādhyāya : On musical notes
2. Rāgavivekādhyāya : On musical modes or melodies
3. Prakīrṇakādhyāya : On music in connection with the human voice
4. Prabandhādhyāya : On musical composition
5. Tālādhyāya : On musical time and measure
6. Vādyādhyāya : On instrumental musical
7. Nṛttādhyāya : On dancing and acting

Title : ***Saṅgītaratnākara***

संगीतरत्नाकर

Size : 5¼″ × 5″

Folios : 175

Lines : 10

Script : Devanāgarī

Text : Incomplete

Source : C of S mss in the I O L, London, Vol I, Pt-II

No. : 2383

Tālādhyāya Folios 35, first part as far as Mārgatāprakaraṇa

Rāgavivekādhyāya Folios 12, Fragment

Prakīrṇakādhyāya Folios 15

Prabandhādhyāya Folios 26

Vādyādhyāyas Folios 72

Title : ***Saṅgītaratnākara***

संगीतरत्नाकर

Author : Gaurī-śaṅkar Bhaṭṭa

Mat. : Paper

Size : 6″ × 4″

Leaves : 106

Lines : 20

Letters : 1855

Script : Devanāgarī

Dated : 1870 AD

Source : K M U H H G K S T V, Kashi

Acc. No. : 133 B

Title : ***Saṅgītaratnākara***

संगीतरत्नाकर

Author : Gaurī-śankara

Mat. : Paper

Size : 8" × 6"

Leaves : 26

Lines : 32

Letters : 480

Script : Devanāgarī

Source : K M U H H G K S T V, Kashi

Acc. No. : 101 E

Title : ***Saṅgītaratnākara***

संगीतरत्नाकर

Author : Priyādāsa

Mat. : Paper

Size : 8″ × 6″

Leaves : 40

Lines : 24

Letters : 1518

Script : Devanāgarī

Dated : 1839 AD

Source : K M U H H G K S T V, Kashi

Acc. No. : 273 E

Title : ***Saṅgītaratnākara***

संगीतरत्नाकर

Author : Śārṅgadeva

Mat. : Palmleaf

Folios : 47

Language : Sanskrit

Script : Malayalam

Source : Kerala Univ. Lib., Trivandrum

Ms. No. : 246

Title : ***Saṅgītaratnākara***

संगीतरत्नाकर

Author : Śārṅgadeva

Mat. : Palmleaf

Folios : 147

Language : Sanskrit

Script : Malayalam

Source : Kerala Univ. Lib., Trivandrum

Ms. No. : 8912A

Title : ***Saṅgītaratnākara***

संगीतरत्नाकर

Author : Śārṅgadeva

Source : A C of mss in the L of H H the M of U, Udaipur, 1943, S B L

No. : 811

Title : ***Saṅgītaratnākara***

संगीतरत्नाकर

Author : Śārṅgadeva

Source : A C of mss in the L of H H the M of U, Udaipur, 1943, S B L

No. : 810

Title : ***Saṅgītaratnākara***

संगीतरत्नाकर

Author : Śārṅgadeva

Size : 6" × 5½"

Folios : 12

Dated : Sam. 1839

Source : Nagpur Univ. Lib., Nagpur

Acc. No. : 1511

Title : ***Saṅgītaratnakara***

संगीतरत्नाकर

Author : Gaurī-śaṅkara Bhaṭṭa

Dated : Sam. 1924

P. Year : 1929

Source : Nagari Pracharini Sabha, Varanasi, Vol II

S. No. : 101 F

Title : ***Saṅgītaratnākara***

संगीतरत्नाकर

Author : Unknown

Leaves : 173 – 193, 219

Granths : 200

Text : Incomplete

Source : O I, Baroda

Acc. No. : 10296

Title : ***Saṅgītaratnākara***

संगीतरत्नाकर

Author : Unknown

Leaves : 71 – 78

Granths : 140

Source : O I, Baroda

Acc. No. : 973

Title : ***Saṅgītaratnākara***

संगीतरत्नाकर

Author : Śārṅgadeva

Leaves : 42
Granths : 700
Source : O I, Baroda
Acc. No. : 1347

Title : ***Saṅgītaratnākara***
संगीतरत्नाकर
Author : Śārṅgadeva
Leaves : 71
Granths : 1801
Source : O I, Baroda
Acc. No. : 1983

Title : ***Saṅgītaratnākara***
संगीतरत्नाकर
Author : Śārṅgadeva
Leaves : 25
Granths : 950
Source : O I, Baroda
Acc. No. : 1986

Title : ***Saṅgītaratnākara***
संगीतरत्नाकर
Author : Śārṅgadeva
Leaves : 50
Granths : 900
Source : O I, Baroda
Acc. No. : 2084

Title : ***Saṅgītaratnākara***
संगीतरत्नाकर
Author : Śārṅgadeva
Leaves : 88
Granths : 1800
Source : O I, Baroda
Acc. No. : 2194

Title : ***Saṅgītaratnākara***
संगीतरत्नाकर
Author : Śārṅgadeva
Leave : 1
Granths : 25
Dated : Śaka 1298
Source : O I, Baroda
Acc. No. : 7615

Title : ***Saṅgītaratnākara***
संगीतरत्नाकर
Author : Śāṛṅgadeva
Pages : 80
Lines : 5
Script : Grantha
Source : L of S mss in P L of S I, Madras, 1880, Vol I
S. No. : 1174

Title : ***Saṅgitaratnākara***
संगीतरत्नाकर
Author : Śārṅgadeva

Pages : 200

Lines : 8

Script : Kadjān Grantha

Source : L of S mss in P L of S I, Madras, 1880, Vol I

S. No. : 4647

Title : ***Saṅgītaratnākara***

संगीतरत्नाकर

Author : Śārṅgadeva

Pages : 65

Lines : 8

Script : Malayalam

Source : L of S mss in P L of S I, Madras, 1880, Vol I

S. No. : 2726

Title : ***Saṅgītaratnākara***

संगीतरत्नाकर

Author : Śārṅgadeva

Source : L of S mss in P L of S I, Madras, 1880, Vol I

S. No. : 7436

Title : ***Saṅgītaratnākara***

संगीतरत्नाकर

Author : Śārṅgadeva

Source : L of S mss in P L of S I, Madras, 1880, Vol I

S. No. : 3063

Title : ***Saṅgītaratnākara***

संगीतरत्नाकर

Author : Unknown

Source : L of S mss in P L of S I, Madras, 1880, Vol I

S. No. : 8314

Title : ***Saṅgītaratnākara***

संगीतरत्नाकर

Author : Unknown

Commentary: Kalānidhi

Source : L of S mss in P L of S I, Madras, 1880, Vol I

S. No. : 8315

Title : ***Saṅgītaratnākara***

संगीतरत्नाकर

Author : Śārṅgadeva

Mat. : Paper

Size : 23.6 × 11 cm.

Folios : 21

Lines : 10

Illustration : 35

Script : Devanāgarī

Text : Complete

Dated : 19th century

Source : R O I, Jodhpur, Pt.-I

S. No. : 2499

Acc. No. : 2528

Title	: *Saṅgītaratnākara*
	संगीतरत्नाकर
Author	: Nicyaṅa Śārṅgadeva
Mat.	: Paper
Lines	: 87
Script	: Devanāgarī
Text	: Incomplete
Source	: Skt. College Banaras, Allahabad, 1911
G. No.	: 3073

Title	: *Saṅgītratnākara*
	संगीतरत्नाकर
Author	: Nicyaṅa Śārṅgadeva
Mat.	: Paper
Lines	: 22
Script	: Devanāgarī
Text	: Incomplete
Source	: Skt. College Banaras, Allahabad, 1911
S. No.	: 3075

Title	: *Saṅgītratnākara*
	संगीतरत्नाकर
Author	: Nicyaṅa Śārṅgadeva
Mat.	: Paper
Lines	: 49
Script	: Devanāgarī
Text	: Incomplete
Source	: Skt. College Banaras, Allahabad, 1911
S. No.	: 3096

Title	: *Saṅgītaratnākara*
	संगीतरत्नाक़र
Author	: Śārṅgadeva
Mat.	: Palmleaf
Size	: 12¾″ × 1¼″
Pages	: 59
Leaves	: 211
Lines	: 3 - 8
Granths	: 4000
Script	: Telugu
Text	: Incomplete
Dated	: First leaf of 13th century AD
Source	: D C of the S mss in the T M S S M L, Tanjore, Vol XVI
S. No.	: 10731
B. No.	: 11496

It is reputed that this work has six commentaries of which only five are known, these are by:

1. Kallinātha
2. Siṁhabhūpāla
3. Kumbhakarṇa
4. Gaṅgārāma
5. Haṁsabhūpāla

Des. No.

Copies : 17332 B. No.11492
Palmleaf Telugu
Incomplete I-VI
10733 B. No. 11493
Palmleaf Telugu
Incomplete
10734 B. No.11495
Palmleaf Telugu
Incomplete Beginning is missing
10735 S.S. 58
Palmleaf Grantha
Incomplete wants I
10736 B. No.11494
Palmleaf Grantha
Incomplete II-VII
10737 B. No.11589b
Palmleaf Grantha
Incomplete VII
10738 B. No.11539a
Palmleaf Grantha
Incomplete VII
10739 B. No.11498d
Palmleaf Grantha
Incomplete Fragment
10740 B. No.11497
Palmleaf Grantha
Incomplete Fragment
10741 B. No.11543b
Palmleaf Grantha
Incomplete Fragment
10742 B. No.11544
Palmleaf Grantha
Incomplete Fragment
10748 B. No.11556
Palmleaf Grantha
Incomplete Fragment

Title : ***Saṅgītaratnākara***
संगीतरत्नाकर

Author : Śārṅgadeva

Source : T A C C, Wiesbaden, 1962, Pt-I

S. No. : 63

Title : ***Saṅgītaratnākara***
संगीतरत्नाकर

Author : Śārṅgadeva (Son of Soḍhala)

Source : T A C C, Wiesbaden, 1962, Pt-II

S. No. : 21

Title : ***Saṅgītaratnākara***
संगीतरत्नाकर

Author : Śārṅgadeva

Source : T A C C, Wiesbaden, 1962, Pt-III

S. No. : 5

Title : ***Saṅgītaratnakara***
संगीतरत्नाकर

Author : Śārṅgadeva

Folios : 8

Script : Devanāgarī

Source : V V R I, Hoshiarpur

Acc. No. : 1265

Title : ***Saṅgītaratnākaracandrikā***
संगीतरत्नाकरचन्द्रिका

Author : Unknown

Ms W P : H. H. the Mahārājā of Travancore

Source : L of S mss in P L of S I, Madras, 1880, Vol I

S. No. : 6258

Title : ***Saṅgītaratnākara Deśītālādhyāya***

संगीतरत्नाकर देशीतालाध्याय

Author : Śārṇgadeva

Mat. : Paper

Size : 26.5 × 10.9 cm.

Pages : 8

Lines : 13

E × tent : 42

Script : Devanāgarī

Text : Complete

Dated : V. S. 1750

Source : L C of S & P mss in M S P C, L D B S V, Ahmedabad

S. No. : 6362

Acc. No : 1562

Title : ***Saṅgītaratnākare Vādyādhyāya***

संगीतरत्नाकरे वाद्याध्याय

Author : Kallinātha

Mat : Paper

Size : 25 × 13.5 cm.

Folios : 3 - 40

Lines : 11

Letters : 28

Script : Devanāgarī

Text : Incomplete

Dated : Sam. 1794

Source : Gujarat Vidya Sabha, Ahmedabad

S. No. : 2646

Acc. No. : 2669

Title : ***Saṅgītaratnākaraḥ***

संगीतरत्नाकरः

Author : Śārṇgadeva

Mat. : Palmleaf

Size : 27 × 4 cm.

Pages : 300

Language : Sanskrit

Script : Telugu

Source : G O M L, Triplicane, Madras

Title : ***Saṅgītaratnākaraḥ***

संगीतरत्नाकरः

Author : Śārṇgadeva

Mat. : Paper

Size : 21 × 17 cm.

Pages : 167

Language : Sanskrit

Script : Telugu

Source : G O M L, Triplicane, Madras

Title	: ***Saṅgītaratnākaraḥ***
	संगीतरत्नाकर:
Author	: Śārṅgadeva
Mat.	: Palmleaf
Size	: 44 × 4.5 cm.
Pages	: 192
Language	: Sanskrit
Script	: Telugu
Source	: G O M L, Triplicane, Madras

Title	: ***Saṅgītaratnākaraḥ***
	संगीतरत्नाकर:
Author	: Śārṅgadeva
Mat.	: Paper
Size	: 27 × 21.5 cm.
Pages	: 222
Language	: Sanskrit
Script	: Telugu
Source	: G O M L, Triplicane, Madras

Title	: ***Saṅgītaratnākaraḥ***
	संगीतरत्नाकर:
Author	: Śārṅgadeva
Mat.	: Palmleaf
Size	: 34 × 2.5 cm.
Pages	: 13
Language	: Sanskrit
Script	: Grantha
Source	: G O M L, Triplicane, Madras

Title	: ***Saṅgītaratnākaraḥ***
	संगीतरत्नाकर:
Author	: Śārṅgadeva
Mat.	: Paper
Size	: 29.5 × 19 cm.
Pages	: 258
Language	: Sanskrit
Script	: Telugu
Source	: G O M L, Triplicane, Madras

Title	: ***Saṅgītaratnākaraḥ***
	संगीतरत्नाकर:
Author	: Śārṅgadeva
Mat.	: Palmleaf
Size	: 19.5 × 2.5 cm.
Pages	: 37
Language	: Sanskrit
Script	: Telugu
Source	: G O M L, Triplicane, Madras

Title	: ***Saṅgītaratnākaraḥ***
	संगीतरत्नाकर:
Author	: Śārṅgadeva
Mat.	: Paper
Size	: 33 × 21 cm.
Pages	: 55
Language	: Sanskrit
Script	: Telugu
Source	: G O M L, Triplicane, Madras

Title	:	***Saṅgītaratnākaraḥ***
		संगीतरत्नाकरः
Author	:	Śārṅgadeva
Mat.	:	Paper
Size	:	19.1 × 15 cm.
Pages	:	6
Language	:	Sanskrit
Script	:	Telugu
Source	:	G O M L, Triplicane, Madras

Title	:	***Saṅgītaratnākaraḥ***
		संगीतरत्नाकरः
Author	:	Somanātha
Mat.	:	Palmleaf
Size	:	40.7 × 3.8 cm.
Pages	:	34
Language	:	Sanskrit
Script	:	Telugu
Source	:	G O M L, Triplicane, Madras

Title	:	***Saṅgītaratnākaraḥ with Telugu Ṭīkā***
		संगीतरत्नाकरः तेलुगू टीका के साथ
Author	:	Śārṅgadeva
Mat.	:	Paper
Size	:	21.5 × 17 cm.
Pages	:	16
Language	:	Sanskrit
Script	:	Telugu
Source	:	G O M L, Triplicane, Madras

Title	:	***Saṅgītaratnākaraḥ Āndhraṭīkopetā***
		संगीतरत्नाकरः आन्ध्रटीकोपेता
Author	:	Śārṅgadeva
Mat.	:	Paper
Pages	:	59
Sheets	:	178
Lines	:	3 - 4
Granths	:	1660
Script	:	Devanāgarī
Text	:	Incomplete
Source	:	D C of the S mss in the T M S S M L, Tanjore, Vol XVI
S. No.	:	10744
B. No.	:	11506

This book has a Aandhraṭīkā which is in Telugu language. Author of this commentary is unknown.

Copies	:	10745
B. No.	:	11507
Pamleaf	:	Telugu
Incomplete	:	10746
B. No.	:	11508
Pamleaf	:	Telugu
Incomplete	:	10747
B. No.	:	11509
Pamleaf	:	Telugu
Incomplete	:	10748

S.S. : 57
Pamleaf : Telugu
Incomplete

Title : ***Saṅgītaratnākaraḥ***
संगीतरत्नाकरः
Author : Śārṅgadeva
Mat. : Paper
Size : 13.5″ × 6.7″
Folios : 17 - 29
Lines : 11
Letters : 51
Script : Devanāgarī
Source : Varanaseya Skt. Visvavidyalaya Lib., Varanasi
S. No. : 45507

Title : ***Saṅgītaratnākaraḥ***
संगीतरत्नाकरः
Author : Śārṅgadeva
Mat. : Paper
Size : 12.5″ × 4.5″
Folios : 2 - 50
Lines : 9
Letters : 42
Script : Devanāgarī
Source : Varanaseya Skt. Visvavidyalaya Lib., Varanasi
S. No. : 45508

Title : ***Saṅgītaratnākaraḥ***
संगीतरत्नाकरः
Author : Śārṅgadeva
Mat. : Paper
Size : 12.2″ × 4.8″
Folios : 2-23
Lines : 9
Letters : 38
Script : Devanāgarī
Source : Varanaseya Skt. Visvavidyalaya Lib., Varanasi
S. No. : 45509

Title : ***Saṅgītaratnākaraḥ***
संगीतरत्नाकरः
Author : Śārṅgadeva
Mat. : Paper
Size : 12.5″ × 4.9″
Folios : 2 - 89
Lines : 10
Letters : 46
Script : Devanāgarī
Source : Varanaseya Skt. Visvavidyalaya Lib., Varanasi
S. No. : 45510

Title : ***Saṅgītaratnākara Kalanidhi***
संगीतरत्नाकर कलानिधि
Author : Catura Kallinātha

Size : 10″ × 4¼″

Folios : 102

Illustration : 10

Dated : 1456 -77 AD

Source : B O R I, Poona

Acc. No. : 247/1883-84

Title : ***Saṅgītaratnākara Nartanādhyāya***

संगीतरत्नाकर नर्तनाध्याय

Author : Śārṅgdeva

Mat. : Paper

Size : 26.8 × 11 cm.

Pages : 44

Lines : 14

E × tent : 44

Script : Devanāgarī

Text : Complete

Dated : V. S. 1626

Source : C of S & P mss in M S P C, L D B S V, Ahmedabad

S. No. : 6363

Acc. No : 2270

Title : ***Sangītaratnākara (Piṇḍaprakaraṇa)***

संगीतरत्नाकर (पिण्डप्रकरण)

Author : Śārṅgadeva

Size : 9¼″ × 5¼″

Folios : 8

Illustration : 11

Cond. : Old mss

Source : B O R I, Poona

Acc. No. : 407/1882-83

Title : ***Saṅgītaratnākara Saṭīkā***

संगीतरत्नाकर सटीका

Author : Catura Kallinātha

Folios : 36

Script : Devanāgarī

Source : V V R I, Hoshiarpur

Acc. No. : 1424

Title : ***Saṅgītaratnākara Svaragatādhyāya***

संगीतरत्नाकर स्वरगताध्याय

Author : Unknown

Mat. : Paper

Size : 26.8 × 11.4 cm.

Pages : 21

Lines : 15

E × tent : 35

Script : Devanāgarī

Text : Complete

Dated : V. S. 1650

Source : C of S & P mss in M S P C, L D B S V, Ahmedabad

S. No. : 6364

Acc. No. : 2268

Title	: ***Saṅgītaratnākara (Tālaprakaraṇa)***
	संगीतरत्नाकर (तालप्रकरण)
Author	: Śāraṅgadeva
Mat.	: Paper
Size	: 27 × 11.5 cm.
Pages	: 14
Script	: Devanāgarī
Text	: Complete
Dated	: V. S. 1650
Source	: C of S & P mss in M S P C, L D B S V, Ahmedabad
S. No.	: 6361
Acc. No.	: 2269

Title	: ***Saṅgītaratnākaraṭīkā***
	संगीतरत्नाकरटीका
Author	: Siṅgabhūpala
Size	: 9¾″ × 4¼″
Folios	: 35
Illustration	: 11
Source	: B O R I, Poona
Acc. No.	: 406/1882-83

Title	: ***Saṅgītaratnākaraṭīkā***
	संगीतरत्नाकरटीका
Author	: Siṁhabhūpāla
Source	: T A C C, Wiesbaden, 1962, Pt-I
S. No.	: 79

Title	: ***Saṅgītaratnākaratīkā***
	संगीतरत्नाकरटीका
Author	: Hansabhūpāla
Source	: T A C C, Wiesbaden, 1962, Pt-I
S. No.	: 94

Title	: ***Sangītaratnākaraṭīkā "Kalānidhi"***
	संगीतरत्नाकरटीका "कलानिधि"
Author	: Kallinātha
Leaves	: 66
Granths	: 2400
Text	: Incomplete
Cond.	: Injured
Source	: O I, Baroda
Acc. No.	: 1131

Title	: ***Sangītaratnakaraṭīkā "Kalānidhi"***
	संगीतरत्नाकरटीका "कलानिधि"
Author	: Kallinātha
Leaves	: 70
Granths	: 2200
Text	: Incomplete
Source	: O I, Baroda
Acc. No.	: 2046

Title : ***Saṅgītaratnākaraṭīkā “Saṅgītasudhākara”***

संगीतरत्नाकरटीका
“संगीतसुधाकर”

Author : Siṁhabhūpāla

Leaves : 216

Granths : 6800

Text : Incomplete

Source : O I, Baroda

Acc. No. : 2046

Title : ***Saṅgītaratnākaravyākhyā***

संगीतरत्नाकरव्याख्या

Source : O R I, Mysore

No. : 1379

Title : ***Saṅgītaratnākaravyākhyā***

संगीतरत्नाकरव्याख्या

Author : Unknown

Mat. : Palmleaf

Script : Telugu

Text : Incomplete

Dated : 14th century

Source : D C of the S mss in the T M S S M L, Tanjore, Vol XVI

S. No. : 10750

B. No. : 1150

Copies : 10751

BL. : 11504

Pamleaf : Telugu

Incomplete : III, IV, V, VII 10752

BL. : 6600

Paper : Devanāgarī

Incomplete : IV 10753

BL. : 6601

Paper : Devanāgarī

Incomplete : VI

Title : ***Saṅgītaratnākaravyākhyā***

संगीतरत्नाकरव्याख्या

Author : Siṃha Bhūpāla

Source : Venkatesvara Univ., Tirupati

Title : ***Saṅgītaratnākaravyākhyā Kalānidhi***

संगीतरत्नाकरव्याख्या
कलानिधि

Author : Kallinātha son of Lakṣmīdhara

Mat. : Palmleaf

Folios : 31

Language : Sanskrit

Script : Malayalam

Source : Kerala Univ. Lib., Trivandrum

Ms. No. : 8951 A

Title	: ***Saṅgītaratnākaravyākhyā Kalānidhi***		
	संगीतरत्नाकरव्याख्या कलानिधि		
Author	: Catura Kallinātha		
Mat.	: Palmleaf		
Pages	: 60		
Leaves	: 1 – 23 : 174 - 272		
Lines	: 6 - 7		
Size	: 17¼ × 1½		
Granths	: 4650		
Script	: Telugu		
Text	: Incomplete		
Dated	: Latter half of the 14th century		
Source	: D C of the S mss in the T M S S M L, Tanjore, Vol XVI		
	S. No.	: 10749	
	B. No.	: 11503	
	Copies	: 10750	
	B. No.	: 11505	
	Pamleaf	: Telugu	
	Incomplete	: 10751	
	B. No.	: 11504	
	Pamleaf	: Telugu	
	Incomplete	: 10752	
	B. No.	: 6600	
	Paper	: Devanāgarī	
	Incomplete	: 10753	
	B. No.	: 6601	
	Paper	: Devanāgarī Incomplete	

Title	: ***Saṅgītaratnākaravyā-khyāsetu***
	संगीतरत्नाकरव्याख्यासेतु
Author	: Gaṅgārāma
Mat.	: Paper
Size	: 13¾″ × 7″
Pages	: 59
Sheets	: 107
Lines	: 8 - 10
Text	: Incomplete
Source	: D C of the S mss in the T M S S M L, Tanjore, Vol XVI
S. No.	: 10754
B. No.	: 6598
	Hindi commentary in Brja Bhāṣā only in Ist chapter.
	10757-10782 – 1-6 chapter, 7-9 chapter-II, 10-13 chapters III, 14-19 chapter IV. 20-22 chapter VI, 23-27 chapter VII

Title	: ***Saṅgītaratnamālā***
	संगीतरत्नमाला
Author	: Mammaṭa
Source	: T A C C, Wiesbaden, 1962, Pt-I
S. No.	: 62

Title	:	***Saṅgītaratnāvalī***
		संगीतरत्नावली
Author	:	Somarājadeva
Source	:	T A C C, Wiesbaden, 1962, Pt-I
S. No.	:	63

Title	:	***Saṅgītaratnāvalī***
		संगीतरत्नावली
Author	:	Unknown
Mat.	:	Paper
Size	:	11.4″ × 4.3″
Folios	:	11 - 27, 36, 38–39, 42–48
Lines	:	9
Letter	:	33
Script	:	Devanāgarī
Source	:	Varanaseya Skt. Visvavidyalaya Lib., Varanasi
S. No.	:	45503

Title	:	***Saṅgītaratnāvalī***
		संगीतरत्नावली
Author	:	Somarāja
Source	:	Veṅkatesvara Univ., Ṭirupati

Title	:	***Saṅgītasamayasāraḥ***
		संगीतसमयसारः
Author	:	Pārśvadeva
Mat.	:	Paper
Size	:	33.5 × 3 cm.
Pages	:	48
Language	:	Sanskrit
Script	:	Nandināgarī
Source	:	G O M L, Triplicane, Madras

Title	:	***Saṅgītasamayasāraḥ***
		संगीतसमयसारः
Author	:	Pārśvadeva
Mat.	:	Paper
Size	:	27.1 × 24 cm.
Pages	:	48
Language	:	Sanskrit
Script	:	Devanāgarī
Source	:	G O M L, Triplicane, Madras

Title	:	***Saṅgītasamayasaraḥ***
		संगीतसमयसारः
Author	:	Parśvadeva
Mat.	:	Palmleaf
Size	:	14½″ × 1 3/8″
Leaves	:	57
Lines	:	4-5
Granths	:	1000
Script	:	Grantha
Text	:	Incomplete
Source	:	D C of the S mss in the T M S S M L, Tanjore, Vol XVI

S. No. : 10785

B. No. : 11545

The author in the colophon mentions that he had the title 'Saṅgītākara' and that he was the disciple of one Mahādeva who was the Śiśya of Abhaya.
The Manuscript wants both beginning and end.

Title : ***Saṅgītasamayasārasaṅgrahaḥ***

संगीतसमयसारसंग्रहः

Source : O R I, Mysore

No. : A 67

Title : ***Saṅgītasāra***

संगीतसार

Author : Devīprasāda

Mat. : Paper

Size : 8" × 6"

Leaves : 46

Lines : 36

Letters : 1548

Script : Devanāgarī

Dated : 1843 AD

Source : K M U H H G K S T V, Kashi

Acc. No. : 84 D

Title : ***Saṅgītasāra***

संगीतसार

Author : Mannā Lāla

Mat. : Paper

Size : 8″ × 6″

Leaves : 80

Lines : 44

Letters : 1956

Script : Devanāgarī

Source : K M U H H G K S T V, Kashi

Acc. No. : 229 C

Title : ***Saṅgītasāra***

संगीतसार

Author : Tānasena

Time : Sam. 1888

P. Year : 1901

Source : Nagari Pracharini Sabha, Varanasi, Vol II

S. No. : 12

Title : ***Saṅgītasāra***

संगीतसार

Author : Devīprasāda

Time : Sam. 1900

P. Year : 1929

Source : Nagari Pracharini Sabha, Varanasi, Vol II

S. No. : 84 D

Title : ***Saṅgītasāra***

संगीतसार

Author : Harivallabha

Mat. : Paper
Lines : 43
Language : Hindi
Script : Devanāgarī
Dated : 1748 AD
Source : Skt. College Banaras, Allahabad, 1911
S. No. : 3074

Title : ***Saṅgītasāra***
संगीतसार
Author : Harivallabha
Mat. : Paper
Lines : 33
Language : Hindi
Script : Devanāgarī
Dated : 1748 AD
Source : Skt. College Banaras, Allahabad, 1911
S. No. : 4973

Title : ***Saṅgītasāra***
संगीतसार
Author : Harivallabha
Mat. : Paper
Lines : 26
Language : Hindi
Script : Devanāgarī
Source : Skt. College Banaras, Allahabad, 1911
S. No. : 4974

Title : ***Saṅgītasāra***
संगीतसार
Author : Harivallabha
Lines : 33
Ślokas : 800
Language : Hindi
Script : Devanāgarī
Dated : 1748 AD
Source : Skt. College Banaras, Allahabad, 1902
G. No. : 496

Title : ***Saṅgītasāra***
संगीतसार
Author : Harivallabha
Mat. : Paper
Size : 13.9″ × 5.4″
Folios : 1 - 26
Lines : 10
Letters : 49
Script : Devanāgarī
Source : Varanaseya Skt. Visvavidyalaya Lib., Varanasi
S. No. : 45987

Title : ***Saṅgītasāra***
संगीतसार
Author : Harivallabha
Mat. : Paper

Size : 12.4 × 4.8 cm.

Folios : 1 - 42

Lines : 8

Letters : 43

Script : Devanāgarī

Source : Varanaseya Skt. Visvavidyalaya Lib., Varanasi

S. No. : 45988

Title : ***Saṅgītasārabolī***

संगीतसारबोली

Mat. : Palmleaf

Size : 27 × 14 cm.

Pages : 10

Language : Sanskrit

Script : Oriya

Source : G O M L, Triplicane, Madras

Title : ***Saṅgītasāraḥ***

संगीतसारः

Author : Harivallabha

Mat. : Paper

Size : 12.9 × 4.5 cm.

Folios : 1 - 43

Lines : 9

Letters : 41

Script : Devanāgarī

Source : Varanaseya Skt. Visvavidyalaya Lib., Varanasi

S. No. : 45873

Title : ***Saṅgīta Sārakalikā***

संगीत सारकलिका

Author : Mokṣadevaḥ

Source : Venkatesvara Univ., Tirupati

Title : ***Saṅgītasārāmṛtam***

संगीतसारामृतम्

Author : Tularājaḥ

Mat. : Paper

Size : 10½″ × 4 1/8″

Sheets : 120

Lines : 7 - 8

Script : Devanāgarī

Granths : 1500

Text : Incomplete

Source : D C of the S mss in the T M S S M L, Tanjore, Vol XVI

S. No. : 10786

B. No. : 6699

The author of this work is one of the Maharatta rulers of Tanjore who ruled 1729-1735 AD. The author is one of the step brothers of Shivājī.
Cat- 10787-10803 of 17 copies of the Manuscript with the exception one in

Telugu of all other are in Devanagari.

Title : ***Saṅgītasārāmṛtam***

संगीतसारामृतम्

Author : Tularājaḥ

Source : Venkatesvara Univ., Tirupati

Title : ***Saṅgītasārāmṛtoddhāra***

संगीतसारामृतोद्धार

Author : Tulājī Rāva Bhosale

Edited by : Bhālacandra Sītārāma Sukthaṅkara

Source : British Museum, London

A metrical account of the musical modes.

Title : ***Saṅgīta Saraṇiḥ***

संगीत सरणिः

Author : Nārāyaṇaḥ

Source : Venkatesvara Univ., Tirupati

Title : ***Saṅgītasārasaṅgraha***

संगीतसारसंग्रह

Author : Jagajjyotimalla

Size : 10" × 5"

Folios : 72

Lines : 9

Ślokas : 1539

Language : Nevārī

Source : A C of P & S P mss D L, Nepal, Calcutta,1905

S. No. : 1478

Title : ***Saṅgītasārasaṅgraha***

संगीतसारसंग्रह

Author : Sudarśana Bhaṭṭa

Source : L of S mss in P L of S I, Madras, 1880, Vol I

S. No. : 1052

Title : ***Saṅgītasārasaṅgraha***

संगीतसारसंग्रह

Author : King Jagajjyotimalla

Source : T A C C, Wiesbaden, 1962, Pt-III

S. No. : 7

Title : ***Saṅgītasārasurādhyāya***

संगीतसारसुराध्याय

Author : Harivallabha

Mat. : Paper

Size : 10½" × 7"

Leaves : 14

Lines : 17

Letters : 250

Script : Devanāgarī

Source : K M U H H G K S T V, Kashi
Acc. No. : 173 B

Title : ***Saṅgītasāriṇīḥ***
संगीतसारिणीः
Author : Nārāyaṇa
Mat. : Paper
Size : 27.5 × 24.5 cm.
Pages : 123
Language : Sanskrit
Script : Devanāgarī
Source : G O M L, Triplicane, Madras

Title : ***Saṅgītasāroddhāra***
संगीतसारोद्धार
Author : Kīkarāja
Size : 13 1/8" × 7¾"
Folios : 16
Illustration : 15
Source : B O R I, Poona
Acc. No. : 838/1886 -92

Title : ***Saṅgītasāroddhāra***
संगीतसारोद्धार
Author : Haribhaṭṭa
Source : T A C C, Wiesbaden, 1962, Pt-I
S. No. : 76

Title : ***Saṅgītasāroddhāra***
संगीतसारोद्धार
Author : Sudhākalaśa
Leaves : 128
Granths : 955
Source : O I, Baroda
Acc. No. : 13271

Title : ***Saṅgītasāroddhāra***
संगीतसारोद्धार
Author : Kīkarāja (Son of Sajjana)
Source : T A C C, Wiesbaden, 1962, Pt-II
S. No. : 15

Title : ***Saṅgītaśāstra***
संगीतशास्त्र
Author : Unknown
Mat. : Paper
Size : 26.3 × 10 cm.
Pages : 9
Lines : 17
Extent : 50
Script : Devanāgarī
Text : Complete
Dated : V. S. 1650
Source : C of S & P mss in M S P C, L D B S V, Ahmedabad
S. No. : 6360
Acc. No. : 5562

Title	: ***Saṅgītaśāstra***
	संगीतशास्त्र
Author	: Śārṅgadhara
Ms W P	: Śaṅkarācārya maṭha of Kumbhaghoṇam
Source	: L of S mss in P L of S I, Madras, 1880, Vol I
S. No.	: 3883

Title	: ***Saṅgītaśāstram***
	संगीतशास्त्रम्
Author	: Vimlā
Leaves	: 35, 57 - 95
Granths	: 1000
Text	: Incomplete
Dated	: 17th century
Source	: O I, Baroda
Acc. No.	: 2505

Title	: ***Saṅgītaśāstradugdhām-budhiḥ***
	संगीतशास्त्रदुग्धाम्बुधिः
Source	: O R I, Mysore
No.	: V 991

Title	: ***Saṅgītaśāstraṭīkāgrantha***
	संगीतशास्त्रटीकाग्रन्थ
Author	: Unknown
Source	: B I S M H G C, Poona
No.	: 22863

Title	: ***Saṅgītaśāstre Nāmavidhāna Prathama***
	संगीतशास्त्रे नामविधान प्रथम
Author	: Unknown
Mat.	: Paper
Size	: 20.5 × 10.5 cm.
Folios	: 5
Lines	: 9
Letters	: 25
Script	: Devanāgarī
Text	: Complete
Dated	: Sam. 1642
Source	: Gujarat Vidya Sabha, Ahmedabad
S. No.	: 2647
Acc. No.	: 5431

Title	: ***Saṅgītasiddhānta***
	संगीतसिद्धान्त
Author	: Rāmānandatīrtha
Source	: T A C C, Wiesbaden, 1962, Pt-I
S. No.	: 77

Title	: ***Saṅgītaśikṣā***
	संगीतशिक्षा
Author	: Kirorī Mohana Dāsa
Source	: British Museum, London
	An Oriya treatise on Hindu music. It illustrated from

Sanskrit Text.

Published from in 1899.

Title : ***Saṅgītaśiromaṇi***

संगीतशिरोमणि

Author : Sulutusuhi

Size : 10″ × 4″

Folios : 2 - 16

Language : Sanskrit

Source : Asiatic Society, 1, Park Street, Calcutta-16

Title : ***Saṅgītaśiromaṇi***

संगीतशिरोमणि

Language : Sanskrit

Source : Sangeet Natak Academy Lib.

Title : ***Saṅgītaśiromaṇiḥ***

संगीतशिरोमणिः

Author : Unknown

Source : Venkatesvara Univ., Tirupati

Title : ***Saṅgītasudha***

संगीतसुधा

Author : Raghunāthabhūpa

Size : 14½ × 1½ cm.

Folios : 230

Illustration : 7

Script : Malayalam

Source : A D C of S mss in the C O L, Trivandrum

S. No. : 1228

C.O.L. No. : 2193

Title : ***Saṅgītasudhā***

संगीतसुधा

Author : Raghunāthabhūpa

Size : 13½ × 8½ cm.

Folios : 662

Illustration : 20

Script : Devanāgarī

Source : A D C of S mss in the C O L, Trivandrum

S. No. : 1229

C.O.L. No. : 397

Title : ***Saṅgītasudhā***

संगीतसुधा

Author : Raghunātha Bhūpāla

Mat. : Paper

Size : 27.5 × 24.5 cm.

Pages : 194

Language : Sanskrit

Script : Grantha

Source : G O M L, Triplicane, Madras

Title : ***Saṅgītasudhā***

संगीतसुधा

Author : Raghunāthabhūpa

Size : 13¼ × 1⅞ cm.

Folios : 159

Illustration : 7

Source : A D C of the S mss in the H H M P L, Trivandrum

S. No. : 1419

Title : ***Saṅgītasudhā***

संगीतसुधा

Author : Ragunāthabhūpa

Mat. : Palmleaf

Language : Sanskrit

Script : Malayalam

Source : Kerala Univ. Lib., Trivandrum

Ms. No. : 1419

Title : ***Saṅgītasudhā***

संगीतसुधा

Author : Bhīma Narendra

Source : T A C C, Wiesbaden, 1962, Pt-I

S. No. : 78

Title : ***Saṅgītasudhā (Voume-II)***

संगीतसुधा *(वाल्यूम्-II)*

Author : Haripālaḥ

Source : Venkatesvara Univ., Tirupati

Title : ***Saṅgītasudhākara***

संगीतसुधाकर

Author : Kāshīnātha

Pages : 62

Source : British Museum, London

No. : 14055 e 4 (1)

A metrical work on the modes of music. He was son of Śrīrāma. Its published from Bombay, Poona in 1917.

Title : ***Saṅgītasudhākara***

संगीतसुधाकर

Author : Śrī Harapāladeva

Size : $14^{3/8} \times 2$ cm.

Folios : 40

Illustration : 10

Source : A D C of the S mss in the H H M P L, Trivandrum

S. No. : 1420

Title : ***Saṅgītasudhākara***

संगीतसुधाकर

Author : Haribhūpāla

Mat. : Palmleaf

Language : Sanskrit

Script : Malayalam

Source : Kerala Univ. Lib., Trivandrum

Ms. No. : 1420

Title	: ***Saṅgītasudhākara***
	संगीतसुधाकर
Author	: Vicāracaturamukha Śrī Haripāla
Mat.	: Paper
Folios	: 71
Language	: Sanskrit
Script	: Tamil
Source	: Kerala Univ. Lib., Trivandrum
Ms. No.	: 2182 A

Title	: ***Saṅgītasudhākara***
	संगीतसुधाकर
Author	: Vicāracaturamukha Śrīharipāladeva
Leaves	: 106
Granths	: 2
Source	: O I, Baroda
Acc. No.	: 1507 (b)

Title	: ***Saṅgītasudhākara***
	संगीतसुधाकर
Author	: Vicāracaturamukha Śrīharipāladeva
Leaves	: 143
Granths	: 2000
Source	: O I, Baroda
Acc. No.	: 9891

Title	: ***Saṅgītasudhākara***
	संगीतसुधाकर
Author	: Unknown
Ms W P	: H H the Mahārājā of Travancore
Source	: L of S mss in P L of S I, Madras, 1880, Vol I
S. No.	: 6259

Title	: ***Saṅgītasudhākara***
	संगीतसुधाकर
Author	: Haripāladeva
Mat.	: Palmleaf
Size	: 18½″ × 1¼″
Leaves	: 56
Lines	: 6
Granths	: 1200
Script	: Telugu and Grantha
Text	: Incomplete
Source	: D C of the S mss in the T M S S M L, Tanjore, Vol XVI

S. No.	: 10804
B. No.	: 11529 b
Copies	: 10805
B. No.	: 11529
Palmleaf	: Telugu
Incomplete	: 10806
B. No.	: 11528
Palmleaf	: Na Incomplete

Title : ***Saṅgītasudhākara***

संगीतसुधाकर

Author : Haripāladeva

Folios : 66

Script : Grantha

Source : V V R I, Hoshiarpur

Acc. No. : 5624

Title : ***Saṅgītasudhākaraḥ***

संगीतसुधाकरः

Author : Haripāla

Size : 11 × 8¾ cm.

Folios : 62

Illustration : 18

Script : Devanāgarī

Source : A D C of S mss in the C O L, Trivandrum

S. No. : 1230

C.O.L. No. : 580

Title : ***Saṅgītasudhākaraḥ***

संगीतसुधाकरः

Author : King Haripāladeva

Mat. : Paper

Size : 27.3 × 21.6 cm.

Pages : 37

Language : Sanskrit

Script : Devanāgarī

Source : G O M L, Triplicane, Madras

No. : 184

Title : ***Saṅgītasudhākaraḥ***

संगीतसुधाकरः

Author : King Haripāladeva

Mat. : Paper

Size : 27.5 × 24.5 cm.

Pages : 60

Language : Sanskrit

Script : Devanāgarī

Source : G O M L, Triplicane, Madras

Title : ***Saṅgītasudhākaraḥ***

संगीतसुधाकरः

Source : O R I, Mysore

No. : A 843

Title : ***Saṅgītasudhākaraḥ***

संगीतसुधाकरः

Source : O R I, Mysore

No. : 105

Title : ***Saṅgītasudhākaraḥ (Voume II)***

संगीतसुधाकरः

Author : Raghunātha Bhūpāla

Source : Venkatesvara Univ., Tirupati

Title : ***Saṅgītasundara***

संगीतसुन्दर

Author : Sadāśiva Dīkṣita

Source : T A C C, Wiesbaden, 1962, Pt-I

S. No. : 80

B. No. : 61 b

Title : ***Saṅgītasūryodaya***

संगीतसूर्योदय

Author : Lakṣmīnārāyaṇa

Size : 43.3 × 4 cm.

Mat. : Palmleaf

Pages : 103

Language : Sanskrit

Script : Telugu

Source : G O M L, Triplicane, Madras

Title : ***Saṅgītasūryodaya***

संगीतसूर्योदय

Author : Lakṣmīnārāyaṇa

Size : 27.2 × 24.2 cm.

Mat. : Paper

Pages : 172

Language : Sanskrit

Script : Devanāgarī

Source : G O M L, Triplicane, Madras

Title : ***Saṅgītasūryodayaḥ***

संगीतसूर्योदयः

Author : Lakṣamaṇa

Source : Venkatesvara Univ., Tirupati

Title : ***Saṅgītasvaralakṣaṇam***

संगीतस्वरलक्षणम्

Source : O R I, Mysore

No. : 4464

Title : ***Saṅgītasvaraprastāra-sāgara***

संगीतस्वरप्रस्तारसागर

Author : Nāradamuni

Source : British Museum, London

No. : 14055 e e 2

A manual of music in Sanskrit verses with Telugu interpretation exposition. pp. x, 604, Madras, 1914.

Title : ***Saṅgītataraṅgiṇī***

संगीततरंगिणी

Author : Unknown

Size : 6.8" × 1.3"

Folios : 60

Language : Oriya

Source : Bhuvaneswar Museum, Bhuvaneswar

Title : ***Saṅgītavidyādarpaṇa***

संगीतविद्यादर्पण

Author : Veṅkatasvāmī Nāyudū

Source : British Museum, London

A manual of music comprising Sanskrit verses with Telugu explanation dissertation.

Title : ***Saṅgītavihāra***

संगीतविहार

Author : Gaurīśaṅkara

Mat. : Paper

Size : 8″ × 6″

Leaves : 12

Lines : 20

Letters : 1960

Script : Devanāgarī

Dated : 1867 AD

Source : K M U H H G K S T V, Kashi

Acc. No. : 101 F

Title : ***Saṅgīta Vinodaḥ***

संगीत विनोदः

Author : Anūpa Siṃha

Source : Venkatesvara Univ., Tirupati

Title : ***Saṅgītaviṣayaḥ***

संगीतविषयः

Size : 15 × 1¼ cm.

Folios : 58

Illustration : 5

Script : Telugu

Source : A D C of the S mss in the G O M L, Madras, Vol XXVIII

No. : 16053

Title : ***Saṅgītaviṣayaḥ***

संगीतविषयः

Size : 15 × 1¼ cm.

Folios : 60

Illustration : 6

Script : Telugu

Source : A D C of the S mss in the G O M L, Madras, Vol XXVIII

No. : 16054

Title : ***Saṅgītaviṣayaḥ***

संगीतविषयः

Mat. : Paper

Size : 20 × 15 cm.

Pages : 16

Language : Sanskrit

Script : Telugu

Source : G O M L, Triplicane, Madras

Title : ***Saṅgītaviṣayaḥ***

संगीतविषयः

Mat. : Palmleaf

Size : 38.5 × 3 cm.

Pages : 25

Language : Sanskrit

Script : Telugu

Source : G O M L, Triplicane, Madras

Title : ***Saṅgītaviṣayaḥ***

संगीतविषयः

Mat. : Palmleaf

Size : 43.1 × 3.5 cm.

Pages : 71

Language : Sanskrit

Script : Telugu

Source : G O M L, Triplicane, Madras

Title : ***Saṅgītaviṣayaḥ***

संगीतविषयः

Mat. : Palmleaf

Size : 25 × 3 cm.

Pages : 13

Language : Sanskrit

Script : Grantha

Source : G O M L, Triplicane, Madras

Title : ***Saṅgītaviṣayaḥ with Malayalam commentary***

संगीतविषयः मलयालम व्याख्या के साथ

Mat. : Paper

Size : 26.5 × 24 cm.

Pages : 38

Language : Sanskrit

Script : Devanāgarī and Malayalam

Source : G O M L, Triplicane, Madras

Title : ***Saṅgītaviṣayako Granthaḥ***

संगीतविषयको ग्रन्थः

Author : Unknown

Mat. : Paper

Size : 12.2″ × 4.2″

Folios : 2, 4 - 13, 73 - 86

Lines : 9

Letters : 38

Script : Devanāgarī

Source : Varanaseya Skt. Visvavidyalaya Lib., Varanasi

S. No. : 45512

Title : ***Saṅgītavṛttaratnākaraḥ***

संगीतवृत्तरत्नाकरः

Author : Viṭthala

Size : 9¾″ × 4⅞″

Leaves : 17

Granths : 300

Script : Devanāgarī

Source : D C of the S mss in the T M S S M L, Tanjore, Vol XVI

S. No. : 10676

B. No. : 6657

Title	:	***Saṅgītopniṣad***
		संगीतोपनिषद्
Author	:	Sudhākalaśa
Source	:	T A C C, Wiesbaden, 1962, Pt-I
S. No.	:	83

Title	:	***Saṅgītopniṣatsāra***
		संगीतोपनिषत्सार
Author	:	Soma
Source	:	T A C C, Wiesbaden, 1962, Pt-I
S. No.	:	84

Title	:	***Saṅgītopaniṣatsarvoddhāra***
		संगीतोपनिषत्सर्वोद्धार
Author	:	Sudhākalaśamaṇi
Mat.	:	Paper
Size	:	30 × 11.8 cm.
Pages	:	28
Lines	:	13
Ex× tent	:	42
Script	:	Devanāgarī
Text	:	Complete
Dated	:	V. S. 1599
Source	:	C of S & P mss in M S P C, L D B S V, Ahmedabad
S. No.	:	6365
Acc. No	:	554

Title	:	***Saṅgītopaniṣatsarvod-dhāraḥ***
		संगीतोपनिषत्सर्वोद्धारः
Author	:	Sudhākalaśaḥ
Source	:	Venkatesvara Univ., Tirupati

Title	:	***Saṅgītopaniṣatsāra***
		संगीतोपनिषत्‌सार
Author	:	Unknown
Leaves	:	12
Granths	:	130
Dated	:	Sam. 1937
Source	:	O I, Baroda
Acc. No.	:	4550

Title	:	***Saṅgrahacūdāmaṇi***
		संग्रहचूडामणि
Author	:	Unknown
Source	:	Venkatesvara Univ., Tirupati

Title	:	***Saṅgrahaprakāśaṭīkā***
		संग्रहप्रकाशटीका
Author	:	Keśavamiśra
Ms W P	:	Lib. of H. H. the Raja of Kochin
Source	:	L of S mss in P L of S I, Madras, 1880, VOL I
S. No.	:	3064

Title	:	***Saṅgṛhītalatikā***
		संगृहीतलतिका
Author	:	Dātārāma
Dated	:	Sam. 1936
P. Year	:	1929 AD
Source	:	Nagari Pracharini Sabha, Varanasi, Vol II
S. No.	:	90

Title	:	***Santanāmāvalīḥ***
		सन्तनामावलीः
Author	:	Unkown (Son of Jayarāma)
Mat.	:	Palmleaf
Size	:	37 × 3 cm.
Pages	:	3
Language	:	Sanskrit
Script	:	Grantha
Source	:	G O M L, Triplicane, Madras

Title	:	***Saptatālavivaraṇam with Telugu meaning***
		सप्ततालविवरणम् तेलुगू अर्थ के साथ
Mat.	:	Palmleaf
Size	:	38.2 × 3 cm.
Pages	:	2
Language	:	Sanskrit
Script	:	Telugu
Source	:	G O M L, Triplicane, Madras

Title	:	***Sārasaṁhitā (Also called Pañcamasārasaṃhitā)***
		सारसंहिता (पञ्चमसारसंहिता)
Author	:	Nārada
Size	:	35 × 16 cm.
Folios	:	8
Language	:	Sanskrit
Source	:	National Lib., Belvedere, Calcutta-27

Title	:	***Sārasaṁhitā***
		सारसंहिता
Author	:	Nārada
Folios	:	7
Illustration	:	8
Script	:	Bengali
Source	:	N of S mss Pub. by G of B, Calcutta, 1871, Vol II
No.	:	540

Title	:	***Sarasvatī Hṛdayālaṅkāraḥ (Volume-II)***
		सरस्वती हृदयालंकारः (वाल्यूम्-*II)*
Author	:	Nānādevaḥ
Source	:	Venkatesvara Univ., Tirupati

Title	:	***Sarvārthasārasaṅgraha***
		सर्वार्थसारसंग्रह
Author	:	Unknown

Ms W P : T. Rāmarāva of Tanjore
Source : L of S mss in P L of S I, Madras, 1880, Vol I
S. No. : 8411

Title : ***Sarvasvaralakṣaṇa***
सर्वस्वरलक्षण
Author : Unknown
Ms W P : H. H. the Mahārājā of Travancore
Source : L of S mss in P L of S I, Madras, 1880, Vol I
S. No. : 6270

Title : ***Saumyanārāyaṇa Pperumāl Kummai***
सौम्यनारायण पेरूमाल् कुम्मै
Author : Haridāsa
Mat. : Palmleaf
Size : 46.2 × 3.8 cm.
Pages : 6
Language : Tamil
Script : Tamil
Source : G O M L, Triplicane, Madras

Title : ***Saumyanārāyaṇa Pperumāl Kummai Śobhanappāṭṭu***
सौम्यनारायण पेरूमाल् कुम्मै शोभनपाट्टु
Author : Unknown
Mat. : Palmleaf
Size : 46.2 × 3.8 cm.
Pages : 1
Language : Tamil
Script : Tamil
Source : G O M L, Triplicane, Madras

Title : ***Sima-Ul-Ilhān***
सिम–उल–इलहान
Author : Unknown
Size : 8.7″ × 4.5″ : 6.5″ × 2.5″
Leaves : 169
Lines : 15
Source : A D C of the O mss in the D L, Bahawalpur
No. : 266 (1)

Title : ***Singhāra Sātha etc.***
सिंघार साथ आदि
Author : Śāha Mohammad Anwar
Size : 18.5 × 10.5 cm.
Pages : 122
Language : Hindi
Script : Urdu
Cond. : Worm eaten & Damaged
Dated : 1060 AH (1707 Sam.)
Source : State Central Lib., Hyderabad

Title : ***Siṅgīśvarasvāmi-pārijātanāṭakam***
सिंगीश्वरस्वामिपारिजातनाटकम्
Author : Kumāraswāmī

Mat. : Palmleaf
Size : 39.5 × 3.8 cm.
Pages : 210
Language : Tamil
Script : Tamil
Source : G O M L, Triplicane, Madras

Title : ***Śirūttoṇḍarayakṣagānam***
शिरूत्तोण्डरयक्षगानम्
Author : Jñānaprakāśan
Mat. : Palmleaf
Size : 40 × 3 cm.
Pages : 164
Language : Tamil
Script : Tamil
Source : G O M L, Triplicane, Madras

Title : ***Sītakalyāṇam***
सीताकल्याणम्
Author : Unknown
Mat. : Palmleaf
Size : 38.7 × 2.5 cm.
Pages : 108
Language : Tamil
Script : Tamil
Source : G O M L, Triplicane, Madras

Title : ***Śivakīrtanāni***
शिवकीर्तनानि
Mat. : Palmleaf
Size : 44 × 3.7 cm.
Pages : 9
Script : Grantha
Source : G O M L, Triplicane, Madras

Title : ***Śravaṇanāṭakam***
श्रवणनाटकम्
Author : Unknown
Mat. : Paper
Size : 33 × 22.9 cm.
Pages : 150
Language : Tamil
Script : Tamil
Source : G O M L, Triplicane, Madras

Title : ***Śrīkṛṣṇa Nīlāmṛta Nāṭaka***
श्रीकृष्ण नीलामृत नाटक
Author : Haribandhu
Size : 14.5″ × 1″
Pages : 70
Language : Oriya
Source : Utkal Univ. Lib., Bhuvaneswar

Title : ***Śrīkṛṣṇa Phaktavātsalya Nāṭikā***
श्रीकृष्ण फक्तवात्सल्य नाटिका
Author : Rāmacandra Gajapati

Size : 13″ × 9.2″

Pages : 30

Language : Sanskrit

Source : Bhuvaneswar Museum, Bhuvaneswar

Title : ***Śrīmatvikṭoriyāmāhātmya***

श्रीमत्विक्टोरियामाहात्म्य

Author : Śaurīndu Mohana Ṭhākura

Dated : 1896 AD

Source : British Museum, London
A Sanskrit poem set to music, with an English translation of 60 years of Victoriyā.

Title : ***Śrīrādhā Mādhāva Bihāra***

श्रीराधा माधव बिहार

Author : Bhūpata Rai

Size : 20 × 12 cm.

Pages : 164

Language : Hindi

Script : Urdu

Source : State Central Lib., Hyderabad
This work was written in fine Nastaliq script, gold ruled margins, headings of rāgas in red, two complete water colour illustrations and a few incomplete outlines. The work composed in Mohammad Śāha's reign.

Title : ***Sṛṅgārahāraḥ***

श्रृंगारहारः

Author : Hammīradeva

Source : Venkatesvara Univ., Tirupati

Title : ***Śṛṅgaratnākara***

श्रृंगरत्नाकर

Author : Śṛṅgdeva

Leaves : 298

Letters : 10

Lines : 37

Cond. : Damaged and Incomplete

Source : R on the S for S mss in the B P, Bombay

S. No. : 978

Title : ***Sudāmācaritaṃ***

सुदामाचरितम्

Author : Tukārāmasvāmī

Mat. : Palmleaf

Size : 35 × 2.5 cm.

Pages : 4

Language : Sanskrit

Script : Grantha

Source : G O M L, Triplicane, Madras

Title : ***Suguṇavilāsaṃ Kīrttanaṃ***

सुगुणविलासम् कीर्तनम्

Author : Unknown

Mat. : Paper
Size : 20.3 × 16.5 cm.
Pages : 215
Language : Tamil
Script : Tamil
Source : G O M L, Triplicane, Madras

Title : ***Śukrabhāratam with Telugu meaning***

शुक्रभारतम् तेलुगू अर्थ के साथ

Mat. : Palmleaf
Size : 38.3 × 3 cm.
Pages : 65
Script : Grantha
Source : G O M L, Triplicane, Madras

Title : ***Sūlādī***

सूलादी

Author : Unknown
Mat. : Palmleaf
Leaves : 85
Granths : 2750
Script : Telugu
Source : D C of the S mss in the T M S S M L, Tanjore, Vol XVI
S. No. : 10906
B. No. : 11586

Title : ***Sūlādī***

सूलादी

Author : Unknown
Mat. : Palmleaf
Script : Telugu
Source : D C of the S mss in the T M S S M L, Tanjore, Vol XVI
S. No. : 10907
B. No. : 11559
Copies : 10908
B. No. : 11560
Palmleaf : Telugu 10909
B. No. : 11561
Palmleaf : Telugu 10910
B. No. : 11562
Palmleaf : Telugu

Title : ***Sumatibodha***

सुमतिबोध

Author : Unknown
Ms. W P : With Paravastu Veṅkaṭaraṅgācārayār of Vizagpatam
Source : L of S mss in P L of S I, Madras, 1880, Vol I
S. No. : 8357

Title : ***Sundara Singhāra***

सुन्दर सिंघार

Author : Mahā Kib Rai (Kib Rāj)
Size : 17 × 10.5 cm
Pages : 131
Language : Hindi

Script : Urdu

Text : Incomplete at end

Dated : 1688 AD

Source : State Central Lib., Hyderabad

In this work heading in red, in between the lines Urdu meanings of certain Hindi words are given. It was composed in Śāha Jahān reign by Kib Rāj of Gwalior, who was honoured by the title of Mahā Kib Rai by the emperor. In this book is Hindi poetry, Chhand, Dohā and Kavitta pertaining to music.

Title : ***Sundaravilāsam***

सुन्दरविलासम्

Author : Unknown

Mat. : Palmleaf

Size : 50.2 × 3.2 cm.

Pages : 108

Language : Tamil

Script : Tamil

Source : G O M L, Triplicane, Madras

Title : ***Surāgacandrodaya***

सुरागचन्द्रोदय

Author : Puṇḍrīka Viṭhthala

Mat. : Paper

Size : 26.8 × 11.4 cm.

Pages : 10

Lines : 14

Extent : 40

Script : Devanāgarī

Text : Incomplete

Dated : V. S. 1650

Source : C of S & P mss in M S P C, L D B S V, Ahmedabad

S. No. : 6366

Acc. No : 2271

Title : ***Surāgacandrodaya***

सुरागचन्द्रोदय

Author : Puṇḍaīka Viṭhṭhala

Leaves : 16

Granths : 520

Dated : Śaka 1767

Source : O I, Baroda

Acc. No. : 11098

Title : ***Surāgacandrodaya***

सुरागचन्द्रोदय

Author : Puṇḍaīka Viṭhṭhala

Leaves : 54

Granths : 500

Text : Incomplete

Source : O I, Baroda

Acc. No. : 4554

Title	:	***Svarakalādilakṣaṇam***
		स्वरकलादिलक्षणम्
Author	:	Unknown
Mat.	:	Palmleaf
Language	:	Sanskrit
Script	:	Malayalam
Source	:	Kerala Univ. Lib., Trivandrum
Ms. No.	:	1421

Title	:	***Svaramelakalānidhi***
		स्वरमेलकलानिधि
Author	:	Rāmāmātya
Leaves	:	2 - 32
Granths	:	190
Dated	:	Sam. 1628
Source	:	O I, Baroda
Acc. No.	:	4551

Title	:	***Svaramelakalānidhi***
		स्वरमेलकलानिधि
Author	:	Unknown
Ms. W P	:	With Paravastu Veṅkaṭaraṅgācārayār of Vizagpatam
Source	:	L of S mss in P L of S I, Madras, 1880, Vol I
S. No.	:	8369

Title	:	***Svaramelakalānidhi***
		स्वरमेलकलानिधि
Author	:	Rāmāmātya
Source	:	T A C C, Wiesbaden, 1962, Pt-II

Title	:	***Svaramelakalānidhi***
		स्वरमेलकलानिधि
Author	:	Rāmāmātya
Source	:	T A C C, Wiesbaden, 1962, Pt-I
S. No.	:	93

Title	:	***Svaramelakalānidhiḥ***
		स्वरमेलकलानिधिः
Mat.	:	Paper
Size	:	33.5 × 21 cm.
Pages	:	13
Language	:	Sanskrit
Script	:	Telugu
Source	:	G O M L, Triplicane, Madras

Title	:	***Svaramelakalānidhiḥ***
		स्वरमेलकलानिधिः
Mat.	:	Paper
Size	:	26 × 20 cm.
Pages	:	4
Language	:	Sanskrit
Script	:	Telugu

Source : G O M L, Triplicane, Madras

Title : ***Svaramelakalānidhiḥ***

स्वरमेलकलानिधिः

Mat. : Paper

Size : 22.5 × 14 cm.

Pages : 42

Language : Sanskrit

Script : Devanāgarī

Source : G O M L, Triplicane, Madras

Title : ***Svaramelakalānidhiḥ***

स्वरमेलकलानिधिः

Author : Rāmāmātya

Mat. : Palmleaf

Size : 40.8 × 3.7 cm.

Pages : 16

Language : Sanskrit

Script : Telugu

Source : G O M L, Triplicane, Madras

Title : ***Svaramelakalānidhiḥ***

स्वरमेलकलानिधिः

Author : Rāmāmātya

Mat. : Palmleaf

Size : 41 × 3 cm.

Pages : 26

Language : Sanskrit

Script : Telugu

Source : G O M L, Triplicane, Madras

Title : ***Svaramelakalānidhiḥ***

स्वरमेलकलानिधिः

Author : Rāmāmātya

Mat. : Paper

Size : 19.1 × 16 cm.

Pages : 36

Language : Sanskrit

Script : Telugu

Source : G O M L, Triplicane, Madras

Title : ***Svaramelakalānidhiḥ***

स्वरमेलकलानिधिः

Source : O R I, Mysore

No. : 3278

Title : ***Svaramelakalānidhiḥ***

स्वरमेलकलानिधिः

Source : O R I, Mysore

No. : A 68

Title : ***Svaramelakalānidhiḥ***

स्वरमेलकलानिधिः

Author : Rāmāmātya

Mat. : Palmleaf

Size : 17⅞″ × 1″

Leaves : 28

Lines : 4

Granths : 400

Script : Telugu

Text : Complete 1-5 Prakaraṇa

Dated : 1550 AD

Source : D C of the S mss in the T M S S M L, Tanjore, Vol XVI

S. No. : 10807

B. No. : 11565

The author belongs to the Toḍaramala family.

Copies : 10808

B. No. : 11566 Telugu

Complete : 10809

B. No. : 11564 Grantha

Incomplete : 10810

B. No. : 14830 Devanāgarī Incomplete

Title : ***Svaraprastāra***

स्वरप्रस्तार

Author : Unknown

Ms. W P : With H. H. The Mahārājā of Travancor

Source : L of S mss in P L of S I, Madras, 1880, Vol I

S. No. : 6293

Title : ***Svaraprastāraḥ***

स्वरप्रस्तारः

Source : O R I, Mysore

No. : SV 115

Title : ***Svararāgasudhārasa***

स्वररागसुधारस

Author : Unknown

Mat. : Palmleaf

Folios : 1

Language : Sanskrit

Source : Kerala Univ. Lib., Trivandrum

Title : ***Svararāgasudhārasaḥ***

स्वररागसुधारसः

Author : Somanārya

Mat. : Palmleaf

Size : 38.3 × 3 cm.

Pages : 17

Language : Sanskrit

Script : Telugu

Source : G O M L, Triplicane, Madras

Title : ***Svararāgasudhārasaḥ with Telugu meaning***

स्वररागसुधारसः तेलुगू अर्थ के साथ

Author : Somanārya

Mat : Palmleaf

Size : 36.6 × 3.1 cm.

Pages : 60

Language : Sanskrit

Script : Telugu

Source : G O M L, Triplicane, Madras

Title : ***Svararāgasudhārasaḥ***

स्वररागसुधारसः

Author : Unknown

Source : Venkatesvara Univ., Tirupati

Title : ***Svararāgasudhārasamu***

स्वररागसुधारसमु

Author : Somanātha

Mat. : Paper

Size : 22 × 16.5 cm.

Pages : 246

Language : Sanskrit and Telugu

Script : Telugu

Source : G O M L, Triplicane, Madras

Title : ***Svarasamuccaya***

स्वरसमुच्चय

Author : Unknown

Ms. W P : With Pola Lakṣamanāvadhvaṃ of Vizagpatam

Source : L of S mss in P L of S I, Madras, 1880, Vol I

S. No. : 7159

Title : ***Svaratālādilakṣaṇa***

स्वरतालादिलक्षण

Author : Unknown

Size : 13½ × 8½ cm.

Folios : 132

Illustration : 17

Script : Malayalam

Source : A D C of S mss in the C O L, Trivandrum

S. No. : 1231

C.O.L. No. : 355

Title : ***Svaratālādikṣanam with Malayalam commentary***

स्वरतालादिलक्षणम् मलयालम व्याख्या के साथ

Author : Unknown

Size : 7¾ × 1¾ cm.

Folios : 83

Illustration : 8

Source : A D C of the S mss in the H H M P L, Trivandrum

S. No. : 1421

Title	: ***Svaratālādilakṣaṇaṃ with Malayalam commentary*** **स्वरतालादिलक्षणम् मलयालम व्याख्या के साथ**
Author	: Unknown
Size	: 7½ × 1⅝ cm.
Folios	: 22
Illustration	: 7
Source	: A D C of the S mss in the H H M P L, Trivandrum
S. No.	: 1422

Title	: ***Svaratālādilakṣaṇaṃ with Tamil commentary*** **स्वरतालादिलक्षणम् तमिल व्याख्या के साथ**
Author	: Unknown
Mat.	: Paper
Folios	: 34
Language	: Sanskrit
Script	: Tamil
Source	: Kerala Univ. Lib., Trivandrum
Ms. No.	: 2182 A

T

Title : ***Taddhitonnaṃ***

तद्धितोन्नम्

Author : Unknown

Mat. : Palmleaf

Size : 15″ × 1¼″

Leaves : 3

Lines : 6

Granths : 22

Script : Grantha

Text : Complete

Source : D C of the S mss in the T M S S M L, Tanjore, VOL XVI

S. No. : 10848

B. No. : 11516 (b)

Deals with the details of the letters (na), (dhi), (to), (na) with Telugu meaning.

The significance of the symbols used is given and a philosophical interpretation is given to them. One of the manuscripts says that it is a portion of Abhinava-darpaṇa.

Copies : 10849

Palmleaf : Grantha

Complete : 10850

Palmleaf : Grantha Complete

Title : ***Tāla Camuttīraṃ***

ताल चमुत्तीरम्

Author : Cūdamaṇi

Size : 8¾ × 1$^{3/8}$ cm.

Folios : 22

Illustration : 11

Source : D C of T M in M D U V S, I L, Adyar, Madras-26

Acc. No. : 2069 (874)

Title : ***Tālacandrikā***

तालचन्द्रिका

Author : Virūpākṣa

Size : 14 × 1½ cm.

Folios : 9

Illustration : 11

Script : Grantha

Source : A D C of S mss in the C O L, Trivandrum

S. No. : 1223

C.O.L. No. : 1901

Title	:	***Tālacandrikā***
		तालचन्द्रिका
Mat.	:	Paper
Size	:	33 × 26 cm.
Pages	:	14
Script	:	Devanāgarī
Source	:	G O M L, Triplicane, Madras

Title	:	***Tāladaśapramāṇadīpikā***
		तालदशप्रमाणदीपिका
Author	:	Govinda
Source	:	T A C C, Wiesbaden, 1962, Pt-I
B. No.	:	61 b

Title	:	***Tāladaśāraṇapraṇadīpikā***
		तालदशारणप्राणदीपिका
Author	:	Govindakavi
Pages	:	84
Language	:	Telugu
Source	:	Andhra Univ. Lib, A. P.

Title	:	***Tāladaśaprāṇaḥ with Telugu meaning***
		तालदशप्राणः तेलुगू अर्थ के साथ
Author	:	Unknown
Mat.	:	Paper
Size	:	22 × 66 cm.
Pages	:	5
Script	:	Telugu
Source	:	G O M L, Triplicane, Madras

Title	:	***Tāladaśaprāṇaḥ with Telugu meaning***
		तालदशप्राणः तेलुगू अर्थ के साथ
Mat	:	Palmleaf
Size	:	38.3 × 3 cm.
Pages	:	16
Script	:	Telugu
Source	:	G O M L, Triplicane, Madras

Title	:	***Tāladaśāprāṇalakṣaṇamu***
		तालदशाप्राणलक्षणमु
Size	:	$14^{3/10''} \times 1^{2/5''}$
Lines	:	39
Illustration	:	6
Granths	:	802
Source	:	A D C of the T mss in the T M S S M L, Waltair, 1933, A U S-11
No.	:	720 - 721
B. No.	:	11616

Title	:	***Tāladaśāprāṇalakṣaṇamu***
		तालदशाप्राणलक्षणमु
Author	:	Unknown
Pages	:	52

Language : Telugu

Source : Andhra Univ. Lib., A. P.

Title : ***Tāladaśāprāṇapradīpikā***

तालदशाप्राणप्रदीपिका

Author : Govinda Kavi

Size : 15½" × 1 3/10"

Lines : 41

Illustration : 5

Granths : 800

Source : A D C of the T mss in the T M S S M L, Waltair, 1933, A U S-11

No. : 719

B. No. : 11600

Title : ***Tālādhyāya***

तालाध्याय

Author : Nandikeśvara

Source : T A C C, Wiesbaden, 1962, Pt-I

S. No. : 5 B

Title : ***Tālādhyāya (From the Saṅgītaratnākara)***

तालाध्याय (संगीतरत्नाकर से)

Author : Śārṅgadeva

Source : T A C C, Wiesbaden, 1962, Pt-I

S. No. : 6 A

Oxf. No. : 199 b

Title : ***Tālādhyāyaḥ with Telugu meaning***

तालाध्यायः तेलुगू अर्थ के साथ

Author : Unknown

Mat. : Paper

Size : 30 × 22 cm.

Pages : 7

Script : Telugu

Source : G O M L, Triplicane, Madras

Title : ***Tālādhyāyaḥ with Telugu meaning***

तालाध्यायः तेलुगू अर्थ के साथ

Author : Unknown

Mat. : Palmleaf

Size : 37 × 3 cm.

Pages : 14

Script : Telugu

Source : G O M L, Triplicane, Madras

Title : ***Tāladhyāyaḥ with Telugu meaning***

तालाध्यायः तेलुगू अर्थ के साथ

Author : Unknown

Mat. : Paper
Size : 34.8 × 22.5 cm.
Pages : 97
Script : Devanāgarī
Source : G O M L, Triplicane, Madras

Title : ***Tālādilakṣaṇam***
तालादिलक्षणम्
Source : O R I, Mysore
No. : 343

Title : ***Tāladīpikā***
तालदीपिका
Author : Gopatippa Bhūpāla
Mat. : Paper
Size : 27.4 × 21 cm.
Pages : 8
Script : Devanāgarī
Source : G O M L, Triplicane, Madras

Title : ***Tāladīpikā***
तालदीपिका
Author : Sāluva Tippabhūpāla
Mat. : Palmleaf
Size : 17¼" × 1 3/8"
Leaves : 79
Lines : 6
Granths : 1650
Script : Telugu
Text : Incomplete
Source : D C of the S mss in the T M S S M L, Tanjore, VOL XVI
S. No. : 10830
B. No. : 11522
It has an Āndhra-Tīka.
Copies : 10831
B. No. : 11536c
Pamleaf : Telugu Incomplete

Title : ***Tāladīpikā***
तालदीपिका
Author : Tippa Bhūpāla
Source : T A C C, Wiesbaden, 1962, Pt-I
B. No. : 60 b

Title : ***Tāladīpikā***
तालदीपिका
Author : Tippa Bhūpālaḥ
Source : Venkatesvara Univ., Tirupati

Title : ***Tāladīpikā***
तालदीपिका
Author : Gopatiṇṇadeva
Folios : 65
Script : Grantha
Source : V V R I, Hoshiarpur
Acc. No. : 5624

Title : ***Tālalakṣaṇa***

ताललक्षण

Author : Kohalācārya
Size : 9" × 7¼"
Folios : 13
Lines : 22
Script : Devanāgarī
Source : C of S mss in the I O L, London, VOL I, Pt-II
No. : 3089

A treatise by Kohalācārya on musical time and measure; wrongly marked as beginning of Bharata-Śāstra in the heading of the pages; and apparently copied from the same South-Indian Manuscript as the next one. Both Manuscripts are very incorrect.

Cf. Burnell, Tanjore Ms., pp. 60, 61 (Arjunabharata)

Title : ***Tālalakṣaṇa***

ताललक्षण

Size : 13½" × 8½"
Folios : 142
Lines : 19
Script : Telugu
Source : C of S mss in the I O L, London, VOL I, Pt-II
No. : 3025

The same treatise Tālalakṣaṇa, with a Telugu commentary.

Title : ***Tālalakṣaṇa***

ताललक्षण

Mat. : Palmyra
Size : 17" × 1¼"
Folios : 26
Lines : 6
Script : Telugu
Dated : 19th century
Source : C of S mss in the I O L, London, Vol II
S. No. : 7904
Acc. No. : 3895

A treatise on Tālalakṣaṇa in Sanskrit verses with telugu exposition.
The manuscript is very inaccurate as regard its Sanskrit leaf.

Title : ***Tālalakṣaṇa***

ताललक्षण

Author : Unknown
Source : T A C C, Wiesbaden, 1962, Pt-I
B. No. : 61 b

Title : ***Tālalakṣaṇam***

ताललक्षणम्

Mat. : Palmleaf
Size : 34 × 3.5 cm.
Pages : 15
Script : Telugu
Source : G O M L, Triplicane, Madras

Title	:	***Tālalakṣaṇam***
		ताललक्षणम्
Mat.	:	Palmleaf
Size	:	38 × 2.3 cm.
Pages	:	15
Script	:	Grantha
Source	:	G O M L, Triplicane, Madras

Title	:	***Tālalakṣaṇam***
		ताललक्षणम्
Mat.	:	Paper
Size	:	27.1 × 24.1 cm.
Pages	:	8
Script	:	Devanāgarī
Source	:	G O M L, Triplicane, Madras

Title	:	***Tālalakṣaṇam***
		ताललक्षणम्
Mat.	:	Paper
Size	:	34.5 × 22 cm.
Pages	:	13
Script	:	Devanāgarī
Source	:	G O M L, Triplicane, Madras

Title	:	***Tālalakṣaṇam with Telugu meaning***
		ताललक्षणम् तेलुगू अर्थ के साथ
Mat.	:	Palmleaf
Size	:	34 × 3.5 cm.
Pages	:	125
Script	:	Telugu
Source	:	G O M L, Triplicane, Madras

Title	:	***Tālalakṣaṇam***
		ताललक्षणम्
Mat.	:	Paper
Size	:	30 × 20 cm.
Pages	:	78
Script	:	Telugu
Source	:	G O M L, Triplicane, Madras

Title	:	***Tālalakṣaṇaṃ***
		ताललक्षणम्
Author	:	Unknown
Mat.	:	Palmleaf
Size	:	12½" × 1¼"
Leaves	:	27
Lines	:	4
Granths	:	350
Script	:	Telugu
Text	:	Complete
Source	:	D C of the S mss in the T M S S M L, Tanjore, VOL XVI
S. No.	:	10837
B. No.	:	11598
Copies	:	10838-10845
		All incomplete 10841 Devanāgarī

Title	:	***Tālamālā***
		तालमाला
Author	:	Unknown
Size	:	33.5 × 8.9 cm.
Leaves	:	6
Language	:	Sanskrit
Script	:	Bengali
Source	:	B H U, Varanasi
S. No.	:	5526

Title	:	***Tālanirṇaya***
		तालनिर्णय
Author	:	Unknown
Size	:	12.7" × 1.4"
Folios	:	9
Language	:	Sanskrit
Source	:	Bhuvaneswar Museum, Bhuvaneswar

Title	:	***Tālaprakaraṇa***
		तालप्रकरण
Mat.	:	Palmleaf
Size	:	25 × 3 cm.
Pages	:	33
Script	:	Telugu
Source	:	G O M L, Triplicane, Madras

Title	:	***Tālaprakaraṇa with Telugu meaning***
		तालप्रकरण तेलुगू अर्थ के साथ
Mat.	:	Paper
Size	:	20 × 16 cm.
Pages	:	15
Script	:	Telugu
Source	:	G O M L, Triplicane, Madras

Title	:	***Tālaprakaraṇa with Telugu meaning***
		तालप्रकरण तेलुगू अर्थ के साथ
Mat.	:	Paper
Size	:	34.5 × 22 cm.
Pages	:	14
Script	:	Devanāgarī
Source	:	G O M L, Triplicane, Madras

Title	:	***Tālaprastāra***
		तालप्रस्तार
Author	:	Keśavamiśra
Ms. W P	:	Lib. of H. H. the Raja of Kochin
Source	:	L of S mss in P L of S I, Madras, 1880, VOL I
S. No.	:	2850

Title	:	***Tālaprastāra***
		तालप्रस्तार
Author	:	Unknown
Source	:	T A C C, Wiesbaden, 1962, Pt-I
B. No.	:	60 b

Title	:	***Tālaprastāra***
		तालप्रस्तार
Author	:	Unknown
Folios	:	2
Script	:	Grantha
Source	:	V V R I, Hoshiarpur
Acc. No.	:	5624

Title	:	***Tālaprastāraḥ***
		तालप्रस्तारः
Mat.	:	Paper
Size	:	27 × 24 cm
Pages	:	16
Script	:	Devanāgarī
Source	:	G O M L, Triplicane, Madras

Title	:	***Tālaprastāraḥ***
		तालप्रस्तारः
Author	:	Unknown
Mat.	:	Palmleaf
Size	:	17½" × 1⅝"
Leaves	:	15
Lines	:	3 - 4
Granths	:	100
Script	:	Telugu
Text	:	Complete
Source	:	L of S mss in P L of S I, Madras, 1880, VOL I
S. No.	:	10832
B. No.	:	11597
Copies	:	10833-10836 Palmleaf Te., Gra., Te., Gra. Complete

Title	:	***Tālasamuttīram***
		तालसमुत्तीरम्
Author	:	Unknown
Mat.	:	Paper
Size	:	26.7 × 23.5 cm.
Pages	:	146
Language	:	Sanskrit & Tamil
Script	:	Tamil and Grantha
Source	:	G O M L, Triplicane, Madras

Title	:	***Tālasarvasvasārasaṅgraha***
		तालसर्वस्वसारसंग्रह
Author	:	Unknown
Size	:	10" × 1.7"
Folios	:	51
Language	:	Sanskrit
Source	:	Bhuvaneswar Museum, Bhuvaneswar

Title : ***Tālavādyavidhānam***

तालवाद्यविधानम्

Author : Unknown

Mat. : Palmleaf

Folios : 1

Language : Sanskrit

Script : Malayalam

Source : Kerala Univ. Lib., Trivandrum

Ms. No. : 8959

Title : ***Tālavicāraḥ***

तालविचारः

Author : Unknown

Mat. : Paper

Size : 9.3" × 4.7"

Folios : 2 - 15

Lines : 10

Letters : 30

Script : Devanāgarī

Source : Varanaseya Skt. Visvavidyalaya Lib., Varanasi

S. No. : 45520

Title : ***Tālavidhānam with Telugu meaning***

तालविधानम् तेलुगू अर्थ के साथ

Mat. : Paper

Size : 30 × 20 cm.

Pages : 26

Script : Telugu

Source : G O M L, Triplicane, Madras

Title : ***Tālavidhānam with Telugu meaning***

तालविधानम् तेलुगू अर्थ के साथ

Mat. : Paper

Size : 30" × 22"

Pages : 7

Script : Telugu

Source : G O M L, Triplicane, Madras

Title : ***Tālavidhānaṃ with Malyalam meaning***

तालविधानम् मलयालम अर्थ के साथ

Mat. : Paper

Size : 27.2 × 24.6 cm.

Pages : 20

Script : Devanāgarī and Malayalam

Source : G O M L, Triplicane, Madras

Title : ***Tālaviṣayaḥ***

तालविषयः

Mat. : Palmleaf

Size : 37 × 3 cm.

Pages : 14

Script : Telugu
Source : G O M L, Triplicane, Madras

Title : ***Tālaviṣayaḥ with Telugu Meaning***
तालविषयः तेलुगू अर्थ के साथ
Mat. : Paper
Size : 25 × 3 cm.
Pages : 13
Script : Grantha
Source : G O M L, Triplicane, Madras

Title : ***Tālaviṣayaḥ with Telugu Meaning***
तालविषयः तेलुगू अर्थ के साथ
Mat. : Paper
Size : 30" × 20"
Pages : 26
Script : Telugu
Source : G O M L, Triplicane, Madras

Title : ***Tālaviṣayaḥ***
तालविषयः
Mat. : Paper
Size : 34.8" × 22.5"
Pages : 97
Script : Devanāgarī
Source : G O M L, Triplicane, Madras

Title : ***Tānanighanṭuḥ***
ताननिघण्टुः
Author : Unknown
Mat. : Palmleaf
Leaves : 41
Granths : 1300
Script : Telugu
Source : D C of the S mss in the T M S S M L, Tanjore, VOL XVI
S. No. : 10904
B. No. : 11594
No. : 1

Title : ***Tanjuman-Ul-Hind***
तंजुमन–उल–हिन्द
Author : Unknown
Folios : 145[b]-169[a]
Dated : 1157 AH
Source : A D C of the O mss in the D L, Bahawalpur

Title : ***Taraṅgaḥ***
तरंगः
Author : Unknown
Size : 17 × 1½ cm.
Folios : 90
Illustration : 7
Script : Grantha
Source : A D C of S mss in the C O L, Trivandrum
S. No. : 1222
C.O.L. No. : 824

Title : ***Taraṅgacandrodayam***

तरंगचन्द्रोदयम्

Author : Rāmacandrendra Sarasvatī

Mat. : Paper

Size : 34.2" × 21.5"

Pages : 16

Script : Devanāgarī

Source : G O M L, Triplicane, Madras

Title : ***Tentirupperaik-Kulaikkāṭṭarperil pātal***

तेन्तिरूप्पेरैकुलैकाट्टरपेंरिल् पाडल्

Author : Unknown

Mat. : Palmleaf

Size : 21.5 × 3.8 cm.

Pages : 3

Language : Tamil

Script : Tamil

Source : G O M L, Triplicane, Madras

Title : ***Terūrndanāṭakam***

तेरूर्न्दनाटकम्

Author : Perumālayyar

Mat. : Palmleaf

Size : 43.2 × 3.2 cm.

Pages : 46

Language : Tamil

Script : Tamil

Source : G O M L, Triplicane, Madras

Title : ***Tirūkkaccūr Noṇḍi Nāṭakam***

तिरूकच्चूर नोण्डि नाटकम्

Author : Madurakaviray

Mat. : Palmleaf

Size : 38.2 × 2.5 cm.

Pages : 64

Language : Tamil

Script : Tamil

Source : G O M L, Triplicane, Madras

Title : ***Tirūkkurūnikuḍi Nambi Utsavappāṭṭu***

तिरूक्कुरूणिकुदि नम्बि उत्सवपाटटु

Author : Unknown

Mat. : Palmleaf

Size : 47 × 4.5 cm.

Pages : 3

Language : Tamil

Script : Tamil

Source : G O M L, Triplicane, Madras

Title : ***Tirūnālaippovār Carittira Kkīrttnai***

तिरूनालैपोवार चरित्तिर कीर्तनै

Author : Unknown

Mat. : Palmleaf
Size : 29.8 × 3.2 cm.
Pages : 8
Language : Tamil
Script : Tamil
Source : G O M L, Triplicane, Madras

Title : ***Treatise of Hindu Music***
ट्रीटाइज ऑफ हिन्दू म्यूजिक
Author : Raushal Zamīr
Dated : 1094 AH
Source : C of the P mss in the B M, London, 1881, Vol II
No. : 793
Technical tunes are in Sanskrit. It is divided into three parts-
I. Gītikāṇḍa
II. Vādyakāṇḍa
III. Nṛtyakāṇḍa

Title : ***Tuhfat-Ul-Abrār***
तुहफत–उल–अबरार
Author : Unknown
Folios : 236 - 39a
Dated : 1157 AH
Source : A D C of the G mss in the D L, Bahawalpur
No. : 266 (3)

Title : ***Tuhfat-Ul-Hind***
तुहफत–उल–हिन्द
Author : Mirzā Khān Mohammad
Size : 11.75 × 8 cm.
Folios : 300
Letters : 16
Dated : 1675 - 76 AD
Source : Asiatic Society of Bengal, Calcutta, 1926
No. : 640
On music and others arts.

Title : ***Tuhfat-Ul-Hind***
तुहफत–उल–हिन्द
Author : Mirzā khān b Fakiruddin Mohammad
Mat. : Paper
Size : 290 × 175 ; 210 × 105 mm.
Folios : 312
Illustration : 17
Cond. : Good
Dated : 1661 AD
Source : Asiatic Society of Bengal, Cal., 1924, Vol I
No. : 1630
Treatise on Indian music, fine arts etc.

Title : ***Tuhfat-Ul-Hind***
तुहफत–उल–हिन्द
Author : Mirzā Jān Ibn Fakīruddīn Muhammad
Size : 8" × 5"

Pages : 381

Language : Persian

Text : Complete

Source : Maulana Azad Lib., A M U, Aligarh

Title : ***Tuhfatun Nagamāt***

तुहफतुन् नगमात

Author : Md. Ruhullaha Bin Śāhavajīullah

Mat. : Paper

Size : 20.5 × 11.7 cm.

Pages : 31

Script : Nastaliq

Text : Complete

Source : G O M L, Triplicane, Madras

Title : ***Tuhjutul Nagamāt***

तुहजुतुल नगमात

Language : Persian

Source : Sangeet Natak Academy Lib.

Title : ***Tulasīdāsanāṭakam***

तुलसीदासनाटकम्

Author : Unknown

Mat. : Paper

Size : 33.3 × 21.2 cm.

Pages : 36

Language : Tamil

Script : Tamil

Source : G O M L, Triplicane, Madras

Title : ***Turaicai-C-Cupramaṇiya Svāmīkaḷnūtu English note***

तुरैचैच्चुरमणिय स्वामिगल्नूटु

Author : Mahavidvān Mīnākṣī Sundaraṃ Pillai

Size : 18 × 1 1/8 cm.

Folios : 3

Illustration : 5

Source : D C of T M in M D U V S, I L, Adyar, Madras-26

Acc. No. : 2070 (839)

U

Title	: ***Umāpatīya***
	उमापतीय
Size	: 8" × 10¼"
Pages	: 30
Lines	: 15 - 16
Script	: Devanāgarī
Dated	: 1925 AD
Source	: C of S mss in the I O L, London, Vol II
S. No.	: 7903
Acc. No.	: 3842
	The Umāpatīya, a treatise on several musical topics- Tālalakṣaṇa, Maddalakṣaṇa, Nṛttalakṣaṇa, Śirobhedalakṣaṇa; and Aṅgābhinayalakṣaṇa.

Title	: ***Urūkkumāṅgatanāṭakam***
	उरूकुमांगतनाटकम्
Author	: Unknown
Mat.	: Palmleaf
Size	: 41.2 × 3.5 cm.
Pages	: 162
Language	: Tamil
Script	: Tamil
Source	: G O M L, Triplicane, Madras

Title	: ***Uṣāniruddha Nāṭaka***
	उषानिरुद्ध नाटक
Author	: Candraśekhara Rāyaguru
Size	: 8.1" × 1"
Folios	: 78
Language	: Oriya
Source	: Utkal Univ. Lib., Bhuvaneswar

Title	: ***Usūl-Ī-Nagamāt-Ī-Āsafī***
	उसूल–ई–नगमात–ई–आसफी
Author	: Gulām Raza Sābir Alī
Size	: 32 × 18 cm.
Pages	: 86
Language	: Persian
Source	: State Central Lib., Hyderabad

Title	: ***Usūl-Ī-Nagamāt-Ī-Āsafī***
	उसूल–ई–नगमात–ई–आसफी
Author	: Gulām Razā Sābir Alī
Size	: 21 × 16 cm.
Pages	: 183
Language	: Persian
Cond.	: Damaged
Dated	: 1323 AH
Source	: State Central Lib., Hyderabad

Title	: ***Usūl-Ī-Nagamāt-Ī-Āsafī***
	उसूल–ई–नगमात–ई–आसफी
Author	: Gulām Razā Sābir Alī

Size : 23 × 15 cm.
Pages : 266
Language : Persian
Cond. : Badly damaged
Source : State Central Lib., Hyderabad

Title : ***Usūl-Nagamāt-Ī-Āsafī***
उसूल–नगमात–ई–आसफी
Author : Gulām Razā Sābir Alī
Size : 33.5 × 20.7 cm.
Pages : 101
Language : Persian
Source : State Central Lib., Hyderabad

Title : ***Usūl-Un-Nagmāt-Ul-Āsafī***
उसूल–उन–नगमात–उल–आसफी
Author : Gulām Rīdā
Size : 9" × 6:7" × 3½"
Folios : 129
Letters : 10-16
Language : Nasttaliq
Dated : 1076 AH 1665 AD
Pub. By : Imperial Lib., Calcutta
Source : C of the P mss in the Būhār Library, Vol I
No. : 235

Title : ***Usūl-Un-Nagmāt-Ul-Āsafī***
उसूल–उन–नगमात–उल–आसफी
Author : Gulam Rīda
Size : 9" × 6:7" × 3½"
Folios : 120
Language : Persian
Source : National Lib., Belvedere, Calcutta-27

Title : ***Usūl-Un-Nagmāt-Ul-Āsafī (Part-I)***
उसूल–उन–नगमात–उल–आसफी
Author : Rāyacanda
Size : 8¾" × 5½:7" × 4"
Folios : 99
Language : Persian
Source : National Lib., Belvedere, Calcutta-27

Title : ***Usūl-Un-Nagmāt-Ul-Āsafī (Part-II)***
उसूल–उन–नगमात–उल–आसफी
Author : Unknown
Size : 8½" × 6:6" × 3 ½"
Folios : 63
Language : Persian
Source : National Lib., Belvedere, Calcutta-27

Title : ***Uttararāmāyaṇanāṭṭakaṃ***
उत्तररामायणनाटकम्
Author : Unknown
Mat. : Palmleaf
Size : 34.2 × 3.7 cm.
Pages : 354
Language : Tamil
Script : Tamil
Source : G O M L, Triplicane, Madras

V

Title	: ***Vadirājakīrtanam***
	वदिराजकीर्तनम्
Author	: Vadirāja
Mat.	: Palmleaf
Size	: 37 × 3 cm.
Script	: Grantha
Source	: G O M L, Triplicane, Madras

Title	: ***Vādyanirūpuṇa***
	वाद्यनिरूपण
Author	: Kiśhora Canda Rājendra
Size	: 13.3" × 1.4"
Folios	: 14
Language	: Sanskrit
Source	: Bhuvaneswar Museum, Bhuvaneswar

Title	: ***Vaiṣṇavāmṛta Goṣṭhi Rūpaka***
	वैष्णवामृत गोष्ठी रूपक
Author	: Jayadeva
Size	: 16.3" × 1.3"
Folios	: 7
Language	: Sanskrit
Source	: Bhuvaneswar Museum, Bhuvaneswar

Title	: ***Valliyammai Nāṭakam***
	वल्लियम्मै नाटकम्
Author	: Kumārappill
Mat.	: Palmleaf
Size	: 28 × 2.8 cm.
Pages	: 120
Language	: Tamil
Script	: Tamil
Source	: G O M L, Triplicane, Madras

Title	: ***Varṇalaghuvyākhyānam***
	वर्णलघुव्याख्यानम्
Author	: Rāma
Mat.	: Palmleaf
Size	: 31.5 × 3.5 cm.
Script	: Grantha
Source	: G O M L, Triplicane, Madras

Title	: ***Vasantatilakā Bhāṇa***
	वसन्ततिलका भाण
Author	: Varadācārya

Size : 10" × 1.6"
Folios : 48
Language : Sanskrit
Source : Bhuvaneswar Museum, Bhuvaneswar

Title : *Veṇīsaṃhāra Nāṭaka* वेणीसंहार नाटक
Author : Bhaṭṭanarayaṇa
Size : 16.5" × 1.4"
Folios : 50
Language : Sanskrit
Source : Bhuvaneswar Museum, Bhuvaneswar

Title : *Veṇīsaṃhāra Nāṭaka* वेणीसंहार नाटक
Pages : 32
Dated : 1893 AD
Source : British Museum, London
No. : 14080

Title : *Veṅkatācala Kīrttanaikal* वेंकटाचल कीर्तनैकल
Author : Unknown
Mat. : Palmleaf
Size : 17.8 × 3.2 cm.
Pages : 98
Language : Tamil
Script : Tamil
Source : G O M L, Triplicane, Madras

Title : *Veṅkatācala Perumāl Peril Kīrttanam* वेंकटाचल पेरूमाल् पेरिल कीर्तनम्
Author : Pāśaikkavirayar
Mat. : Palmleaf
Size : 40.1 × 25 cm.
Pages : 8
Language : Tamil
Script : Tamil
Source : G O M L, Triplicane, Madras

Title : *Vidagdhamādhava Nāṭaka with Bengali translation* विदग्धमाधव नाटक बंगाली अनुवाद के साथ
Author : Rūpagosvāmī
Size : 11.5" × 1.3"
Folios : 164
Language : Sanskrit
Source : Bhuvaneswar Museum, Bhuvaneswar

Title : *Vīṇālakṣaṇam* वीणालक्षणम्
Author : Parameśvara
Leaves : 6

Extent : 150
Dated : Sam. 1994
Source : O I, Baroda
Acc. No. : 10010 (b)

Title : ***Vīṇāprapāṭhaka***
वीणाप्रपाठक
Author : Unknown
Leaves : 15
Granths : 180
Dated : Sam. 1994
Source : O I, Baroda
Acc. No. : 5351

Title : ***Vināyaka Bharataḥ***
विनायक भरतः
Author : Unknown
Source : Venkatesvara Univ., Tirupati

Title : ***Vīramāraṅkatainātakam***
वीरमारंकटैनाटकम्
Author : Unknown
Mat. : Palmleaf
Size : 21 × 16.5 cm.
Pages : 544
Language : Tamil
Script : Tamil
Source : G O M L, Triplicane, Madras

Title : ***Viṭhṭhalīyaḥ***
विठ्ठलीयः
Author : Viṭṭhala
Size : 6½" × 4¾"
Leaves : 6
Granths : 65
Script : Devanāgarī
Source : D C of the S mss in the T M S S M L, Tanjore, Vol XVI
S. No. : 10677
B. No. : 6656

Y

Title	:	***Yatsārikāgānam***
		यत्सारिकागानम्
Mat.	:	Palmleaf
Size	:	41.5 × 2.6 cm.
Pages	:	3
Script	:	Telugu
Source	:	G O M L, Triplicane, Madras

Title	:	***Yayātivilāsam***
		ययातिविलासम्
Author	:	Varadarāja
Mat.	:	Palmleaf
Size	:	47 × 2.5 cm.
Pages	:	254
Language	:	Tamil
Script	:	Tamil
Source	:	G O M L, Triplicane, Madras